Drugs and Money

DRUGS AND MONEY

Laundering Latin America's Cocaine Dollars

Robert E. Grosse

Westport, Connecticut
London

Library of Congress Cataloging-in-Publication Data

Grosse, Robert E.
    Drugs and money : laundering Latin America's cocaine dollars / Robert E. Grosse.
        p.   cm.
    Includes bibliographical references and index.
    ISBN 0–275–97042–6 (alk. paper)
    1. Money laundering—Latin America.   2. Cocaine industry—Latin America.   3. Money
laundering—Latin America—Case studies.   4. Narcotics dealers—Latin America—Case
studies.   5. Money laundering—Prevention.   I. Title.
HV8079.M64G75   2001
364.16'8—dc21   00–032409

British Library Cataloguing in Publication Data is available.

Library of Congress Catalog Card Number: 00–032409
ISBN: 0–275–97042–6

First published in 2001

Praeger Publishers, 88 Post Road West, Westport, CT 06881
An imprint of Greenwood Publishing Group, Inc.
www.praeger.com

Printed in the United States of America

The paper used in this book complies with the
Permanent Paper Standard issued by the National
Information Standards Organization (Z39.48–1984).

10 9 8 7 6 5 4 3 2

Contents

Acknowledgments

I would like to thank the many people who contributed to the development of this book. I cannot include all of them, some because of necessary anonymity and others because I cannot recall all of their contributions. I apologize to those whom I have left out. Undoubtedly, the initiating forces behind my work in this area were Bruce Bagley, Colombia expert and protagonist in the country's efforts to deal with the drug problem, and Lynn Summers, both of whom invited me to participate in analyses of economic aspects of narcotics trafficking and money laundering.

Next, I would like to thank the several student assistants who worked with me in tracking down articles, books, and government documents on these subjects. They include Michael Crowe, Kumar Venkataramany, Steve Bettink, Pari Thirunavukkarasu, and others at Thunderbird and at the University of Miami. I would especially like to thank Georgia Lessard of the Thunderbird presentation graphics department for her superb work in creating the figures and tables in this book.

For the most part, I cannot explicitly recognize those who provided me with information about money laundering schemes from the law enforcement community and from the launderers themselves. Since they know who they are, I simply express my appreciation for their insights and willingness to share information. I can mention a couple of them by name, and through them thank the rest implicitly. Mike McDonald, formerly of the IRS Criminal Investigation Division in Miami, regaled me with many stories of amazing money laundering schemes, some of which appear in these pages; and Charles Intriago, editor of the newsletter *Money Laundering Alert*, provided me on several occasions with access to useful documents and an interpretation of government regulations and policies. Quite a few Colombian bankers and businesspeople helped me to understand the laundering processes, but due to concern for their personal safety I cannot mention their names here.

Introduction and Explanation of Scope

Money laundering is as old as illicit business, since criminals have to get their ill-gotten gains into clean financial instruments in order to use them in the legitimate business system. The process by which cocaine traffickers take dollars generated from street sales of cocaine or crack and convert them into bank accounts, airplanes, securities investments, and other uses is the topic of this book.

The whole subject is pretty hard to figure out for a non-participant. Imagine the problem of trying to hide the source of a suitcase full of perhaps $U.S. 400,000 in $5, $10, and $20 bills when the drug trafficker (or his or her money launderer accomplice) needs to convert cocaine sales into "legitimate" financial instruments such as bank deposits or investments. This is the task that has led government enforcement agencies to a point of attack in their efforts to reduce the flow of illicit narcotics to U.S. consumers. It is also the problem that faces drug cartel members as they make their sales.

Part of the purpose of this book is to describe and illuminate a wide variety of narcotics money laundering schemes. These ventures are almost unimaginably creative and extensive. From shipping suitcases of dollars to Mexico to buying gold with drug cash in California to faking the export of clothing from Colombia to Panama, the clandestine activities of the launderers are truly fascinating. The amounts of money involved are often staggering—hundreds of millions of dollars in most of the cases described here. All of the stories relate to the laundering of narcotics proceeds, mostly cocaine-derived dollars produced from the activities of Colombian and Mexican drug traffickers.

A second purpose of this book is to consider some of the concerns raised by money laundering. One major concern is for banks and other financial intermediaries that want to try to avoid becoming involved in a money laundering process. Some guidance is offered to the banker who needs to be informed about money laundering and capable of implementing policies to reduce its likelihood. Another concern is to understand the social costs and benefits produced by money laundering. It has been said that the rapid development of Miami in the 1980s was due directly to the hundreds of millions of cocaine dollars invested in real estate and businesses there by the "cocaine cowboys."[1] While this is an overstatement, it is important to think carefully about both the costs of the illegal activity and its spillover benefits. These issues are raised in Part III of this book.

The discussion is divided into three parts. Part I examines the broad terrain of laundering drug money. Chapter 1 explains what money laundering is, with a particular emphasis on the laundering of narcotics revenues generated from cocaine production, transport, and sale. This chapter also presents several scenarios that are textbook "money laundering 101" kinds of narcotics money laundering schemes. Chapter 2 describes the process of the production of cocaine, from coca plants growing in Peru and Bolivia to refining in Colombia to the delivery of cocaine hydrochloride and crack in the United States. Chapter 3 looks in some detail at the way in which foreign exchange black markets in Latin America are used to launder the drug cash. Chapter 4 gives a history of money laundering in the context of U.S. laws and court cases during the 1970s, 1980s, and 1990s and demonstrates the growing and evolving complexity of money laundering as the participants seek to foil law enforcement efforts and make their money ever cleaner. It is used as a framework for proceeding with the description of various money laundering schemes that have cropped up over the past 30 years.

Part II forms the bulk of this book, in which a number of truly wild tales are told about money laundering ventures. Chapter 5 provides some simple and early examples of the operation of parts of a laundering process—for example, the smurfing of drug dollars into bank accounts and the shipment of cash hidden in stereos and water heaters. In Chapter 6, the famous case of La Mina, the jewelry store/gold dealer group that laundered money for the Medellin cartel, is used to show the full chain of cocaine trafficking, which produces revenues in cash, which is then moved into and through the legal financial system in the U.S. and abroad.

Other chapters describe the Cali cartel's laundry operating through European bank accounts, the precious metals venture of Stephen Saccoccia, which was used to buy jet aircraft for transporting cocaine, and other cases focusing on non-bank laundering devices, such as money remitters, car dealers, and even interior decorators. As part of the system through which money laundering takes place, financial havens occupy an important place. The way in which Panama has been used for this purpose, especially during the regime of General Manuel Noriega, demonstrates the difficulties in dealing with the problem. Likewise, not central as a money laundering venture but indicative of the scope of the problem is the involvement of Raul Salinas, brother of then-President Carlos Salinas of Mexico, in a scheme related to Mexican trafficker Jose Garcia Abrego. The cases build in size and complexity over the course of the 30-year period that is covered, up to the recent (1998–99) case called "Operation Casablanca," which involved a huge cocaine trafficking–money laundering venture through Mexico and California.

Part III deals with some managerial, technical, and policy concerns. First, in Chapter 14, the question of measuring the size of money laundering is explored in the context of Mexico. Second, in Chapter 15, the involvement of Colombia in virtually every phase of this issue is reviewed, and some suggestions are offered with respect to policy responses that could alter the current situation. Next, in Chapter 16, the concerns of financial institutions and others whose businesses become enmeshed with the activities of money launderers are considered. This chapter describes the major problems banks face in trying to avoid being used in money laundering ventures, and it suggests some bank policies and methods for dealing with that problem. Chapter 17 comments on the social costs of the narcotics trade and related money laundering, plus the costs and benefits of various government policies that deal with these issues. It also offers some conclusions to the entire issue.

The Appendix contains a set of forty recommendations made by the multilateral government organization, the Financial Action Task Force, for government policies to deal with the problem of money laundering. While the scope of the recommendations is broader than only narcotics-related money laundering, the points are key steps that are being implemented by national governments increasingly in the past five years. Added cooperative efforts will make more of the recommendations into realities in the near future.

NOTE

1. The "cocaine cowboys" were Colombian nationals who earned fortunes in the drug trade and then pursued highly visible, luxurious lifestyles as dramatized in the television show *Miami Vice*. They often drove fancy cars, wore gold chains and rings, and partied on south Miami Beach and in Coconut Grove.

Part I

What Is Money Laundering?

Chapter 1

The Basic Money Laundering Arrangement

Money laundering is the means used to convert funds that proceed from illegal activities, such as narcotics trafficking, prostitution, casino gambling skimming, and many others, into financial uses that involve legal instruments (such as bank deposits, investments in stocks and bonds or real estate, etc.). The Financial Crimes Enforcement Network (FinCEN) defines money laundering in three parts, from the initial disposition of funds received for drugs to the concealment of illicitly gotten funds in the legal economy. Each step in the laundering process is described briefly here.

First, the *placement* of cash into the banking system is the step in which the money launderer disposes of the criminally derived cash proceeds. Cash is the most common medium of exchange used in drug transactions, and drug traffickers quickly accumulate large volumes of cash. Because checks, credit cards, and other non-cash means are commonly accepted in legitimate financial transactions in today's society, carrying out a large cash transaction may draw undesired attention to the criminal desiring to use his or her illegally acquired money. Accordingly, the drug trafficker will employ a money launderer to *place* the funds into the financial system unnoticed, or to physically transport the cash outside of the United States (for example, to Mexico or to Panama). Placement is the money laundering stage that is most vulnerable to detection.

After the funds enter the financial system, the launderer further separates the illicit proceeds from his or her illegal source through *layering*. This layering occurs through a series of financial transactions which, in their frequency, volume, and/or complexity, resemble legitimate financial transactions. For example, the use of a gold dealer who can sell gold to the drug trafficker enables the trafficker to obtain a financial instrument (gold) that can readily be converted into a bank deposit through sale to another gold dealer or user, and thus move another step away from the initial drug cash. (The gold dealer can even fake the existence of the gold by creating a false invoice, receiving and depositing the cash, and then sending money from his or her bank account to the drug trafficker through a wire transfer or by writing a check on the account.) The ultimate goal of the layering stage is to make tracing the funds back to their original criminal source as difficult as possible.

Finally, *integration* of the funds into the legal economy moves away from the financial transfers and into the realm of real or financial assets or purchases. This is accomplished in such a way that the funds appear to be derived from a legitimate source, such as earnings from an ongoing export-import business or the purchase of stocks and bonds by foreign investors. Integration is the final stage of the process of providing a legitimate explanation for the criminally derived funds. By this stage, distinguishing between licit and illicit funds is extremely difficult. Following successful integration, the launderer/trafficker may reinvest the profits into the criminal enterprise, invest in other assets, or use the funds to support a luxurious lifestyle.

GETTING DIRTY MONEY INTO THE BANKING SYSTEM

In the present context focusing on Andean narcotics trafficking, the most frequently observed means of money laundering are various methods to convert cash dollars into bank accounts. More completely, narcotics traffickers buy or grow their coca, marijuana, or opium poppies and pay their suppliers with funds, typically local currency (for example, pesos). They then ship the narcotics to customers, typically in industrial countries such as the United States or a European Union country. The traffickers subsequently sell the narcotics to local retailers, who pay with cash received from their customers/users. The net result is that the traffickers are faced with receipts of large amounts of cash payments, in many cases hundreds of thousands of dollars at a time. It is this cash that needs initial laundering (placement) into the legal financial system.

A common means for converting the direct cash payments for cocaine, heroin, or marijuana into bank deposits is through a process of *smurfing*, which utilizes numerous individuals who take portions of the cash and deposit it in small quantities (less than $10,000 per deposit, to avoid U.S. reporting requirements) in various banks. A single individual or smurf may deposit $100,000 in one day at two dozen banks, with each deposit under $5,000 to avoid attracting attention.

This smurfing activity was rampant during the 1980s and 1990s, as traffickers, especially in cocaine, earned huge sums from their sales in U.S. cities. As one might imagine, law enforcement officials tried to put a stop to this practice, but the traffickers responded creatively to the threat. For example, when banks were required to report cash transactions of $10,000 or more,[1] the traffickers simply instructed their smurfs to deposit amounts less than that, but to do it multiple times to achieve the same result.

Next, when banks were instructed not only to report cash transactions of

Figure 1.1
The First Steps of Money Laundering

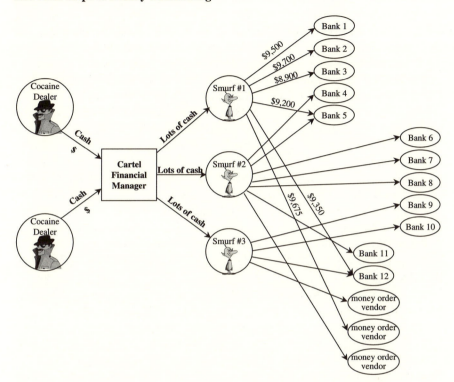

$10,000 or more but also to report *structured* transactions of multiple deposits of less than that amount (beginning in 1986), the traffickers switched to having their smurfs purchase monetary instruments, such as money orders, and then they deposited these items into bank accounts. By avoiding the direct use of cash in banks, the money launderers were able to shift the problem from the banks to providers of money orders and traveler's checks, such as Western Union, American Express, and the U.S. Postal Service. Now the authorities have to scrutinize the business of these issuers of monetary instruments, even though the basic process remains the same. The smurfs have to purchase money orders in amounts less than $10,000 to avoid reporting requirements, but the sellers of these instruments have thus far been less pressured by the authorities to look for suspicious transactions (see Figure 1.1).[2]

Of course, an alternative to this process is to funnel the cash through a business that typically would generate large volumes of cash from its ongoing activities. Large cash receipts are common in businesses such as gambling (from horse racetracks to casinos[3] to bingo parlors), jewelry stores, and cash transfer services.[4] Large cash receipts may also arise in more mundane businesses such as maid service, barber shops, lawn care, and other personal services. These businesses can "legitimately" claim the need to deposit large quantities of cash into banks on a regular basis and can comply with cash deposit reporting requirements as well. Obviously, having access to this kind of business is a gold mine for a narcotics trafficker, who can readily move drug money through it.

Of course, the process is not quite as simple for a barber shop or a lawn care service. When cash in amounts of $500 to $1,000 are involved, it is easy to justify these deposits as the outcome of a day's or a week's work in such a service. When the amounts reach $100,000 or more, it is a bit more difficult to believe that the barber (or maid service) is doing such a booming business to produce that level of cash on a weekly or even a monthly basis. For this reason, money launderers have to be more creative in arranging their false business fronts. Jewelry stores or gold vendors make better fronting operations, since sales of such items can easily arrive at sums of hundreds of thousands of dollars, and only a few transactions need to be claimed in cash to justify very large amounts of money.

Yet another common means for getting narcotics trafficking proceeds into the banking system is through physically shipping the cash overseas and then depositing it into bank offices in other countries. One can imagine the idea of taking the money to a less hostile environment to deposit it—but can you imagine carrying the literally tons of cash involved? A million dollars in $20 bills occupies a space about the size of two suitcases and weighs about 114 pounds. Even this would be somewhat manageable, but remember that the money launderer has to count the money, divide it into bills of the same denomination, and then ship it overseas—not to mention recounting it at the foreign bank location.

These concerns are compounded by another occasional complication that occurs in such business. Counterfeit bills sometimes surface in the context of money laundering, and then the launderer is faced with the embarrassment of explaining not only why he or she is carrying hundreds of thousands of dollars in cash but also why some of the cash is fake! This occurred in the early 1990s in Cali, Colombia, when a local source began producing counterfeit $100 bills. This outbreak of fake bills then hit the press, and people became very leery of accepting U.S. $100 bills—the preferred currency of the narcotics trafficker.

Despite these hindrances, money laundering has been widely practiced through the offshore financial center in Panama and Caribbean financial havens such as the Cayman Islands and the Bahamas.[5] Even today it is possible for a drug trafficker or money launderer to fly into one of these island locations with a Cessna or a Gulfstream airplane loaded with U.S. cash and deposit it into a bank with little concern about the source of the money. It is good business for the receiving bank, because the trafficker is likely to be very insensitive to the rate of return on the deposit but very concerned about getting the money safely into a bank. With no laws prohibiting the receipt of U.S. dollar deposits and no limits on the transfer of this cash to the United States (once it has been recorded in the bank), the process is just a mechanical one of moving the money back to the United States.

This activity has spread far beyond the financial havens of the Caribbean. During the 1990s, Mexico rose in importance as a laundering center as law enforcement became more severe in South Florida and to some extent in the Caribbean locations. In this case, the border towns along the Texas and California borders in particular have functioned as major money laundering sites. This business operates in parallel to the underground activity of Mexican nationals, who work and/or live in the United States and send funds to relatives in Mexico. The many thousands of undocumented and documented Mexican workers in the U.S. Southwest provide a solid base for the money transmitting business, taking dollars from the United States and passing them on as dollars or pesos to Mexican recipients. Narcotics trafficking cash fits in comfortably with this other business.

THE LINK BETWEEN THE NARCOTICS TRAFFICKER AND THE MONEY LAUNDERER

So far our discussion has focused on the process of getting money that is generated from illegal activity into the legal financial system. The process is a bit more complex than suggested, since the narcotics trafficker and the money launderer generally are not members of the same organization. That is, traffickers typically contract with various money laundering specialists who sell their services for a fee. The cocaine proceeds are earned by the trafficker, but they are moved into the financial system by the money launderers. Figure 1.2 portrays this relationship.

Notice that the money laundering takes place entirely outside of the direct participation of the narcotics trafficker—though of course using his or her money. The funds once deposited into the banking system may be kept in the United States, wire transferred to a less hostile jurisdiction such as Panama or Nassau, or used to invest in some other instrument, such as stocks or bonds. The trafficker could carry out this further transformation of the funds by directly instructing the bank to make the transfer or by having the money launderer carry out the transfer. At this stage, the money has already been laundered, so it becomes a question of putting it into a form that can be held safely until the trafficker wants to use it for some other purpose.

Also, once placed into a bank deposit, the money is very difficult to capture from the view of law enforcers. Unless the link to narcotraffic has been established and the funds frozen by this time, the laundered proceeds are free to be moved as any other funds in the system. If subsequent law enforcement leads to the linking of funds with narcotrafficking, then the trail may become hot once again. To preclude such tracing of funds, launderers and/or narcotraffickers may move through more elaborate schemes of money transfer (layering).

For example, a common shift in the laundering process that occurred in the

Figure 1.2
The Full Cocaine Trafficking–Money Laundering Cycle

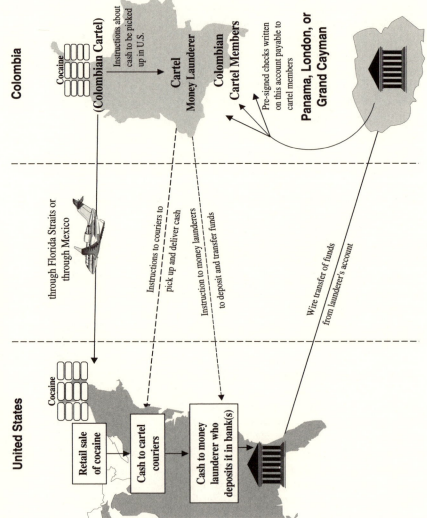

period after the indictment of General Noriega in Panama in Februrary 1988 used London or Luxembourg as a transfer point for funds. (Chapter 10 gives an example of this phenomenon, in the context of the Mora/Jurado smuggling organization and a group of Colombian clothing exporters.) The initial smurfing of cash into bank accounts in the United States proceeded as described. Then, to avoid the U.S. authorities, traffickers would often instruct the launderers to wire transfer funds to Panamanian bank accounts. With the U.S. indictment and subsequent fall of General Noriega, these accounts were seen (rightly) as more likely to be examined by U.S. enforcement agencies. For that reason, the funds were wire transferred to European destinations such as London, the largest financial center, and Luxembourg, another financial center with less rigorous enforcement.

This path led to the establishment of narcotraffickers' accounts in European financial centers. While less accessible physically than the close-to-home banking centers in Panama or Miami, the European locations have the desirable feature of not being subject to the direct supervision and surveillance of U.S. authorities. Also, as with other wealthy individuals, narcotraffickers find that diversification into non-U.S. financial instruments and currencies provides useful safety for their wealth by reducing currency risk and/or by obtaining higher returns than in the United States.

NON-U.S. DESTINATIONS FOR NARCODOLLARS

The movement of drug money into the legal financial system may likewise pass through other locations. The closest destinations for the Andean cocaine traffickers in Latin America are places such as Caracas, Venezuela, and Panama. A bit further away but still outside of the direct surveillance of the U.S. authorities are locations such as São Paulo, Brazil, and Buenos Aires, Argentina, which are desirable because they are large financial centers with millions of dollars of transactions taking place daily and physical cash moving in and out as well. Due to the relative lack of confidence in Latin American economies and government policies, local investors often prefer to hold some of their wealth in U.S. dollars, so they readily buy dollars in cash or in other financial instruments to protect this wealth. As a consequence, the supply and demand for U.S. dollars is quite significant, despite the fact that the dollar is not legal tender (except in Panama, where it is legally used in place of the domestic currency, the balboa, in daily business activity, and now in Argentina).

The volume of narcodollars in cash that moves through Latin American financial centers is probably much less than that which moves through the U.S. system, simply because the dollars are earned in the United States from drug sales, and they only leave the United States when physically shipped elsewhere. The funds moved through wire transfers or the shipment of monetary instruments such as money orders tend to go to locations such as major international financial centers in Panama or London, not to Buenos Aires. Even so, with major traffickers residing in Latin American countries, it is certain that some of their wealth is being held in Latin American financial markets. In the largest center of cocaine trafficking, Colombia, it is estimated that as much as 10 percent of ownership of private-sector assets in the country belongs to narcotraffickers. This translates into $U.S. 3 billion of banking system assets, though much of this wealth is held in real estate and other physical assets rather than in bank deposits.

NON-CASH LAUNDERING STRATEGIES

In addition to the means of shifting illegally earned dollars into the banking system, alternative uses of the funds include investment in normal financial assets such as stocks and bonds as well as not-so-normal assets such as airplanes, cars, and other expensive items. The normal process takes place usually through an initial entry into the banking system, as already described. Then the funds are transferred into a stockbroker account to purchase financial assets such as stocks, bonds, mutual funds, and even U.S. Treasury securities. Or, alternatively, the funds are spent to buy luxury items, such as cars and airplanes.

This use of the money is sometimes tied to the drug trafficking process. For example, traffickers have used drug proceeds to buy executive jet airplanes, which are then used to transport cocaine from Latin America to U.S. destinations. Depending on the willingness of the airplane vendor to accept cash payment, the narcodollars may pass directly from the street into the hands of the vendor, or they may be first laundered through a bank account and then spent to purchase the plane. Since it is not common to pay the $U.S. 1 million-plus cost of an airplane in cash, the trafficker will either have to pay a significantly higher price for the plane or launder the funds through a bank initially before making the purchase.

Another alternative that has been used in large-scale laundering schemes is to operate through an automobile dealership. The dealer claims automobile purchases in cash, when cars are actually being sold for normal means of payments such as checks or credit card payments. The cash is then brought in from drug sales and deposited into a bank as (falsely claimed) proceeds from auto sales. This process may also be accompanied by false invoicing, so some car sales actually are completely fictitious, except for the narcodollars that are brought to the bank. This scheme was used by the AutoWorld dealership in Miami during the early 1990s, when over $100 million was laundered for traffickers in the Medellin cartel.[6]

HYPOTHETICAL MONEY LAUNDERING SCHEMES

To clarify the often complicated steps involved in narcotics money laundering, it might be interesting to take a look at the business from the perspective of a direct participant. Let us take three or four points of view and see how the schemes might work.

Suppose that you are a U.S. drug trafficker earning $100,000 per week in revenues from your cocaine sales in Detroit. You get your supply of cocaine from an unknown but reliable Colombian source, whose intermediary is Eduardo. Every couple of weeks, Eduardo delivers to you the 35 kilos of cocaine, and you are instructed to give Jose LNU (last name unknown) the $500,000 that is the agreed-upon price. Faithfully, you collect cash from your group of distributors and pass on part of the money in a gym bag to Jose, keeping the difference between your cost and your sale price, which is about $100,000 each week. Now what do you do?

You cannot merely take the cash to a bank and deposit $100,000 unless you want the bank to file a Currency Transaction Report (CTR), in which you will declare the money to be proceeds of cocaine trafficking. This will land you in jail quickly. Instead, you might take the cash to 11 banks and deposit about $9,000 in an account in each one. If you have the time and the inclination, this could work. If any one of these banks figures that your activity is suspicious, and you do not have a good reason for the repeated cash deposits, then your actions may be recorded on a Suspicious Activity Report. Also, if anyone is able to discover and demonstrate that you are making the multiple deposits, you can be prosecuted for structuring cash deposits to evade the CTR reporting requirement.

Now you may decide to pass the buck, so to speak, and get together a team of employees to take the cash and deposit it in various banks. Alternatively, they could take the cash and buy traveler's checks or money orders, which you could then deposit in a bank. In either event, you could hire three people, have each one take $33,000 or so each week, and then make regular $3,000 deposits in 11 banks each. This activity could be reasonably easy to justify based on lots of made-up but plausible stories about obtaining the money from some retail business that generates the cash. If you go the route of buying money orders, you might also have to justify to the bank your reasons for bringing in multiple checks for deposit on a repeated basis, which could be viewed as suspicious at some point. None of this is foolproof!

How about another scenario? Suppose that, due to the consolidation of the banking industry in recent years, you are an unemployed banker. You are looking for work, and you have been trained to recognize money laundering schemes at your former bank. You also know of a few former bank clients whose suspicious activity had caused the bank to close their accounts. You contact each of them and find that one would be willing to have your help in laundering—I mean depositing into a bank—a few thousand dollars on an occasional basis.

Your first step is to decide whether or not you want to get into this illegal business. There are not too many stories of money launderers getting killed by cocaine cowboys, but there are quite a few stories of them ending up in jail. You figure that the odds of getting caught are, on average, only about 5–10 percent, and you are much better than the average launderer, so you decide to go for it.

The next step is to line up a plausible business activity that will enable you to open the bank accounts you want and to use them on a continuing basis, since you expect the business to continue for a while, at least until you get rich. A jewelry store is the best front you can think of, since it is the type of business that commonly attracts large cash transactions. You even figure that it might be fun to open a jewelry store, to have a "legitimate" front. Accordingly, you find a fairly quiet and somewhat run-down location in your hometown of San Francisco, and you rent a store that has been unoccupied for some time. You then check out the other jewelry stores in the area, ask a few questions, and invest $20,000 in a wide array of costume jewelry to get started. It is already apparent that you need help to run this business, along with the intended money laundry, so you recruit your girlfriend to help you.

Now you are ready to go. The contact offers to deliver to you an initial order of $50,000 of cash that he wants you to get into a Bank of America account in Los Angeles. You readily accept, and you receive the money on Tuesday. By Friday, you have deposited all of it in your bank account. On Monday, you transfer the funds to your customer's account at BofA in Los Angeles, keeping the 8 percent fee that had been agreed upon.

The customer is satisfied with this result and offers to deliver $75,000 the next day. You again agree, and subsequently carry out the deposits without a hitch and transfer the money to the requested account, this time at a different bank and location for your client. Eight percent isn't bad! You now have $10,000 of income for the past three weeks.

The plot thickens when your client asks you to take $250,000 the next week. How are you going to handle this large jump in "revenue" of your jewelry store? The initial answer is to open another bank account at a different bank in San Francisco, claiming the same jewelry business as the source of your cash. This way you can operate on a similar basis as with the initial bank, but now your volume can double without alerting anyone. Good idea!

You begin to have some doubts when you wonder what will happen if the client's cash conversion needs grow even bigger. Should you go to a smurfing operation? No, too risky. Should you try to structure deposits at more banks? Perhaps. How about taking the cash to Mexico? This idea was described in the newspaper last week, and although the Mexican drug trafficker involved had been apprehended and thrown in jail, it sounded like a good scheme. Your good friend Francisco is also unemployed, and he has spent a lot of time in his hometown of Tijuana.

Francisco agrees to take $60,000 with him to Tijuana and to deposit it in a bank there. Once the funds have been deposited, Francisco agrees to transfer them to the client's account for you. This works out just fine, and Francisco seems to be a good partner in the venture.

How about one final scenario? Suppose that you are a Colombian narcotics trafficker, and you are doing about $10 million a month in cocaine sales in the United States through your wholesale distributor there. It is a little late to start thinking about laundering the money now, and indeed you have already established a relationship with one money laundering organization that has successfully taken care of your needs over the past year. However, one seizure of cash and another seizure of cocaine have left you $2 million poorer, and you want a new arrangement to parallel your existing one, and perhaps eventually to replace it. Who do you go to?

The initial answer is probably to find another Colombian money exchanger who has an established infrastructure in the United States for receiving cash and getting it into banks there and abroad. There are a couple dozen of these entrepreneurs around, and in your hometown of Bogotá, you know three of them, all of whom have worked for you before and one now.

Since the level of law enforcement on this activity in Bogotá is minimal, you feel no need to look to money exchangers in other locations. By putting out feelers in the community, you find four additional recommended money exchangers. Your trusted lieutenant interviews each of them, checks on their reliability and prices, and picks one. After testing him out with successive deliveries of $250,000 and $600,000 over a three-week period, you are satisfied with the service. Now you have an additional alternative for laundering your cash. The only problem is the money exchanger's steep 15 percent charge for carrying out the process. It seems like only yesterday that the laundering organizations charged just 7–8 percent for the job. Even though the launderer is getting the funds into your Luxembourg bank account successfully, the costs of operating are getting out of control.

These examples show in sketchy form the kinds of concerns that each of the money laundering participants has and some alternatives that are available in the laundering process. While the examples certainly demonstrate the basics that money launderers encounter in their business, they also fail to show the incredibly large range of alternatives used to launder drug money and the many problems that these people run into.

IN SUMMARY

The process of laundering money derived from narcotics trafficking has developed from simple deposits of large quantities of cash into banks in U.S. cities to a highly complex series of transfers and conversions of drug-derived cash into non-cash monetary instruments and movement to locations in Europe and Latin America. The vast majority of the funds remain in the United States, since the greenback is legal tender in this country, and it must ultimately be used here in the legal financial system. Even so, the huge underground economies in many countries of the world, especially in Latin America, often use U.S. dollars as a major currency of transaction, so the dollars need not find their way back to the United States in a short period of time.

To see how the money becomes available for laundering, let us next take a look at the Andean cocaine business.

NOTES

1. This rule was established in the Bank Secrecy Act of 1970, but enforcement of the rule only became extensive during the 1980s.

2. The rules on reporting cash transactions have applied to non-bank institutions since the passage of the Money Laundering Suppression Act in 1994. Explicit attention is now paid to issuers of money orders and to casinos and other institutions that deal in large quantities of cash.

3. It is interesting to note that casinos are likely targets of money launderers, since they generate large cash inflows. At the same time, casinos are likely sources of money to be laundered, as unscrupulous managers may skim funds from casino operations and divert them to personal accounts. Thus, this business in particular is subject to large opportunities for money laundering activity.

4. Cash transfer has been the source of numerous money laundering cases in the United States during the past decade. Exchange houses that offer the service of exchanging dollars for foreign currency, as well as simple money transfer services that move dollars to distant locations, have been used in money laundering ventures. When large volumes of cash form the basic business, it is easy to see how more money could be added to the pot for laundering. This concern was addressed directly by the Money Laundering Suppression Act of 1994.

5. Panama and the Cayman Islands, along with the Bahamas, are well recognized havens for money laundering, as noted in the annual *International Narcotics Control Strategy Report* (U.S. Department of State, various years) country sections and in many other publications. See, for example, John Dinges, *Our Man in Panama* (New York: Random House, 1990).

6. Many of the known structures for money laundering are discussed in Financial Action Task Force (FATF), *Report on Money Laundering Typologies* (Paris: FATF, February 10, 1999).

Chapter 2

The Andean Cocaine Business

INTRODUCTION

In 1993, Colombian law enforcement agents finally caught up with Pablo Escobar, and a SWAT team shot him to death in a brief gun battle in his home in Medellin. He died, appropriately enough, with a pistol blazing in each hand. Escobar represented the last key member of the Medellin cartel leadership, after the Ochoa brothers, Jorge Luis and Fabio, had been captured and jailed, Jose Gonzalo Rodriguez Gacha (the Mexican) had been gunned down in a battle with police, and Carlos Lehder had much earlier been captured and extradited to the United States, where he remains in prison. This seemed to mark the end of an era of violent and open opposition to Colombian laws and flamboyant lifestyles of the chief cocaine cowboys.

At the same time law enforcement moved to focus on the Cali cartel, another group of large-scale cocaine traffickers was headquartered in the rival city of Cali, to the south and west of Medellin in the valley of the Cauca River. The Cali cartel members followed a much lower visibility strategy of operations, seldom calling attention to themselves by staging Hollywood-style assassinations or using the media to brag about their exploits. Despite this lower profile method of operating, the Cali cartel was recognized as a major force in the drug trafficking industry, and law enforcement agents had long ago identified the key leaders of the group. During 1994 and 1995, most of the leaders of this group, including Jose Santacruz Londoño, Gilberto Rodriguez Orajuela, and Miguel Rodriguez Orajuela, were captured and jailed as well.

From these brief stories it may appear that the problem of Andean cocaine trafficking has been largely resolved. Indeed, no new cartels in Colombia have achieved the market share or notoriety of the Cali and Medellin groups of the recent past. However, the amount of coca leaf produced in the Andean countries was approximately 264,000 metric tons in 1997, compared to 291,000 tons in 1987 and to similar quantities in the intervening years[1]—still clearly in the same range. There seems to be no noticeable decline in cocaine trafficking, despite the successful efforts to stop the drug cartel leaders.

Law enforcement officials in both Colombia and the United States are quick to point out that, while the two cartels have diminished in importance, they have been replaced by numerous smaller organizations. And in fact, while the cartels received much of the notoriety for cocaine trafficking, all along there have been dozens or more trafficking groups of various sizes. The cartels never really controlled the cocaine trafficking, though they were for some time the dominant players in the wholesale business between growers of coca in Bolivia and Peru and consumers in the U.S. market.

The highly uncentralized nature of the cocaine trafficking business is underscored by the dozens of successful law enforcement efforts that capture kilos upon kilos of cocaine and regularly find new suppliers on one end of the shipments, and often new distributors on the other. Even in the heyday of the Medellin cartel, shipments of cocaine that were known to enter the United States were often combined cargoes of multiple traffickers, shipped together to take advantage of the availability of a trustworthy pilot or boat captain.

The new reality of cocaine trafficking in the Americas shows a much wider range of traffickers and money launderers, from Argentina to Mexico, and in the Caribbean as well. Figure 2.1 depicts this business.

The Andean countries no longer dominate the transportation phase of the cocaine business, though they still monopolize the production of coca leaf. In the mid-1990s, the focus of shipments moved to Mexico and the Caribbean islands away from Colombia. The largest trafficking groups still appear to be based in Colombia, but Mexican cartels are now growing to challenge that dominance.

As a result of the deterrence efforts of various governments, the traffic of cocaine has moved significantly into Mexico instead of passing directly from Colombia into the United States. This shift in logistics reflects the U.S. government's somewhat successful effort to reduce the amount of cocaine shipped through South Florida, which led the nation in imports of this drug during the 1980s. Since about 1990, approximately two-thirds of Andean cocaine shipments have entered the United States through the Southwest from numerous points in Mexico. This border is much more difficult to patrol for U.S. law enforcement than the more limited one in Florida, and once in the United States, the drugs are shipped just as efficiently throughout the country.

By the end of the 1990s, greater law enforcement efforts in the Southwest led to a return to greater cocaine trafficking through the Florida Straits, and also through the Caribbean islands, such as the Dominican Republic and the Bahamas. The Dominican Republic was especially useful to traffickers, since it is located only a few miles from Puerto Rico, which is part of the United States.

Figure 2.1
Cocaine Flows, Latin America to the United States

Once drugs have been smuggled into Puerto Rico, it is more difficult to interdict them, since there is no requirement for passing through customs when products are shipped to the mainland from there. This phenomenon produced a large-scale increase in law enforcement efforts in Puerto Rico in the late 1990s.

Traffic in heroin from Colombia became substantial in the early 1990s, so overall drug trafficking through Colombia is unquestionably still a huge and growing multinational business. Heroin has not at all replaced cocaine in the traffickers' activities, but it has definitely supplemented the former drug. Estimates show that Colombian opium production reached 65 metric tons in 1995 (compared to 2,650 tons produced in Myanmar that year). The dollar value of this production is approximately 10 times that of a similar weight of cocaine, but even so the impact in Colombia or in the United States is fairly small at this time.

To offer a better idea of how the money arises from drug trafficking, it is helpful to look at the process of producing and distributing cocaine. This way, the laundering of money derived from trafficking can be seen as the final step in the business chain.

PRODUCTION OF COCA

The process of producing coca leaves, from which cocaine is derived, is such a traditional agricultural story that it is hard to believe that this crop is at the center of such a controversy. Coca production is known to have taken place at least from the time of the Inca empire in Peru, Ecuador, and Bolivia.[2] The coca plant grows wild in the Andes Mountains, and chewing coca leaves was found to have the effect of satisfying the appetites of manual laborers as they worked during the time of the Incas. Similarly, the leaves were found to reduce the feeling of nausea that often affects hikers at high altitudes. In the high Andean Mountains, this relief was and is a welcome solution to an age-old problem.

Beyond these uses, coca leaves have traditionally been used to make coca tea, which has a pleasant if somewhat bitter taste. The tea produces the same stomach-settling effect and in general serves as a means of warming tea drinkers at altitudes in the high Andes, ranging up to 15,000 feet above sea level. These uses of the coca plant have been known and followed by the Andean Indians for more than five centuries.

Coca production takes place in many locations along the Andes Mountains. Figure 2.2 shows the estimated concentrations of coca production in the Peruvian and Bolivian Andes. During the 1980s, when the cocaine business became so huge globally, the Upper Huallaga River Valley in the region around Tingo Maria apparently became the largest coca production center in Latin America. Figure 2.2 supports this assertion, and stories abound concerning the coca growers and cocaine cowboys in the Alto Huallaga region (described later in this chapter). It was boasted in 1990 that Tingo Maria had the largest concentration of auto dealers in Peru, while the town had no paved streets! Despite drug

Figure 2.2
Coca Cultivation in South America

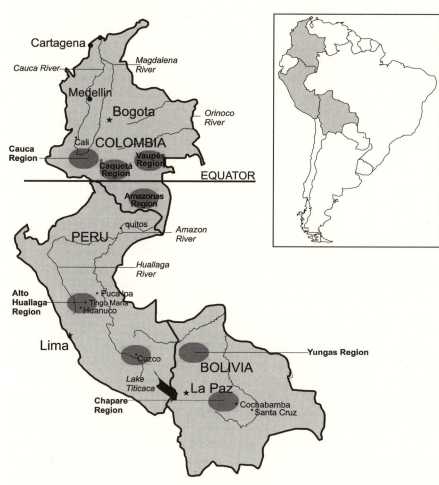

enforcement, crop substitution, and other government efforts, the Alto Huallaga region was the world's leading supplier of coca leaf in the late 1990s.

Coca plantations have become numerous on the eastern slopes of the Andes in Peru, away from law enforcement's ability to intervene and building on the traditional crop. The same is true for the Cochabamba region in the Andes of Bolivia, where Incas long grew coca for domestic consumption. With the boom in the cocaine business, many farmers have been lured into producing enormous quantities of coca. In both countries, the isolation of the growing regions continues to hinder attempts by government authorities to slow the drug trafficking and also to substitute alternative crops (which generally are so meager in value that they really do not substitute at all).

One of the really striking difficulties of fighting the drug war is the problem of reducing the production of coca plants. Obviously, governments would like to see farmers grow coffee or potatoes or some other crop rather than coca. The economics involved are staggering. By growing coca plants, farmers earn about 10 times what they could obtain from other crops. Table 2.1 shows an estimate of these alternatives in the early 1990s.

The crops shown in the table are more exotic alternatives; if traditional potatoes or coffee were included, these would demonstrate an even worse comparison to the profitability of coca growing.

To get a better idea of how money and products move through the cocaine production and distribution chain, let us next look at the process through which coca plants grown in the Alto Huallaga, Chapare, or other regions in the Andes, are converted into cocaine hydrochloride.

The processing of coca into cocaine involves two major steps. First, the narcotic must be extracted from the coca leaves. Initially the leaves are dried to remove as much moisture from them as possible. Then they are soaked in a solution of sulfuric acid and water. The liquid is drained off from large soaking vats and mixed with an alkaline solution of calcium oxide or sodium carbonate. A thick, alkaloid, whitish fluid is the result. This fluid is mixed with kerosene to take out impurities, and as it settles, the kerosene separates from the top of the mixture.

In a second stage of processing, the mixture is placed into another solution of water and sulfuric acid, producing a clear liquid. Sodium carbonate is again added to the liquid, and a dirty white substance settles from this process—coca paste. The paste is then placed on a fine cloth mesh to allow the liquid to drain off. The coca leaves are run through this process two or three times to ensure that the maximum amount of coca paste is produced. This is then the raw material from which cocaine is subsequently distilled.

The second major step in cocaine production is mixing the coca paste with acetone, ether, and hydrochloric acid. This process is extremely corrosive, so high-quality containers and processing equipment are needed. Glass or porcelain containers are the most commonly used to allow for the successful processing of the coca paste. The paste is first dissolved in acetone and then heated to evaporate the acetone. The cleaned coca paste is then remixed with a solution of ether, more acetone, and hydrochloric acid. From this process a whitish sludge appears. It is then heated by placing lightbulbs above the mixture. When it dries, it becomes a white powder—cocaine hydrochloride.

This second stage of cocaine processing was done principally in Colombia during the 1980s, when cocaine production was more limited and centralized. The Colombian distributors of the drug typically received coca paste in air shipments from Peru and Bolivia and then carried out the second stage of processing into cocaine hydrochloride in their own laboratories in isolated locations in Colombia.

As shown in Figure 2.1, the cocaine flows mainly into Florida. The distri-

Table 2.1
Internal Rate of Return (net cash flow/costs) for Some Alternative Crops

Crop	Internal Rate of Return	Data Area	Data Year	Year at Positive Cash Flow
Coca	165.4			2
Annatto (Achiote)	20.0	Pucallpa, Peru	January 1992	4
Araza	20.2	Pucallpa, Peru	November 1991	6
Banana (export)	53.8	Colombia		2
Black pepper	22.9	Pucallpa, Peru	January 1991	5
Macadamia	54.0	Colombia		5
Orange	29.0	Pucallpa, Peru	February 1992	5
Passion fruit	41.9	Peru	March 1992	4
Peach palm	82.2	Ucalyi, Peru	January 1992	2
Pineapple	40.3	Pucallpa, Peru	January 1992	2
Rice	22.3	Tarapoto, Peru	March 1992	1

Sources: H. Villachica, C. Lescano, J. Lazarte, and V. Chumbe, "Estudio de Oportunidades de Inversion en Desarrollo e Industrializacion de Culti-vos Tropicales en Pucallpa," Perfil de proyecto para la planta de coloantes naturales y para la planta de conservas de palmito, Convenio FUNDEAGRO, Region Ucayali, Lima, Peru, 1992.

Coca—H. Villachica, "Crop Diversification Bolivia, Colombia, and Peru: Potential to Enhance Agricultural Production," contractor report prepared for the Office of Technology Assessment, April 1992.

Banana—J. Arbelaez, "El Cultivo de Platano en Zona Cafetera, Federacion National de Cafeteros," Bogotá, Colombia, 1991, p. 40.

Macadamia—O. Rincon, "El Cultivo de Macadamia, Federacion National de Cafeteros," Bogotá, Colombia, 1990, p. 29.

bution channels have expanded greatly in recent years to pass through the Southwest into the United States and from Colombia directly to European countries.[3] Also, as law enforcement efforts complicate traffickers' production of cocaine hydrochloride, the processing laboratories have spread to additional locations in Colombia, Brazil, Peru, and Venezuela.

NOTES

1. These data come from the U.S. Department of State, *International Narcotics Control Strategy Report* (Washington, D.C.: U.S. GPO, March 1998).

2. Edmundo Morales, *Cocaine: White Gold Rush in Peru* (Tucson: University of Arizona Press, 1989). It is traced back 4,000 years in W. Bray and C. Dollery, "Coca Chewing and High Altitude Stress: A Spurious Correlation," *Current Anthropology* 24, no. 3 (1993), pp. 269–282. This section describing the cocaine production process is largely based on Morales' detailed discussion of the subject.

3. Cocaine trafficking in Europe has also moved through Eastern European points such as Warsaw and Prague. This phenomenon has become signficantly greater since the fall of the Berlin Wall in 1989.

Chapter 3

Foreign Exchange Black Markets
in Latin America

A main avenue for laundering drug dollars is through the foreign exchange (forex) black market in many countries of the world. In Latin America in particular, these markets are well established and fairly widely used. The entrance of drug money into the black markets simply expanded their use rather than creating new markets. In this context we address two questions. The first is: What are these black markets, and how do they work? The second is: How are black markets used by money launderers in the process of converting drug money into clean investments or purchases? Let us start by defining the markets and their characteristics.

WHAT ARE FOREIGN EXCHANGE BLACK MARKETS?

A foreign exchange black market is a market for the purchase/sale of foreign currency that operates outside of the legal financial system of a country. That is, it is an illegal source (or use) of foreign currency that buyers and sellers choose to utilize for various reasons—from tax evasion to operation of a contraband business to escape from onerous and sometimes conflictive governmental regulations.

A foreign exchange *black* market can be distinguished from a foreign exchange *parallel* market. Parallel markets are simply foreign exchange markets that operate parallel to the official market that is carried out through a country's commercial banking system. Parallel markets may be legal or illegal, but they involve non-bank middlemen. Black markets are parallel markets that explicitly operate outside of the legal rules in the country.

The illegality of the black market typically stems from the fact that transactions are not reported to legally required governmental agencies, such as the tax authorities. Even if a non-bank—such as a travel agency or a stockbroker firm—operates a legally constituted business of that type, such a firm may operate a sub-rosa business in foreign exchange without reporting it, thus one reason for the existence of a foreign exchange black market is tax evasion by the users.

Another reason for the existence and illegality of forex black markets are the limits on uses of foreign exchange imposed by some governments. In some cases, residents of a country are forbidden to hold foreign exchange (with specified exceptions) as part of a national macroeconomic policy. Under this condition, residents may need to resort to the black market to obtain foreign exchange for whatever purposes they may have, such as buying restricted imports or holding funds in a more desirable currency. A third reason for the existence and illegality of forex black markets stems from the ban on moving funds overseas imposed by some governments. To limit balance of payments problems and to conserve foreign exchange reserves, governments may try to restrict outgoing foreign investment. To escape this limitation, residents may resort to the black market for obtaining foreign exchange *and* for moving it overseas.

A final reason for the existence and illegality of forex black markets is that they may be used for financing illegal business activities such as narcotics production and distribution or prohibited weapons transactions. Since dealing in these contraband goods may involve transfers of funds through black markets, the purchase or sale of currency in the black market may link other users to such contraband activities.[1]

In sum, there are four principal reasons—individually or in combination—why foreign exchange black markets may involve illegal activities: (1) they are unreported and thus they evade taxes; (2) they specifically evade rules that prohibit holding foreign exchange; (3) they specifically evade rules that prohibit taking funds overseas: and (4) they are used in the financial side of illegal businesses such as narcotics production and distribution.

These black markets are contrasted to parallel markets where non-bank firms are specifically *permitted* to deal in foreign exchange. For example, in Chile, residents have been allowed to hold dollar-denominated financial instruments and non-banks have been allowed to deal in foreign exchange since 1981.[2] Likewise, in the Dominican Republic, since 1987 the foreign exchange market has been essentially open—although some black market foreign exchange dealing is known to be done in conjunction with the operation of the underground economy. In Colombia, residents have been permitted to buy and sell foreign exchange freely since 1993, though the black market remained very active at the end of the 1990s.

WHY DO FOREX BLACK MARKETS EXIST?

The reasons for the existence of forex black markets can be grouped into two categories. First, they are often responses to governmental intervention in the official foreign exchange market to prevent some activities (such as flight capital). Second, they are used to operate underground economies, especially in smuggling contraband goods.

A forex black market typically results from a current or past balance of payments imbalance (deficit), so it is associated with an excess demand for foreign exchange in the local market. This problem is a target of governmental policy, both in terms of controls on access to foreign exchange (which produced the black market) and of domestic monetary policy (which often produces inflation and in turn adds pressure for the devaluation of currency). Thus the underlying balance of payments deficit is the crucial issue that policy makers confront, with the black market being one of its symptoms.

This deficit may be the result of several factors, separately or in combination. An excessive rate of monetary growth can lead to inflation. If that inflation is higher than in other countries, it will lead to demand for foreign currencies, both to buy foreign goods and to hold wealth in more stable currencies. A less developed country may find that investors' confidence in the economic prospects of the country is weak, and that they consequently look to place their investments in other countries (and therefore in other currencies); this again produces excess demand for foreign exchange and contributes to the capital flight that such countries want to avoid. Even without the previous two factors, a country may find that goods produced locally are perceived as inferior in quality to similar goods produced abroad, thus demand arises for foreign exchange to buy higher quality foreign products.

Even if all aspects of the demand side of the foreign exchange market are initially balanced by supply, the equation still may be broken by a decline in prices of key export goods (such as primary minerals and metals and agricultural products, the major export goods of Latin American countries). When an externally driven price cut is imposed on the exporting country (such as in Colombia and Brazil when world coffee prices fall, or in Mexico and Venezuela when world oil prices decline), export earnings drop, and a net demand for foreign exchange is produced.

This situation of excess demand for foreign exchange occurred frequently in the post–World War II period, when governments encountered foreign exchange shortages due to speculation against the currency, when export earnings dropped, and when domestic purchasing exceeded domestic output. In all Latin American countries, this phenomenon occurred frequently during the 1970s and 1980s, and even into the 1990s in various instances (especially in relation to the December 1994 Mexican peso crisis).

A second variety of reasons for the development of parallel, particularly black, markets is the existence of an underground (or informal, or gray, etc.) economy in the country. When some participants in the local economy choose to enter into illegal business activities—such as the sale of contraband products—then a need arises for financial services that circumvent the legal financial system. The underground economy can be as "harmless" as the street vendor phenomenon that exists widely throughout less developed countries. Street vendors obtain contraband products ranging from toothbrushes to television sets and sell them from unregistered places of business (usually from sidewalk tables or literally in the street). Another type of underground economy that has become quite significant in a few countries is the trafficking of narcotics. This business involves products such as marijuana, heroin, and cocaine, which are illegal to produce and sell in the first place, thus requiring the use of nonconventional means of production, distribution, sale, and financing. The black market in foreign exchange provides both of these kinds of business access to the foreign exchange needed to purchase the contraband goods—and in the case of narcotics, the access to local currency that can be bought in exchange for foreign currency earned in the drug trade.

To summarize, foreign exchange black markets exist for two fundamental reasons. First and most widely discussed, governmental controls on access to foreign exchange push into the black market those potential users of the foreign exchange market who are not permitted to buy foreign currency in the official market if they choose to make forex purchases despite government-imposed controls. The second reason has to do with the operation of the underground economy. When some businesses are set up and operated outside of the legal system in a country, they need financial services that circumvent the legal financial system. Thus, a foreign exchange black market develops alongside a domestic financial black market in which transactions are not reported and governmental controls are not able to be applied. This situation is especially notable in narcotics trafficking, in which drug traffickers sell foreign exchange earnings into the black market, and various users of the market buy that foreign exchange.

WHO PARTICIPATES IN FOREX BLACK MARKETS?

Foreign exchange black markets are a form of release valve for those who desire to buy or sell foreign currency but who are prohibited from doing so on terms that they are willing or able to accept in the official market. Since these markets are illegal by definition, they must be operated surreptitiously, often out of the back rooms of businesses that carry out "normal" activities in their front offices or from second-floor offices that likewise are hidden from public view. In addition, just as there are street vendors of products obtained in the underground economy, there are street vendors of foreign exchange. These intermediaries carry out retail sales and purchases of foreign currency in typically small quantities, often at locations frequented by foreign tourists or where large concentrations of underground business exist.

Retail vs. Wholesale

The forex black markets really can be divided into three or four levels of activity, from the small retail transactions of street vendors to the sophisticated, often large-scale transactions of financial intermediaries that provide multiple financial services to their clients. Although the exact characteristics of the market vary to some extent among the countries in Latin America, many clear patterns are discernible. For the sake of consistency, we will use the term *cambista* to refer to the intermediary in the black market foreign exchange transaction, whether the cambista is a large or a small firm, an individual, or somewhere in between. The *casas de cambio*, as larger forex intermediaries are often labeled, are included under this heading.

The retail level of black market foreign exchange dealing is dominated by thousands of small cambistas that follow the street vendor model. They typically operate visibly on city streets near concentrations of potential users such as tourists and contraband sellers. One or a few owners of the retail forex business employ runners who hawk dollars and/or local currency at prices that are completely market determined, in competition with other vendors in close proximity. Typical transactions exchange $U.S. 10–100 for the equivalent of local currency. The owner provides runners with cash to sell and instructions on pricing. The runners try to maximize their own gains while producing sufficient earnings to satisfy their owner/suppliers. The business tends to be cutthroat, and the margins are razor thin. (The street market in the Miraflores district of Lima provided a fascinating lesson in this business during the late 1980s and early 1990s.)

PERU'S BLACK MARKET IN 1990[3]

Figure 3.1 depicts the various participants in Peru's forex black market and its geographic structure. Notice that the black market is centered in Lima, the capital and largest city in Peru. Much of the supply of dollars into the market apparently comes from narcotics trafficking, as discussed below. Additional sources of foreign exchange in the black market include contraband sales at the northern and southern borders with Ecuador and Chile, respectively. Depending on the exchange rate between the Peruvian sol and Ecuador's currency, many different products will be cheaper on one side of the border or the other. When the sol is undervalued relative to the Ecuadorean sucre, then contraband (unreported) exports from Peru take place and sucres as well as dollars enter the Peruvian black market. The same phenomenon occurs on the Chilean border— and the volume of business is greater, since Chile is a larger country and has maintained an overvalued peso frequently during the past two decades.

Demand for dollars in the black market comes primarily from Peruvian businesses that wish to purchase imports without passing through the official market and from Peruvian individuals or families who want to hold part of their wealth in dollars, especially overseas.[4] Thus these purchasers of dollars demand both the foreign exchange and often the placement of the funds in the United States (again depicted in Figure 3.1).

The foreign exchange black market is operated largely through a group of "wholesale" cambistas, or foreign exchangers, who buy dollars where they are

Figure 3.1
Peru's Forex Black Market Participants and Geographical Structure

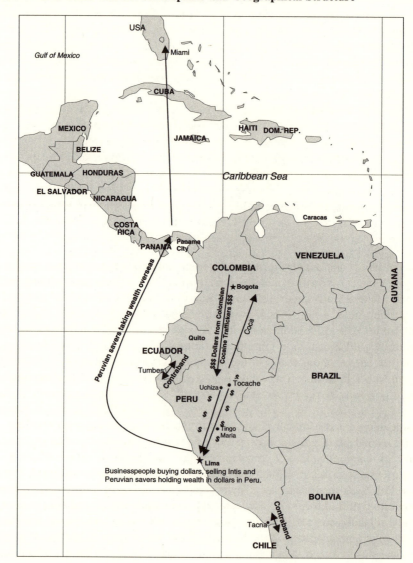

available and sell them to customers for delivery in Peru or elsewhere. These large cambistas account for the greatest part of the value transacted in the market; the thousands of small-scale cambistas who operate on the streets of Lima (including Calle Ocoña) and in stores and homes account for the vast majority of transactions in the market.

The market is linked directly to the Upper Huallaga (pronounced "Why-agga") River Valley, where about 70 percent of Peru's coca farming is carried out.[5] The coca farmers sell both coca leaves and processed cocaine paste to Colombian narcotics traffickers. The Colombians fly airplanes into several villages in the valley (such as Uchiza, Tocache, and several others[6]), where they exchange U.S. currency for the coca. The Peruvian growers in turn sell the dollars to local foreign exchange houses, that in turn sell them to Lima-based exchange houses[7] for local currency. Only about a dozen exchange houses exist in the Upper Huallaga River Valley, and they sell dollars to a similarly small number of large exchange houses from Lima. The Lima-based currency exchangers fly airplane loads of soles to Uchiza, Tocache, and so on when news of a coca shipment to Colombia is received in Lima. They then return to Lima with the dollars several hours later.

THE ALTO HUALLAGA REGION

The "Alto Huallaga" is the southernmost part of the valley cut by the Huallaga River, which winds northward near the town of Tingo Maria (in the Juánuco province) and eventually contributes to the formation of the Amazon River in Iquitos. While Tingo Maria is the only populous town in the area, and one that is to some extent controlled by the Peruvian government, the rest of the region is wild and lightly populated, with only a handful of villages, such as Tocache and Uchiza. The central part of the river valley begins around Tarapoto in the San Martin province.

The Alto Huallaga region lies on the eastern slopes of the Andes Mountains. It is mostly jungle terrain, with no highways and few roads. The total population of the region is less than 100,000 people. The land is not particularly fertile, though it is suitable for the coca plant, which grows quickly and produces coca leaves that can be converted into cocaine as early as the first year of growth.

The economy of this region is almost completely dependent on the production and sale of coca leaves, cocaine paste, and cocaine hydrochloride to Colombian narcotraffickers. No other source of foreign exchange exists there. Before 1980, coca was one of several crops grown locally for local consumption, along with corn, rice, cocoa, and coffee. The farmers lived largely at the subsistence level, having little contact with the rest of the world. It was only with the development of the U.S. market for cocaine that this region came to the attention of outsiders.

The coca leaves that are grown by local farmers are generally processed into cocaine paste in the same region. Until about 1990, most of the processing into cocaine hydrochloride took place in laboratories outside of Peru, depending on the Colombian narcotraffickers. An increasing portion of Peruvian exports is being processed into cocaine hydrochloride locally because of interdiction efforts in Colombia during the late 1980s and early 1990s.

At this stage of the black market, U.S. dollars have been brought into the country by Colombian narcotics traffickers and have been received initially by

Peruvian coca farmers who sell the dollars through their local exchange houses to Lima exchange houses for soles.[8] The Lima exchange houses then complete the process of integrating the dollars into the Peruvian economy by selling them to clients at the wholesale and retail levels. Pictures of cambistas waving calculators to show their price quotes and selling dollars in the street (especially the famous Calle Ocoña) have by now become commonplace in local and international newspapers.

In addition to the direct sale of currency to local clients, the large exchange houses also provide the service of transferring funds to foreign destinations such as Panama and Miami. In this case, the foreign exchange market operates so that the client delivers soles in Lima and subsequently receives a deposit into his or her bank account in the foreign location specified. The charge for this additional service was on the order of 1–2 percent of the value exchanged.[9]

NARCOTRAFFIC SIZE ESTIMATES

The volume of dollars in the narcotraffic grew dramatically over the past decade. Estimates for the period 1980–95 are shown in Table 3.1. Note that most of the value was earned through sales of cocaine base (the intermediate, partly processed product), while smaller percentages of the total came from the sale of coca leaves (the raw material) and the sale of cocaine hydrochloride (the final product).[10]

Estimates from other studies of the value of sales of coca and derivatives during 1988 and 1989 remained consistently above $U.S. 1 billion per year. (See, for example, ½ de Cambio, March 1–15, 1990; p. 18.) Campodónico estimated the income for Peruvian narcotraffickers at $U.S. 1.548 billion for 1988[11]; and Perú Económico (February 1989; p. 6) similarly estimated it at $U.S. 1.5 billion for that year. This value can be compared to the total legal foreign exchange earnings of Peru for 1989 of $U.S. 3.5 billion.[12] Estimates for the late 1990s are similarly greater than $U.S. 1 billion per year, based on annual coca production that has stabilized at about 130,000 metric tons (producing about 300 metric tons of cocaine).

BLACK MARKET SIZE ESTIMATES

While no precise measure of the volume of money transacted in the foreign exchange black market can be obtained, several estimates are available. A major complication in the estimation process is that Peru's economy became greatly "dollarized" during the 1980s; that is, many people chose to hold significant parts of their wealth in dollars, and prices of many goods were quoted in dollars rather than local currency. This situation, along with the availability of dollars through the black market, resulted in a huge supply of dollars being held in cash in Peru. For example, Perú Económico estimated that in 1988, about $U.S. 700 million in cash coming from coca/cocaine exports was retained within Peru.

Table 3.1
Peru's Income from Coca and Cocaine Exports

Year	Value in Millions of Current U.S. Dollars
1980	753
1981	766
1982	642
1983	581
1984	662
1985	989
1986	863
1987	865
1988	544
1989	532
1990	398
1991	388
1992	434
1993	379
1994	540
1995	405

Source: Roberto Steiner, "Colombia's Income from the Drug Trade," *World Development* 26, no. 6 (1998), p. 1026. Based on *International Narcotics Control Strategy Report* annual production estimates.

The black market itself may be the initial source of dollars that enters the system, but these dollars subsequently function as part of the de facto money supply in Peru, without necessarily being exchanged for soles at any time.

One estimate of the size of the total foreign exchange black market was presented in *Actualidad Económica* (October 1988, p. 8). It showed approximately $U.S. 380 million exchanged by retail cambistas and about $U.S. 700 million exchanged by wholesale dealers, for a total of $U.S. 1.08 billion in 1988. A similar estimate of $U.S. 1 billion was given by the director of Peru's Instituto Nacional de Plancación (INP), as quoted in *El Nacional* (July 14, 1987). These figures, when compared to the value of narcodollars entering Peru, demonstrate that virtually all of the black market supply of dollars indeed came from coca and cocaine exports.[13]

Participants (wholesale cambistas) in the black market estimated that the black market in 1988–89 was comprised largely of narcodollars. Because some of the narcodollars earned by Peruvian traffickers are probably *not* brought into the country, it is likely that a portion of the black market is supplied from other sources. Using the *Perú Económico* estimate of narcodollars brought into the country with the $U.S. 1 billion estimate of black market size gives a proportion of about 70 percent for narcodollars in 1988—an estimate that was supported through interviews of large-scale cambistas. During 1990, a decline in sales of coca and derivatives led to a reduction in dollar inflow from that source, at the same time Peruvians were repatriating significant amounts of their overseas dollars to meet financial needs domestically under the severely depressed conditions of the time. Thus, for 1990, the final estimates of narcodollars supplying the black market may be under the estimates for the previous few years.

A second heading of retail vendors of black market foreign exchange are businesses that have other primary operations but that offer small-scale foreign exchange services on the side. Many hotels and restaurants, travel agencies, and other businesses provide such services to retail clients. It should be noted that in some contexts (such as in Colombia and Peru during the late 1980s and early 1990s), hotels and travel agencies were able to obtain official licenses to deal in foreign exchange with their retail clients. These licenses required the hotels and travel agencies to turn in the foreign exchange received from clients to the Central Bank. Thus, often a business would operate a licensed forex business that complied with the rules—as well as an additional forex business that was not licensed or recorded. This dual form of operation may enable the cambista to reduce the risk of being caught and penalized by the government.

A third category of black market foreign exchange intermediary is the medium or large-scale cambista. Although no classification can be exact due to the changing market conditions and difficulties in obtaining complete information about these dealings, a general rule seems to be that a large-scale cambista in the late 1980s and early 1990s was one that transacted deals of $U.S. 10,000 or more per transaction. A medium-sized cambista would be one that operates in the range between the street vendor and the large-scale exchange house. Since the medium-sized cambista really just combines the characteristics of the small- and large-scale cambistas, no separate discussion of this category is offered.

Large-scale cambistas frequently operate legally incorporated financial services firms such as securities brokerages or travel agencies. Then, on the side, they offer services such as the purchase/sale of large quantities of foreign exchange, the transfer of funds to overseas locations, and even overseas investment services—through their unrecorded cambista ventures. These large-scale cambistas tend to dominate the market by moving the largest quantities of funds and being able to influence the price of foreign exchange by their activities in the market.

In their foreign exchange businesses, the large-scale cambistas often function in a manner similar to banks when they deal in large individual transactions. If a request to buy or sell more than (approximately) a million dollars in currrency is received from one client, large-scale cambistas frequently organize "syndications" of cambistas, each one of which takes a participation in the deal and profits accordingly. For example, a transaction for $U.S. 1 million may be sold to nine more cambistas by the initial one; each one takes $U.S. 100,000 to place among clients, and they all share the risks involved.

Types of Users

As noted above, the forex black markets have traditionally been discussed as responses to governmental controls on access to foreign currency in the official market. This implies that users of the black market in this context are business-people who seek to carry out "normal" activities such as importing when import controls prohibit their access to otherwise legal goods or investing when they wish to hold their funds in foreign currency (and often physically outside of the country). These users indeed form an important part of the demand side in black markets in all of the countries studied here, though they are only part of the whole picture. In addition, it is often difficult to define what "otherwise legal" goods really are. (Are they just imported goods in general? If so, what does the tax and tariff evasion employed by such importers do to the "otherwise legal" concept?)

Three broad classes of participants in the foreign exchange black markets can be distinguished at the initial level of analysis. First, there are the intermediaries (cambistas), who make the market by offering to buy and sell foreign exchange from clients who seek such a service. Second, there are people who want foreign exchange outside of the official forex market. These people include importers and those who want to invest in foreign currency instruments—who in each instance choose to use the black market rather than the official market due to restrictions, costs, or other reasons. Third, there are suppliers of foreign exchange into the black market. These suppliers include overseas residents who choose to send funds to their families or friends through the black market, contraband exporters who fail to declare their exports to the authorities, exporters who underinvoice their sales (thus leaving some of their earnings over-seas), and importers who overinvoice their purchases (thus leaving excess foreign exchange overseas beyond what they need to pay suppliers). Suppliers also include those smugglers who earn forex for their overseas sales of narcotics and who choose to remit some of the earnings to their home country. On both the supply and the demand sides are *arbitrageurs*, who seek to take advantage of differences in returns from holding their funds in domestic currency or dollars and shifting back and forth as interest and exchange rates change to favor one side or the other.

Links to the Underground Economy

The foreign exchange black market generally has been importantly linked to the underground economy of Latin American countries during the past two dec-ades (e.g., De Soto, 1986). This sector is estimated to constitute upward of 50 percent of the total economy in countries such as Bolivia, Paraguay, and Peru, and probably not much less in the rest of Latin America during the period 1970–90. The difference between this use of the foreign exchange black market and the previous one is that here the users are not operating at all in the legal economy. That is, all of their business, defined as underground, is unreported to the government, so no taxes are paid, no legal restrictions are applied, and generally the market is "free" except for the risk of getting caught and facing sanctions.[14] The underground economy is the broad extension of the foreign exchange black market to the whole economy, in that it is illegal under the country's laws and enables users to carry out business transactions without any official records.

COLOMBIA'S FOREX BLACK MARKET[15]

The black market in foreign exchange in Colombia has several layers of participants. On the demand side, participants range from individuals seeking to convert $U.S. 10–20 equivalent of pesos into dollars all the way to large companies buying millions of dollars with their pesos. On the supply side, they range from *contrabandistas* seeking to sell their excess dollars received for sales of coffee or cattle in the underground economy all the way to narcotraffickers seeking to convert millions of dollars that they have earned from sales in the United States (and elsewhere). The intermediaries in most black market transactions are cambistas (foreign exchange dealers), who exist at both the retail and wholesale levels.[16] Figure 3.2 depicts the various participants in the market and its geographical structure.

The simplest form of black market foreign exchange dealing occurs in the street market, in which a small-scale cambista buys dollars from foreign tourists and sells them pesos, typically in quantities of $U.S. 10–100. Similar retail transactions occur in the contraband markets in all major Colombian cities, where the "San Andresitos" (contraband sellers[17]) sell imported electronics, clothing, and many other articles that have been brought into the country without being registered, and thus without paying taxes or tariffs.

Another form of simple black market dealing, and the one that stimulated market growth in the late 1960s and early 1970s, is contraband trade along the borders with Venezuela and Ecuador. Since both of these neighboring countries are major oil exporters, they were able to maintain overvalued currencies for many years, making imports cheaper without affecting oil exports (priced in U.S. dollars, not local currency). In contrast, Colombia depends heavily on commodity exports of coffee, sugar, bananas, and cut flowers—all of which respond to local currency devaluations. Frequently during the past 20 years the Colombian peso has been sufficiently low in value relative to the bolivar or sucre, so that all kinds of products were cheaper to import into Venezuela and Ecuador from Colombia than to obtain locally. Thus contraband in many products, especially cattle, moved into these countries in exchange for bolivars, sucres, and

Figure 3.2
Colombia's Black Market Participants and Geographical Structure

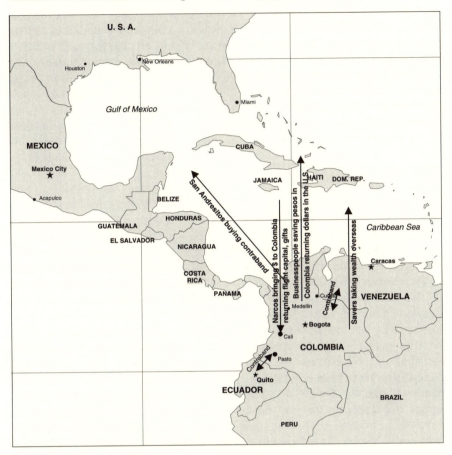

dollars. As Venezuela and Ecuador have moved to establish more open foreign exchange regimes, this kind of contraband trade has slowed greatly.

More complex transactions occur when Colombian gold or emeralds are shipped abroad and paid in dollars. In this case, when the contraband exporter wants to sell dollars to buy pesos for use in Colombia, the foreign exchange originates abroad. The exporter then must either transport the dollars in currency or check to Colombia or contract with a cambista for sale of the dollars to some buyer who can pay with pesos in Colombia. In this case, the dollars are transferred to the buyer's account in the United States, and the pesos are delivered to the gold or emerald exporter in Colombia, either in the form of a check or another financial instrument.[18]

Even more complex transactions occur when the seller of dollars is a narcotics trafficker. In this case, a wide variety of means is used to deliver the dollars.

One mechanism is to physically carry the dollars to Colombia for direct exchange for pesos in cash. Another mechanism is to convert the dollars into money orders or checks in the United States and then ship them to Colombia for sale in exchange for pesos. A third means of selling the dollars is to deposit them in bank accounts in the United States and to arrange for bank transfers into accounts of the purchasers who reside in Colombia. In this instance, the dollar buyer specifies a bank account to receive the dollars and pays in pesos, typically with a personal check, to the cambista in Colombia.[19] Many more processes have been devised to convert the narcodollars into pesos—just as the narcotraffickers have devised numerous means for holding and moving their dollar wealth outside of Colombia. A notable feature of these transactions is that most of the situations involve delivery of dollars *outside* of Colombia, in exchange for pesos delivered in Colombia.

Note that on the demand side for dollars are Colombian businesspeople who seek to obtain dollars for their business needs and/or to hold their wealth over-seas. These two motives are the basic ones in virtually all of the demand for black market dollars. The businesspeople who buy these dollars tend to deal in fairly large quantities of money (e.g., $U.S. 10,000 or more), and they generally want to keep the dollars outside of Colombia.

The cambistas who service the large-scale black market generally operate out of offices or homes, though without advertising, since the business must be carried out surreptitiously.[20] While the Colombian government has been unable to stop the black market from functioning, it nevertheless penalized hundreds of participants each year during the 1980s and 1990s. Penalties ranged from forfeiture of the funds that were passed through the black market to imprison-ment if the funds were not delivered to the Central Bank.[21] Many of the large cambistas function legally as stock market brokers. These firms then operate money exchanges on the side, however, seven of the major securities brokers were forced to leave the Bogotá stock exchange in 1988, apparently due to their business in black market foreign exchange.[22]

In summary, these categories of participants constituted the black market in Colombia at the end of the 1980s and into the early 1990s:

1. Supply

a. narcotraffickers (60%)

b. contrabandistas selling coffee, gold, emeralds (10%)

c. contrabandistas selling cattle, etc., to Venezuela and Ecuador (10%)

d. transfers of funds to their families by Colombians living abroad (10%)

e. return of flight capital by Colombian businessmen (10%)

2. Demand

a. importers who want to escape the costs and bureaucracy of buying dollars legally (30%)

b. importers who buy contraband products (San Andresitos) (25%)

c. wealthy Colombians who want to hold their wealth abroad (30%)

d. Colombians wanting to hold dollars in Colombia (15%)

The percentages noted on both sides of the market represent market shares.

MARKET SIZE ESTIMATES

While no precise measure of the volume of money transacted in the foreign exchange black market can be obtained, several estimates are available. The remarkable point about these estimates is their similarity.

The Central Bank has tried to estimate the size of this market as part of its concern with monetary policy in Colombia. The black market obviously detracts from the Bank's ability to regulate the amount of foreign exchange in the economy and has a consequent impact on domestic money holding as well. A recent estimate of the dollar volume of black market exchanges during the 1980s shows that approximately $U.S. 1.775 billion per year entered the black market from narcotraffic and about $U.S. 525 million per year from return of capital flight (including contraband sales of gold, cattle, and other products overseas).[23] This study presented estimates of annual funds flows for 1981–88; here an annual average for the period is constructed. The drug flow data are taken from reports by the National Narcotics Intelligence Consumers Committee (NNICC), a U.S. governmental organization that pools information from the law enforcement agencies that deal with narcotics trafficking.

A second study using the NNICC data with several additional adjustments reflecting factors such as narcotics seizures, crop eradication, money confiscations, and others produced similar estimates of narcotics money flows on the order of $U.S. 2.5 billion–3 billion per year during the 1980s, according to Eduardo Sarmiento's 1991 study.[24] This study also discussed but did not estimate the sources of black market dollars coming from the underinvoicing of exports (in which case, exporters leave some portion of their receipts overseas, and some of those funds may enter the black market) and from remittances of Colombians living abroad. Sarmiento's estimate was that approximately $U.S. 900 million to $U.S. 1.3 billion of narcodollars annually enter the black market and the "Ventanilla Siniestra" (discussed below). Unfortunately, he did not estimate the size of the total black market.

A third study, presented at a recent conference on the underground economy in Colombia, produced an estimate of $U.S. 2.5 billion in total dollars generated by the underground economy, of which approximately $U.S. 1.5 billion were from narcotics trafficking.[25] According to this study, the rest of the foreign exchange entering Colombia through this market resulted from contraband exports of coffee, cattle, cement, and other products.

A fourth study was undertaken by Miguel Urrutia in 1990.[26] He obtained an estimate of $230–$250 million for the value of narcodollars entering Colombia in 1988. His estimate was based on the value of dollars entering the Colombian Central Bank's Ventanilla Siniestra, which is not part of the black market, though it does probably receive large quantities of narcodollars, as explained by Urrutia. That is, in addition to the narcodollars entering Colombia through the black market, more funds enter through the Ventanilla Siniestra, which are part of the official market in Colombia. Urrutia explicitly did *not* consider the dollars delivered outside of Colombia to Colombians who buy them in the black market, since his concern was to examine the impact of the drug traffic and funds flows *in* Colombia.[27]

A fifth estimate of the size of the black market was obtained from a large-scale cambista in Bogotá. In an interview in May 1990, this cambista estimated a daily volume of about $U.S. 25 million, or about $U.S. 6 billion for 1990. This is about twice the previous estimates, which mainly covered the mid-1980s. He also estimated that about 60 percent of the supply of black market dollars comes from narcotraffic—and virtually all of that (85%) are dollars delivered *outside* of Colombia. The remainder of the foreign exchange supply was estimated as 20 percent from return of flight capital, 10 percent as contraband sales on the Venezuelan and Ecuadorean borders, and 10 percent as transfers to their local relatives from Colombians living overseas. This cambista also provided estimates of the distribution of demand for foreign exchange in the black market: about 30 percent of the foreign exchange was estimated to be purchased by each of three categories of market user—general importers, by San Andresitos, and by flight capitalists—while about 15 percent of the demand was by Colombians wanting to hold dollars domestically in Colombia.

Salomon Kalmanovitz[28] presented an estimate that Colombian narcotraffickers earned approximately $U.S. 4.0 billion per year during the 1980s, of which $3.5 billion annually were taken into Colombia. This estimate, if coupled with the previous estimates of black market volume, would show virtually all of the black market dollars coming from this one source, a result that clearly is overstated due to the known supply of dollars from the other sources mentioned. Kalmanovitz assumes that almost all of the traffickers' incomes are remitted to Colombia, which is at odds with all other discussions of this phenomenon. He estimates that a total of $U.S. 4.6 billion per year were used by various classes of black market purchasers of foreign exchange, *including* the Ventanilla Siniestra. This would place the narcotraffic as providing 76 percent of the total black market dollars.

In sum, it appears that more than $U.S. 2.5 billion entered the black market annually by 1989, and perhaps significantly more according to the estimation of the large cambista. About two-thirds of this money came from narcotics sales, principally cocaine sold in the United States.[29]

Estimates of the earnings of Colombian narcotraffickers in the 1990s show a fairly stable pattern, despite the ebbs and flows of interdiction efforts and crop eradication. Roberto Steiner[30] estimated total earnings of the Colombian traffickers at about $U.S. 2.3–2.7 billion annually during 1990–95. He asserts that *most* of the earnings are repatriated to Colombia, though this is doubtful based on the sources. Thus Steiner estimates that perhaps $U.S. 2 billion of cocaine, marijuana, and heroin income were brought into Colombia annually in the 1990s—a number somewhat higher than estimates for the 1980s, but only due to his assumption of a greater degree of earnings repatriation to Colombia.

THE VENTANILLA SINIESTRA

A foreign exchange phenomenon in Colombia during the 1980s and early 1990s that did *not* belong directly to the black market but similarly took place outside of the commercial banking system was the Central Bank's practice of receiving foreign currency from individuals without demanding evidence of its source. Similar to an amnesty program for failure to comply with taxes or other governmental regulations, this program operated through a special window at the Central Bank, where anyone could turn in foreign exchange and receive pesos without incurring a penalty. Foreign exchange was received from various types of holders, such as tourists and professionals who provided personal services abroad, donations from abroad to Colombian families, and remittances of dividends and interest from abroad. While the program operated since before the narcotics boom, all estimates show that it became a major recipient of narcodollars during the 1980s. This means of exchanging foreign exchange for pesos became known as the Ventanilla Siniestra (the sinister window) because of the suspected narcotics connection.[31] Annual flows of funds that took place through this account are listed in Table 3.2.

Note that the value of services and remittances by 1989 had grown to over $U.S. 1 billion, indicating that a large quantity of narcodollars probably was being "laundered" through this vehicle. These funds did *not* enter the black market, since they were used by the Central Bank for official purposes such as financing legal imports and paying foreign debt—and these dollars were sent physically to the U.S. Federal Reserve Bank branch in Houston, Texas, for crediting the Colombian Central Bank's account.[32,33]

CLASSIFICATION OF COUNTRIES

To clarify the concept of the foreign exchange black market in another way, it may be useful to categorize Latin American countries as those having extensive, highly visible black markets versus those where legal parallel markets operate and where the black market is more limited to contraband buyers and sellers. For example, Chile, Mexico, and Uruguay for many years have permitted non-bank financial institutions to provide foreign exchange services. These intermediaries provide parallel markets for foreign exchange. On the other hand, Brazil, Colombia, and Jamaica until fairly recently have much more strictly limited foreign exchange dealing to the commercial banks (with approval from

Table 3.2
Flows of Funds through the Ventanilla Siniestra

Year	Millions of U.S. Dollars
1970	129.5
1971	130.1
1972	147.2
1973	232.7
1974	253.8
1975	465.4
1976	876.6
1977	922.6
1978	960.1
1979	1,452.6
1980	1,281.2
1981	1,008.2
1982	720.0
1983	489.9
1984	403.8
1985	570.7
1986	945.3
1987	1,042.6
1988	1,149.0
1989	1,269.3

Source: Banco de la Republica series on "servicios laborales y otros."

the Central Bank), and these latter countries had largely relegated non-banks to operating in the black market if they wished to deal in foreign exchange at all. Since the broad economic opening in Latin American countries, beginning in about 1990, almost all have opened up the foreign exchange market to permit legal parallel markets and largely open official markets.

Appendixes 3.1, 3.2, and 3.3 list selected Latin American countries and sketch some of their key foreign exchange rules and regulations in 1985, 1990, and 1995. Note that the most common kinds of restrictions appear on exporters' ability to use their forex earnings and on residents' ability to buy foreign exchange for travel abroad. In addition, most foreign exchange dealing has been restricted to commercial banks, which function under the close supervision of the Central Bank. By 1990, a wave of economic *apertura* had swept Latin America, and many of the restrictions had disappeared. Virtually across the board, residents were permitted to buy and sell foreign exchange freely and to transfer their funds overseas through the legal channels (implying that they would pay taxes on income related to these flows *and* that they would be potentially scrutinized by the Central Bank in the forex transactions). This is particularly notable when comparing Appendixes 3.1 and 3.3, in which the third appendix shows the even less restricted situation by the end of 1995.

KEY CONCLUSIONS

One clear conclusion from the analysis of forex black markets in Latin America is that there is little likelihood of eliminating the foreign exchange black market, even when a government opens the official market to relatively free access. Because of the existence of huge underground economies in each of the countries in the region, the forex black market will continue to fill a need for those people involved in contraband trade as well as narcotics trafficking. In addition, in Brazil, economic policy has not achieved the degree of openness of the other countries, so the black market in that instance fulfills the role of providing alternative access to foreign exchange when the government otherwise heavily restricts it.

When Latin American governments restricted access to foreign exchange in the official market, especially during the 1970s and 1980s, black markets provided an important escape valve for excess demand for foreign currency. Because of a fairly generalized lack of confidence in governmental policies on foreign exchange (and indeed in other areas) during that period of time, recourse to forex black markets was frequent and widespread. The escape valve function of black markets—namely, that these markets enabled firms to obtain needed imported commercial and industrial inputs that were inhibited by bureaucratic rules and enabled individuals to place their wealth in desired forms such as foreign exchange-denominated instruments—may very well have served a useful purpose in the development of these countries. After the sweeping economic apertura throughout Latin America in 1988–91, it is no longer clear whether that function is needed as much.

The institutional structure in each of the countries shows several levels of intermediaries in the forex black market, from street vendors to sophisticated financial intermediaries offering multiple services to their forex clients. The black market exchange rate is largely determined in the wholesale market, where large transactions of many thousands of dollars are the rule. This fact leads to the unfortunate side effect that the small number of market makers in the wholesale market in each country possesses monopolistic pricing power. In fact, repeated market manipulation has been reported in Peru and Colombia, and it is likely to occur elsewhere as well. Nevertheless, the wholesale and retail markets function fairly freely in each instance, and they appear to operate based on logical economic principles (such as maintaining purchasing power parity).

The cost of operating in the black market seems to be fairly well captured by the premium on the exchange rate; that is, the cost of buying dollars in the black market exceeds the cost of buying in the official market by the spread between the two rates. The somewhat higher transactions costs (e.g., search costs, enforcement costs) in the black market are approximately offset by the higher fiscal costs (i.e., paying taxes) of operating in the official market. On the other hand, the risk of operating in the forex market is much more substantial in the black market, since typically funds are committed by the buyer and seller before the intermediary makes payment (in the wholesale market). Also, there is some risk of getting caught and of incurring sanctions, which typically range from a small fine to forfeiture of the funds involved in the black market transaction being sanctioned. According to the available evidence, the ex post risk of getting caught was insignificant during the 1980s and 1990s.

Some interesting economic aspects of the black markets can be seen by carefully examining the key price in the markets, or the exchange rate itself. The black market exchange rate is largely determined by relative inflation. That is, the difference in inflation in the Latin American country versus inflation in the United States (since the dollar is the reference currency) explains over 90 percent of the variation in monthly black market rates for most countries over the 20-year period 1970–90.[34] An additional important influence on the rate in the southern cone countries came from the interest differential on similar financial instruments in the given country versus the United States. Another key influence on the rate in the Andean countries came from the export of the coca leaf and its derivatives during the 1980s.

The overall economic structure of the black markets in Latin America is complex. Unquestionably, the structure must be considered in two periods: the 1970–90 period of generally high regulation and bureaucratic delays versus the period of the 1990s, when liberalization produced fairly open economies throughout Latin America, and foreign exchange markets were characterized by their burgeoning growth and diversification rather than by their limitations.

Appendix 3.1

Foreign Exchange Markets in Latin America: Country Characteristics, 1985*

Country	Government Rules on Forex	Government Rules on Funds Transfer
Argentina	export proceeds must be surrendered to the Central Bank residents may own forex	legal, parallel market permitted to sell forex at free rate residents may hold overseas financial accounts
Brazil	Brazilians may buy up to $300 per month for travel abroad export proceeds must be surrendered to the Central Bank residents may not own forex banks may not hold short positions in forex	residents may not hold overseas accounts
Chile	forex must be transacted within +/–2 percent of the official rate residents may buy at most $1,500 per trip for travel abroad export proceeds must be surrendered to the Central Bank	residents may hold overseas financial accounts
Colombia	all forex proceeds must be surrendered to the Central Bank most forex payments require prior approval by the Central Bank residents may not own forex residents may buy at most $3,000 per year for foreign travel	residents may not hold overseas financial accounts
Dominican Republic	all forex proceeds must be surrendered to the Central Bank; surtaxes charged on exports commercial banks may transact freely in forex residents may own forex in local bank accounts exchange rate set by the Central Bank	residents may hold overseas financial accounts
Ecuador	export proceeds must be surrendered to the Central Bank residents may own forex and hold local forex-denominated accounts	residents may hold overseas financial accounts

Appendix 3.1 (continued)

Country	Government Rules on Forex	Government Rules on Funds Transfer
Jamaica	export proceeds must be surrendered to the Central Bank residents may not hold forex residents may buy at most $56 per year for tourism abroad and $125 per day for business abroad	residents may not hold overseas financial accounts
Mexico	export proceeds must be surrendered to the Central Bank exchange houses may operate in forex with no restrictions residents may own forex and hold local forex-denominated accounts	residents may hold overseas financial accounts
Peru	export proceeds must be surrendered to the Central Bank residents may own forex and hold local forex-denominated accounts	
Venezuela	imports must obtain licenses and permits to purchase forex export proceeds must be surrendered to the Central Bank	residents may hold overseas financial accounts

Note: These are generalized rules on forex dealing in each country. Many exceptions and special cases exist to complicate the application of these rules, and additional rules also apply.

*In every country in 1985 there were at least two exchange markets, an official controlled market for specified transactions and a financial or free market for all other transactions. The official market had a lower peso/dollar exchange rate and was often subject to taxes and fees.

Sources: International Monetary Fund (IMF), *Exchange Regimes and Exchange Restrictions* (Washington, D.C.: IMF, 1986, 1991); International Currency Analysis, *World Currency Yearbook* (New York: International Currency Analysis, 1988–89 edition).

Appendix 3.2

Foreign Exchange Markets in Latin America: Country Characteristics, 1990

Country	Government Rules on Forex	Government Rules on Funds Transfer
Argentina	exchange transactions must be carried out by entities licensed to provide this service unified foreign exchange market	residents may freely transfer funds abroad and hold overseas accounts
Brazil	Brazilians may buy up to $4,000 per month for travel abroad export proceeds must be surrendered to the Central Bank residents may not own forex unless involved in international business banks may not hold short positions in forex more than $5 million total controlled exchange market for some transactions, free market for all others	residents may not hold overseas accounts
Chile	forex must be transacted through registered entities export proceeds must be surrendered to the Central Bank controlled exchange market for some transactions, free market for all others	residents may hold overseas financial accounts
Colombia	forex must be transacted through registered entities controlled exchange market for some transactions, free market for all others	residents may transfer funds abroad and hold overseas accounts
Dominican Republic	essentially unchanged from 1985	residents may hold overseas financial accounts
Ecuador	essentially unchanged from 1985	residents may hold overseas financial accounts
Jamaica	export proceeds must be surrendered to the Central Bank residents may hold forex-denominated bank accounts	residents may not hold overseas financial accounts
Mexico	essentially unchanged from 1985	residents may hold overseas financial accounts

Appendix 3.2 (continued)

Country	Government Rules on Forex	Government Rules on Funds Transfer
Peru	exchange transactions must be carried out by entities licensed to provide this service	residents may freely transfer funds abroad and hold overseas accounts
Venezuela	exchange transactions must be carried out by entities licensed to provide this service unified foreign exchange market	residents may freely transfer funds abroad and hold overseas accounts

Note: These are generalized rules on forex dealing in each country. Many exceptions and special cases exist to complicate the application of these rules, and additional rules also apply.

Sources: International Monetary Fund (IMF), *Exchange Regimes and Exchange Restrictions* (Washington, D.C.: IMF, 1991); International Currency Analysis, *World Currency Yearbook* (New York: International Currency Analysis, 1990–93 edition).

Appendix 3.3

Foreign Exchange Markets in Latin America: Country Characteristics, 1995

Country	Government Rules on Forex	Government Rules on Funds Transfer
Argentina	exchange transactions must be carried out by entities authorized and regulated to provide this service	residents may freely transfer funds abroad and hold overseas accounts
As of 12/31/95	unified foreign exchange market	
	exchange rate is pegged to U.S.$	
	residents may own forex	
	export proceeds can be retained in a "foreign currency account"; such funds need not be repatriated	
	foreign investor access to domestic exchange markets is unrestricted	
	freely negotiated swap and forward transactions are allowed in any currency	
Brazil	no limit on purchase of forex for travel abroad by Brazilian residents	certain residents may hold overseas accounts
As of 2/29/96	export proceeds must be surrendered to the Central Bank	transaction tax of up to 5 percent for foreign borrowing converted into domestic currency
	exchange rate is managed float	
	transaction tax of up to 25 percent for exchange operations for service imports	
	residents may not own forex unless involved in international business	
	banks may buy/sell forex on a forward basis, but must settle within 180 days	
	limits for the short positions of banks determined by June and December financial statement net assets	
	dual (commercial and tourist) exchange rate market; transactions are by authorized entities	
Chile	dual (official and informal) forex market; in the official market,	residents may hold overseas financial accounts

Country	Government Rules on Forex	Government Rules on Funds Transfer
	transactions are through licensed entities	
As of 4/30/96	exchange rate is adjusted based on selected indicators	overseas remittances can be made freely
	residents can own foreign currency	
	an exchange subsidy is available for certain debt obligations	
	exchange proceeds from exports are not subject to surrender	
	any person can purchase up to U.S.$15,000 per month in forex for invisibles	
	windfall receipts from Corporacion del Cobre (CODELCO) copper exports must be deposited at the Central Bank, otherwise no export surrender requirements	
Colombia	forex must be transacted through registered entities	residents may transfer funds abroad and hold overseas accounts
As of 6/30/96	export proceeds of goods that are repatriated must be surrendered in some cases	
	controlled exchange market for some transactions, free market for others	
	residents may deal in forward transactions; residents may not hold foreign currency	
Dominican Republic	exchange rate pegged to U.S.$	residents cannot maintain overseas financial accounts
As of 12/31/95	export proceeds must be surrendered to the Central Bank	
	residents cannot hold foreign currency	
	commercial banks must sell excess forex to the Central Bank after 48 hours	
Ecuador	two exchange rates: free market rate, Central Bank official rate	residents may hold overseas financial accounts

Appendix 3.3 (continued)

Country	Government Rules on Forex	Government Rules on Funds Transfer
As of 12/31/95	forward exchange transactions are permitted	
	residents may hold foreign exchange	
	export proceeds must be surrendered to authorized financial entities	
Jamaica	residents and nonresidents may hold forex-denominated bank accounts	residents may hold overseas financial accounts
As of 12/31/95	export proceeds need not be surrendered	
Mexico	exchange houses may operate in forex without restrictions	residents may hold overseas financial accounts
As of 12/31/95	a forward exchange market exists	no limitations apply to the transfer of forex
	residents may own forex and in some cases hold local forex-denominated accounts	
Peru	residents may own forex and hold local forex-denominated accounts	residents may freely transfer funds abroad and hold overseas accounts
As of 12/31/95	commercial banks may operate in the forward market	
	export proceeds need not be surrendered	
Venezuela*	exchange transactions must be carried out by entities authorized to provide this service	residents may freely transfer funds and hold overseas accounts
As of 7/31/96	exchange rate is managed float	
	residents may own foreign currency	
	the state petroleum company, PDVSA, must surrender export proceeds, otherwise no surrender requirements	
	unified foreign exchange market	

Note: These are generalized rules on forex dealing in each country. Many exceptions and special cases exist to complicate the application of these rules, and additional rules also apply.

*Several significant changes occurred on 4/22/96, such as the unification of two exchange markets and the elimination of export surrender requirements.

Source: International Monetary Fund (IMF), *Exchange Arrangements and Exchange Restrictions* (Washington, D.C.: IMF, 1996).

NOTES

1. This issue has been an especially interesting one in the context of money laundering of Andean cocaine revenues. The U.S. government has confiscated funds owned by numerous people who purchased it in the Colombian or Peruvian currency black markets during the late 1980s. Businesspeople who buy what turns out to be narcotics-related money have found themselves required to demonstrate that they had no knowledge of the source of that money (i.e., that they were "innocent owners") in order to obtain the return of their money. See, for example, *U.S. v. 85 Designated Accounts Containing Monies Traceable to Exchanges for Controlled Substances*, Civil Case #90-1203, Southern District of Florida.

2. Nevertheless, Chile's government prohibited the *transfer* of funds overseas, except for specified purposes, such as servicing foreign debt, until 1988, thus the transfer of funds overseas by non-bank foreign exchange dealers was illegal until the end of the 1980s.

3. Much of this section is based on published articles in the Peruvian press and Peruvian scholarly journals, as cited in the text. An especially detailed exposition appears in Juan Briceño and Javier Martínez, "El Ciclo Operativo del Trafico Ilicito de la Coca y Sus Derivados: Implicaciones in la Liquidez del Sistema Financiero." In Federico Leon and Ramiro Castro de la Mata, *Pasta Basica de Cocaina* (Lima, Peru: CEDRO, 1989), pp. 216–279. Corroborative evidence comes from detailed interviews with Peruvian cambistas in Lima and with wholesale users of their services. Both large-scale foreign exchange dealers (who operate in transactions of approximately $U.S. 10,000 or more) and retail dealers were interviewed, as well as other intermediaries involved.

4. See, for example, "La Paridad y el Dólar Ocoña," *1/2 de Cambio* (October 1–15, 1988), p. 6.

5. This estimate comes from Ines Astete and David Tejada, "Elementos para una economía política de la coca en el Alto Huallaga" (New York: United Nations, October 1988) (Document # AD/PER/86/459 OSP-PNUD). Briceño and Martínez ("El Ciclo Operativo," p. 264) estimate that by 1987, the Alto Huallaga Valley accounted for about 80 percent of total coca production in the country.

6. The Upper Huallaga River Valley runs through the eastern Peruvian jungle, on the slopes of the Andes Mountains. Beginning near the town of Tingo Maria, the river flows northward through the villages of Uchiza, Tocache, Juanjui, Tarapoto, and several even smaller settlements before joining the Marañon River and flowing into Iquitos, where it contributes to form the Amazon. In the Upper Huallaga Valley, traditional crops such as corn, rice, and beans are still grown for local consumption. The only product that generates any foreign exchange earnings in this region is coca.

7. The exchange houses in the Upper Huallaga Valley also sell dollars directly to local branches of commercial banks (except during the July 1987–September 1988 period, when the banks were not permitted to deal with cambistas), which in turn transport the cash to Lima for local use and/or sale to the Central Bank.

8. This process was described in personal interviews with large-scale exchange house operators and corporate treasurers in Peru.

9. This description is based on published accounts of the Peruvian drug trade (e.g., "El Mercado y el Poder," *Actualidad Economica* [October 1988], pp. 8–10), and on interviews of wholesale exchange house managers in Lima during 1990.

10. Briceño and Martínez ("El Ciclo Operativo") actually estimate that $U.S. 1.974 billion were earned by Peruvian narcotraffickers in 1987, of which about $U.S. 500

million were placed directly into overseas accounts without entering Peru. The 1987 estimate is corroborated by a study published in *Actualidad Economica* (October 1988, p. 8), which states that 1987 narcotics exports generated at least $U.S. 1.56 billion for Peruvian traffickers. Two other studies cited in *Actualidad Economica* (November–December 1988, p. 54) estimated a 1988 cocaine-related income for Peruvian narcotraffickers of about $U.S. 1.2 billion.

11. Humberto Campodónico, "La Politica del Avestruz," in Diego Garcia-Sayan (ed.), *Coca, Cocaina, y Narcotrafico* (Lima, Peru: Comision Andina de Juristas, 1989), p. 238.

12. Source: International Monetary Fund, *Direction of Trade Yearbook, 1990* (Washington, D.C.: IMF, 1990), p. 320.

13. This point is made explicitly in the *Actualidad Economica* article (October 1988, p. 8). In *1/2 de Cambio* (October 1–15, 1988, p. 6), it is estimated that over $U.S. 1 billion enter the black market from narcotraffic, while an additional supply of dollars comes from contraband sales to Ecuador and Chile.

14. Again, it should be noted that participants in the black market for currencies or the underground economy in general may operate legally registered businesses at the same time they engage in the unreported, underground activities. Only their unreported business in the black market/underground economy is being characterized here.

15. Much of this section is based on detailed interviews with Colombian cambistas in Colombia and in the United States. Both large-scale foreign exchange dealers (who operate in transactions of approximately $U.S. 10,000 or more) and retail dealers were interviewed, as well as other intermediaries involved. Additional evidence comes from published records of money laundering prosecutions of Banco de Occidente and Bank of Credit and Commerce International.

16. Useful descriptions of the market and its various participants appear in Angela Cuevas, *La Otra Cara del Dolar* (Bogotá: Tercer Mundo, 1986) and Hector Mario Rodriguez, *Los Piratas de la Bolsa* (Bogatá: Peyre, 1988).

17. The San Andresitos are named for the Colombian island of San Andres, which lies off the coast of Nicaragua in the Caribbean Sea. This island is a free port into which products are imported without taxes or tariffs. Subsequently, much of the merchandise is smuggled into the Colombian mainland for sale as contraband by the people from San Andres. Over time, the label "San Andresito" has come to mean any contraband seller in Colombia; in the large cities, these vendors are actually gathered into specific districts where they ply their wares side by side.

18. See, for example, Guillermo Perry, "Minas y Energia," in *Colombia Siglo XXI*, Vol. 2 (Bogotá: Ediciones Impresores, 1990), pp. 129, 159–60.

19. This process of laundering narcodollars is described in detail in the documents presented by parties in the Banco de Occidente legal case. Criminal Case #89-086-A, *U.S. v. Pablo Emilio Escobar-Gaviria et al.*, Northern District of Georgia. Laundering of Colombian cocaine money is also discussed in Max Mermelstein, *The Man Who Made It Snow* (New York: Simon & Schuster, 1990) and in Rodriguez, *Los Piratas de la Bolsa*.

20. The proliferation of cambistas makes it certain that the regulatory authorities are aware of this black market business. Some degree of enforcement of the exchange controls is indeed undertaken. In 1989, some 500 cases were brought against illegal holders of U.S. dollars in Colombia (*Estrategia*, May 1990, p. 5), and in 1988, half a dozen stock brokerage firms were forced to leave the Bogotá exchange, primarily due to their high volume and high visibility activities in black market foreign exchange. See Rodriguez, *Los Piratas de la Bolsa*.

21. These penalties are discussed in Emilio Wills, "Regimen de Control de Cambios

en Colombia—Origen, Evolucion, Aspectos Generales," *Revista de Derecho, Universidad de los Andes* (1990), pp. 127–139. Wills was Superintendent of Exchange Controls at the Central Bank during the Barco administration in the 1980s. An annual statement of the prosecutions underway appears in the *Informe Anual* of the Superintendencia de Control de Cambios.

22. See Rodriguez, *Los Piratas de la Bolsa*, Ch. 5.

23. See Hernando Jose Gomez, "El Tamaño del Narcotráfico y su Impacto Económico," *Economía Colombiana*, nos. 226–227 (February–March 1990), p. 15.

24. See Eduardo Sarmiento, "Economía del Narcotráfico," in Carlos Gustavo Arrieta, Luis Javier Orjuela, Eduardo Sarmiento Palacio, and Juan Gabriel Tokatlian (eds.), *Narcotráfico en Colombia* (2nd ed.) (Bogotá: Universidad de los Andes, 1991).

25. Oscar Borrero, "La Finca Raiz y la Economia Subterranea," *Camacol Seminario*, November 8, 1989.

26. See Miguel Urrutia, "Análisis Costo-Beneficio del Tráfico de Drogas para la Economía Colombiana," *Coyuntura Económica* (October 1990), pp. 115–126.

27. This estimate would be consistent with the others if it truly measures the dollars that physically enter Colombia. The other analyses show that most narcodollars remain outside of Colombia and are exchanged for pesos that are paid in Colombia. Following the large cambista's estimate that 85 percent of the narcotics-related dollars remain outside of Colombia, Urrutia's etimate of the dollars that do enter Colombia would be 15 percent of the total, which in turn would be about $1.533 billion for that year. This is quite similar to the other estimates.

28. See Salomon Kalmanovitz, "La Economía del Narcotráfico en Colombia," *Economía Colombiana*, nos. 226–227 (February–March 1990), pp. 18–28.

29. A final estimate that may be useful to consider in this context comes from a study by Carlos Caballero Argaez, "La Economia de la Cocaina, Algunos Estimativos para 1988," *Coyuntura Economica* 18, no. 3 (Septemper 1988), pp. 179–183. He estimated that the cocaine trade generated about $U.S. 4 billion in revenues for Colombian traffickers, of which about $U.S. 1 billion would have been brought into Colombia through the black market. This estimate is lower than most of the others presented here, primarily because of the author's assumption of a far smaller return of the narcodollars to Colombia.

30. See Roberto Steiner, "Colombia's Income from the Drug Trade," *World Development* 26, no. 6 (1998), pp. 1013–1031.

31. Discussions of the Ventanilla Siniestra appear often in the Colombian press. See, for example, Fernando Gaviria Cadavid, "Cuanto vale el narcotráfico," *La República*, February 18, 1988, pp. E7–E8; see also Silverio Gomez, "Mientras las Exportaciones de Bienes Crecen 11%, La Ventanilla Siniestra está Disparada," *El Tiempo*, April 24, 1989, pp. 1B–4B.

32. Information obtained from the U.S. Treasury, Financial Crimes Enforcement Network (FinCEN) in August 1990.

33. The Colombian government also probably buys proceeds of narcotraffic through its purchases of gold mined in the country. Since the narcotics traffickers are known to have entered the gold business, any gold they sell to the government would indirectly be linked to the narcotics business, though not necessarily to foreign exchange transactions. That is, some of the gold may be purchased by the narcotraffickers for dollars, and more gold is produced by mines controlled by the narcotraffickers. See, for example, Kalmanovitz, "La Economía de Narcotráfico en Colombia," p. 23.

34. See Robert Grosse, *Foreign Exchange Black Markets in Latin America* (New York: Praeger, 1994).

Chapter 4

A Recent History of U.S. Money Laundering Regulations, 1970–98

Money laundering has existed throughout history whenever people tried to hide the nature or sources of their money, income, or wealth. The present focus is on money laundering in the United States that relates to drug trafficking during the last 30 years.

One way to look at this history is to examine the laws and regulations that have been implemented in the United States during this time. Some regulations in other countries are useful to review as well, since they also relate to the U.S. financial flows in the process of laundering. By tracking the legislative history of money laundering as a crime in the United States, we can readily begin in 1970 with the passage of the Bank Secrecy Act and continue through the legislative changes that had occurred through 1998, which assuredly will continue to evolve by the time this book is in print.

A second way to organize this history would be to explore the kinds of money laundering activity that characterized the early years of this period (since 1970) and then to see how the activities have evolved over the past three decades. Interestingly, due to the almost complete lack of prosecutions under the Bank Secrecy Act during its first decade, there were no major shifts in money laundering practice during that decade. That is, money launderers were not forced to seek alternative means of carrying out their activities, since the rules established in the Bank Secrecy Act were not clarified for several years, and then prosecutions under the act were extremely few. By 1980, the situation had changed, and launderers had to develop alternatives to the large-scale dumping of huge quantities of dollar bills into commercial banks. From that time until now, the launderers have developed increasingly sophisticated methods for carrying out their business, often in response to the increasingly hostile legal environment that has developed. Thus the money laundering activities that have characterized narcotics proceeds have developed quite noticeably in response to the regulatory environment.

Whichever way we start the process, money laundering schemes will be seen to evolve in response to regulation and enforcement, so the presentation here follows that basis. (A timeline of regulatory actions appears in Figure 4.1.)

THE BANK SECRECY ACT OF 1970

The Bank Secrecy Act of 1970 (Public Law No. 91-508, Titles I and II, 84 Stat. 1114 [1970]) was enacted to deal with the growing problem of money laundering in the United States at that time. Title II of the Bank Secrecy Act (BSA) is called the Currency and Foreign Transactions Reporting Act. This section required financial institutions to report cash transactions of $10,000 or more. The vehicle for implementing this rule became the Currency Transaction Report, or CTR. U.S. Treasury regulations implemented the CTR in 1971, so there was some delay between the act and the potential for prosecutions.

A second requirement under the act was that institutions and individuals must file a Currency or Monetary Instrument Report (CMIR) when moving $5,000 (later revised to $10,000) or more in currency or monetary instruments into or out of the United States. This document was not created until the following year, so as in the case of CTRs, prosecutions under the BSA were not possible until that time.

Third, individuals must file a Report of Foreign Bank and Financial Accounts (FBAR) annually if they have overseas bank accounts or securities accounts with a value of $5,000 or more. This report was likewise implemented by U.S. Treasury regulations in 1971.

Each of these requirements created penalties for failing to file the reports, and the infractions themselves were illegal. However, the BSA did not make money laundering a federal crime, so even if a narcotics trafficker used the commercial banking system to launder large amounts of funds on a continuing basis, as long as the trafficker filed the required reports nothing in the BSA would restrict or penalize that activity.

Some exemptions were allowed under the act. Most logically, interbank deposits between domestic financial institutions were not subject to the reporting requirement. Also, transactions with certain bank customers that had occasion to receive large amounts of cash on a retail basis—such as grocery stores, department stores, and other retail stores—could be exempt. These exemptions had to be supported in each instance by a statement from the customer certifying the kind of business and the reason for generating the cash deposits. Banks remain responsible for monitoring account activity to make sure it is consistent with the certified purpose.

Few prosecutions occurred in the 1970s.[1] One reason was that the responsibility for filing reports and even the constitutionality of the act were questioned by financial institutions in the first few years of the BSA's existence. In 1972,

Figure 4.1
Time Line of Key Events in First Decade of U.S. Money Laundering Law

1986

- Money Laundering Control Act is signed into law by President Ronald Reagan on October 27, codified as Title 18, USC Secs. 1956 and 1957.

1988

- Anti-Drug Abuse Act of 1988 amends Section 1956, adding "sting" provision, making U.S. tax evasion a prohibited objective and expanding the definition of "financial institution" to include car, boat, and airplane dealers and real estate brokers.
- UN Convention against Illicit Traffic in Narcotics Drugs is proposed.

1989

- G-7 nations create Financial Action Task Force (FATF) in Paris.

1990

- Financial Action Task Force issues "Forty Recommendations" for national action on money laundering.
- U.S. Treasury Department's Financial Crimes Enforcement Network is established.
- Caribbean Financial Action Task Force is created.
- Crime Control Act of 1990 amends Section 1956 to expand the "sting" provision, to include environmental crimes as "specified unlawful activities" and to expand the definition of "monetary instruments."

1991

- U.S. Justice Department establishes the Money Laundering Section.
- European Union issues the Money Laundering Directive.

1992

- Annunzio-Wylie Act of 1992 amends Section 1956 to expand the definition of "financial transaction," to add "specified unlawful activities," and to add conspiracy section. It creates a new crime of conducting "illegal money transmitting business" at Title 18, USC Sec. 1960.
- First civil penalty is imposed under Section 1956.
- U.S. Justice Department issues money laundering guidelines to federal prosecutors.
- Organization of American States adopts a 19-point money laundering proposal.

1994

- Money Laundering Suppression Act is enacted without amendments to money laundering laws.
- Attorney General Janet Reno establishes the Asset Forfeiture and Money Laundering Section in the U.S. Justice Department.

1995

- President Clinton addresses the United Nations on money laundering on October 22 and announces the "blocking" of assets of "specially designated narcotics traffickers."
- U.S. Congress rejects efforts to relax sentencing guidelines for money launderers.

Figure 4.1 (continued)

- Terrorism Prevention Act of 1995 amends Section 1956 to add "specified unlawful activities" relating to financial transactions linked to terrorism.

1996

- New Suspicious Activity Report form for U.S. depository institutions takes effect on April 1.
- FATF revises its "Forty Recommendations."
- Ohio becomes the 30th state to enact a money laundering law.

the California Bankers Association filed a lawsuit to try to disallow the rules on financial reporting established by the BSA, asserting that the rules were onerous and that they violated clients' rights. The initial lawsuit led to a court decision in California that supported the association on their claim for relief from filing the domestic transactions reports but left intact the U.S. Treasury's right to demand the records for international transactions and accounts. Both the U.S. government and the association filed appeals to the decision.

The appeal led to a key U.S. Supreme Court case in 1974 (*California Bankers Association v. Shultz*, 416 U.S. 21 [1974]), which produced the ruling that the BSA did not violate constitutional due process rights, nor Fourth Amendment protection against unreasonable search and seizure, nor Fifth Amendment privilege against self-incrimination. Thus the BSA was constitutionally supported. A subsequent ruling in 1976 (*U.S. v. Miller*, 425 U.S. 435 [1976]) also supported the BSA by stating that bank customers possess no privacy interests protected by the Fourth Amendment with respect to their bank records. In sum, the U.S. Treasury's right to demand the information from commercial banks in pursuit of money launderers, tax evaders, and drug traffickers was upheld.

In the early 1980s, cases in different jurisdictions produced different results on the question of whether or not a client was required to initiate the filing of a CTR, or if only a bank was responsible for meeting the reporting requirement. This issue was not resolved until the passage of new anti-money laundering legislation in 1986.

Throughout the 1970s, the BSA was not frequently used to pursue money laundering activities, mainly because the standards for demonstrating criminal liability were so difficult for law enforcement agencies to prove. Between 1970 and 1984, the U.S. Treasury reported only four cases in which civil penalties were assessed against financial institutions for violation of the BSA, and none against individual bank employees. As a counterpoint, it should be noted that criminal prosecutions of banks and employees, once the underlying criminal activity had been discovered, produced large numbers of prosecutions in the early 1980s. In 1983, the Justice Department reported convicting 239 individuals for criminal money laundering offenses.[2] (This number approximated all of the indictments brought during the previous decade of the existence of the BSA.)

In 1985, the government actively began to prosecute banks for failure to file CTRs under the BSA. This effort led to visible prosecutions in which banks were found guilty of failing to file hundreds of required CTRs and were fined hundreds of thousands of dollars. The Bank of Boston was the first culprit prosecuted in this wave of enforcement activity. It pled guilty to failing to file reports on 1,163 cash transactions worth more than $1 billion. The bank paid a fine of $500,000. Soon after, the case was followed up with prosecutions of Chemical Bank (857 cash transactions worth $26 million), Irving Trust (1,659 cash transactions worth $292 million), Manufacturers Hanover (1,400 cash transactions worth $140 million), and others. Crocker National Bank was prosecuted for 7,877 failures to file on transactions worth $3.98 billion! This last case brought a fine of $2.25 million.

Recognition of the growth and seriousness of the problem of money laundering and of widespread non-compliance with the BSA led to the enactment of new legislation in 1986.

MONEY LAUNDERING CONTROL ACT OF 1986 (PL 99-570)

By the late 1970s, cocaine trafficking had become a major concern of law enforcement in the United States. The Medellin cartel had become infamous, and drug-related assassinations in Colombia were common newspaper fare. In this environment, U.S. enforcement agencies were looking for tools to assist them in dealing with the cocaine problem.

One possible tool was money laundering legislation, which would enable U.S. law enforcement agencies to pursue the money that necessarily accompanies drug trafficking. Enforcement efforts on money laundering were hindered by the fact that the BSA only permitted the Internal Revenue Service (IRS) and U.S. Customs—U.S. Treasury agencies—to prosecute such cases. The Drug Enforcement Administration (DEA) and the Federal Bureau of Investigation (FBI)—Justice Department agencies—were not allowed to pursue such criminal or civil offenses.

A very interesting initiative was undertaken beginning in 1980 to pool law enforcement agencies' efforts in this field. Operation Greenback,[3] based in Miami, was undertaken as a joint IRS–U.S. Customs task force in cooperation with the local U.S. Attorney's office and with a liaison with the DEA as well. This project began by targeting people and companies in South Florida whose names appeared extensively in CTR and CMIR filings. While Operation Greenback was quite successful in pursuing and prosecuting several major money launderers (such as Isaac Kattan and the Great American Bank), it also demonstrated the weakness of the law for dealing with money laundering and cocaine trafficking crimes.

In partial response to the burgeoning drug problem, and as a result of prosecutions under the BSA and Operation Greenback, the U.S. Congress passed the Money Laundering Control Act of 1986 (MLCA). This act made it a federal crime to "promote specified unlawful activity," such as narcotics trafficking, through money laundering. The MLCA also made it a federal crime to "design transactions or transport monetary instruments to conceal or disguise the nature, the location, the source, the ownership, or the control of the proceeds of 'specified unlawful activity.'" As part of the effort to stop the concealment of drug money (and other money derived from "specified unlawful activities"), the MLCA has made it a federal crime to avoid BSA reporting requirements.

It may be useful to look at the MLCA in some detail to understand the specific activities that were defined as illegal—and which have subsequently led money launderers to seek other means of accomplishing their aims. The act adds to Sections 1956 and 1957 of Title 18 of the US Code, and also to Sections 5312–5322 of Title 31 of the U.S. Code (in which the BSA appears and is hereby amended).

In Section 1956, the MLCA makes money laundering a criminal offense. The act allows for the prosecution of defendants who know, or use willful blindness to avoid knowing, that their activities are promoting specified unlawful activity. The specified unlawful activity includes crimes listed in the Racketeer Influenced and Corrupt Organizations (RICO) law—such as Mafia-related bribery and extortion, casino gambling skimming, and so on—as well as federal financial offenses (such as income tax evasion, embezzlement, bank bribery, and illegal arms sales) and foreign drug offenses.

The kinds of transactions that constitute money laundering include domestic banking transactions, such as deposits of cash, and international monetary transactions, such as the transfer of funds into or out of the United States. These transactions include not only bank deposits but also funds transfers, purchases of stocks or other securities, and non-bank activities such as the purchase and sale of property of all kinds (including securities, real estate, cars, airplanes, etc.).

The law as originally written specifically does not apply to foreign transactions or foreign crimes, except for foreign specified unlawful activities such as drug crimes, and fraud against foreign Central Bank ("the BCCI clause"—see Chapter 8) and kidnapping and terrorism. It does include foreign transactions or activities in the event that there is a U.S. citizen involved, or if the transaction(s) includes some stage(s) that passes through the United States. This includes not only financial transfers that move through the United States but also telephone calls or other electronic message transfers to or from the United States in which instructions are given to carry out the money laundering, which itself may occur abroad.

The act also creates another new category of crime, the "Monetary Transaction Crime," which includes any monetary transaction using criminally derived property. It covers any financial transaction of $10,000 or more that affects interstate or international trade through a financial institution involving any property constituting or derived from proceeds obtained from a specified unlawful activity. A person carrying out such a transaction may be prosecuted under this law, just as with the activities that seek to evade BSA requirements and/or to promote the specified unlawful activity.[4]

The MLCA adds to the penalties that may be imposed for violations of the BSA. The civil penalties have been raised from a maximum of a $10,000 fine to a new maximum of a $1 million fine, as well as a $1,000-per-violation fine (for example, for transactions a bank fails to report). Criminal penalties include imprisonment with a new limit of 10 years rather than five years.

Section 4 of the MLCA amended Title 31 of the U.S. Code, making it a crime for a person to cause or attempt to cause a financial institution to not file a required report, to file an incorrect report (paragraph 5313), or to structure a transaction to evade reporting requirements (paragraph 5324). Structuring transactions to avoid reporting under the BSA had become a favorite method of money launderers in the early and mid-1980s to get around the rules. Structuring transactions includes any activity that may be used to evade the reporting requirements; for example, making multiple deposits of $9,900 in cash in a bank rather than depositing more than $10,000 at one time, or depositing similar amounts under $10,000 at several banks to evade having to report the total amount at one bank. This strategy led drug runners and money launderers to use "smurfs," people employed solely to make multiple deposits of less than $10,000 per deposit at multiple banks during a short period of time.[5]

The various crimes identified in the MLCA were explicitly defined as "predicate crimes" eligible for application of the RICO statutes that were developed to deal with organized crime.

THE FINANCIAL ACTION TASK FORCE (FATF)

As a result of the Group of 7 industrial countries' summit in April 1989 in Paris, the member countries agreed to pursue active programs to combat drug trafficking, including efforts to deal with related money laundering. As one of the members of this group, the United States helped design the principles (40 points) that were produced from the follow-up to this summit meeting in April 1990. Subsequently, the United States has moved to incorporate them into law and rules on financial activity. A discussion of the FATF continues at the end of this chapter, under International Cooperation.

CREATION OF FINCEN (1990)

In 1990, the Secretary of the U.S. Treasury authorized the creation of the Financial Crimes Enforcement Network (FinCEN). This organization was charged with coordinating an effort to detect financial crimes in the United States, especially using the tools that had been developed in the BSA and the subsequent anti-money laundering legislation. Initially, FinCEN was asked to assist law enforcement agencies in investigations that they brought to the new agency. Subsequently, since 1994, FinCEN has been the agency to which CTRs,

CMIRs, and FBARs are sent and analyzed for use by all federal enforcement agencies.

In other words, FinCEN does not impose new regulations or policies on money laundering, nor is it an investigative agency. Rather, it functions as the principal record-keeping and watchdog agency, whose studies and findings are intended to be shared by regulatory and law enforcement agencies. FinCEN has become the agency charged with developing new tools to be used in assuring compliance with the BSA and other money laundering laws. So, for example, the development of a reporting form for Suspicious Activities was assigned to FinCEN, and likewise the development of specific guidelines for record keeping on wire transfers was placed under the leadership of FinCEN.[6]

THE 1992 ANTI-MONEY LAUNDERING ACT (ANNUNZIO–WYLIE MONEY LAUNDERING ACT)

By the early 1990s, law enforcement agencies had discovered a number of weaknesses of the MLCA, and they were able to gain congressional support for more stringent regulations. As embodied in the Annunzio–Wylie Act, these new rules included the requirement for financial institutions to "report any *suspicious transactions* relevant to possible violations of law or regulation" (Section 1517 of the act). This meant that commercial banks were now required to file reports of any patterns of activity of clients that the bank viewed as possibly constituting money laundering. The rules included a "safe harbor" provision to protect banks against client or third-party complaints for having designated accounts or transactions as suspicious when they may not subsequently be proven to violate any laws or regulations.

The act also requires financial institutions to carry out anti-money laundering programs in terms of record keeping and training employees to be on the lookout for money laundering activity (Section 1517). The act permits the Department of the Treasury to issue regulations requiring financial institutions to maintain appropriate procedures to guard against money laundering. The U.S. Treasury indicated its intention to issue regulations requiring financial institutions to adopt "know your customer" (KYC) procedures (Section 1513), proposed in 1997.

The act authorized special record-keeping rules on funds transfer transactions (Section 1515), though the rules for record keeping on wire transfers were not proposed until 1993 and not approved until 1994. Since 1994, banks and non-bank financial institutions have had to keep detailed information about both initiators and recipients of wire transfers for values above $3,000 (e.g., name, address, and type of business of each party).

The act also addressed the issue of terminal penalties for financial institutions convicted of money laundering. The Controller of the Currency must notify financial institutions that are convicted of money laundering crimes that it will hold hearings toward the revocation of institutions' licenses and the termination of all of their rights and privileges (Section 1502). The act amended the Federal

Deposit Insurance Corporation (FDIC) charter to require the FDIC to initiate a hearing toward the revocation of deposit insurance for an institution convicted of a money laundering offense and, in the extreme, to take over the operation of a financial institution convicted of a money laundering offense, ordering it to be closed (Section 1503). It amended the International Banking Act of 1978 to direct the Board of Governors of the Federal Reserve System to issue a notice of its intention to commence a termination proceeding upon written notification from the Attorney General that the state branch or agency of a foreign bank has been convicted of a money laundering offense (Section 1507). This was clearly in response to the BCCI embarrassment.

Similar to the penalties on financial institutions, officials of the institutions who may be convicted of money laundering crimes will be suspended and possibly permanently removed from their activities in the institution under the new law (Section 1504).

The act makes it a federal crime to own or to operate an illegal money transmitting business that is operating without an appropriate state license, and it provides for the forfeiture of any property involved in such a crime (Section 1512). This part of the act refers to the practice of some non-bank businesses that have been established in the United States to move funds between the United States and other countries, especially in Latin America. These money transmitters have in some cases proven to be major vehicles for narcotics money laundering (e.g., *U.S. v. Henry Melo*, case CR #97-942 (NG) Eastern District of New York).

And finally, the Annunzio–Wylie Act made it a crime for financial institutions or clients to *structure* the purchase of monetary instruments (such as travelers' checks or money orders), so the financial institution would not file the required reports (especially CTRs). This section also proposed to reduce the minimum level of cash transactions that needed to be reported, prohibiting the structuring of transactions to avoid the record-keeping requirements for the purchase of monetary instruments between $3,000 and $10,000. (Section 1535). The reduction was not approved as far as the filing of CTRs and CMIRs was concerned, however, banks were instructed to maintain records of cash transactions below $10,000, so that law enforcement efforts could utilize such records when appropriate, and banks were instructed to file Suspicious Activity Reports for cash transactions of less than $10,000 when the client's activity indeed appeared suspicious.

RECORD KEEPING AND TRAVEL RULES ON WIRE TRANSFERS (1993)

Rules were recommended by the U.S. Treasury in August 1993 to require financial institutions to collect and retain records on both domestic and foreign funds transfers of $3,000 or more. The final rules were promulgated in 1996, jointly by FinCEN and the Federal Reserve (31 CFR Part 103). The rules apply to all institutions that are required to comply with BSA regulations (such as banks, money transmitters, casinos, stockbrokers, and exchange houses).

These rules require the first financial institution in a wire transfer chain to include in the transmittal order certain information about the transfer and the parties involved. This information includes the true name and street address of the sender and receiver of the funds. Each intermediary institution in the chain must then pass on this information to the next institution in the chain. All financial institutions in the chain must keep these records for at least five years.

Some exceptions are made for transactions within branches of the same institution and for circumstances in which funds transmittal does not permit all information to be collected. However, in such exceptional situations, the institution is required to demonstrate why the exception is appropriate and also to note that the relevant information was not obtained.

MONEY LAUNDERING SUPPRESSION ACT OF 1994

Another loophole in the anti-money laundering rules was closed with the passage of the Money Laundering Suppression Act of 1994 (MLSA). Prior to that time, non-bank financial companies such as Western Union and other money transmitters were not required to be registered with the U.S. Treasury or Federal Reserve. This opening to money launderers for arranging money transfers through unlicensed and unregulated institutions was closed. Now all firms involved in transmitting funds into, out of, or within the United States must be licensed to carry out this activity, and they must explicitly comply with report filings such as CTRs and CMIRs.

The precise definition of the money transmitter activity, as described in Section 8 of the act, is:

Money transmitting service includes accepting currency or funds denominated in the currency of any country and transmitting the currency or funds, or the value of the currency or funds, by any means through a financial agency or institution, a Federal reserve bank or other facility of the Board of Governors of the Federal Reserve System, or an electronic funds transfer network.

Thus, any firm that provides the service of moving funds for clients, when the funds pass through the U.S. commercial banking system, is subject to the rules.

As described in several of the cases in later chapters, this loophole had become an important avenue of money laundering in the United States by the early 1990s. Money transfer businesses in Miami were actively involved in sending funds to families of expatriate Jamaicans, Haitians, and other Caribbean basin nationals from their South Florida locations back to their home country relatives and friends. Because this business was not regulated specifically, it offered an excellent front for narcotics traffickers to launder their money through the same system. Likewise, along the Mexican border, especially in Texas and California, money transmitter businesses sprang up to service Mexican expatriates sending part of their earnings back to families and friends in Mexico, with the same influx of drug money taking advantage of the loosely regulated industry.

The MLSA (in Section 2) also instituted a relaxation of the rules for filing CTRs, which had become an overwhelming burden on the regulators to utilize. That is, so many CTRs were being filed by banks and other institutions by the early 1990s that useful information for pursuing financial crimes was being hidden by the vast quantity of non-suspicious cash activity that banks were required to report under the BSA. The new act allowed banks to exempt a larger range of clients from reporting with CTRs, and it also gave banks the flexibility to designate additional selected clients as exempt from reporting—as long as the bank kept good records regarding the reasons for exempting these clients and maintained at least an annual reevaluation of the clients to ensure that their business was indeed above suspicion.

The MLSA (in Section 9) also clarified the application of the reporting requirements for casinos and other gaming institutions, which by their nature are subject to being used by money launderers as well.

SUSPICIOUS ACTIVITY REPORT (1996)

On April 1, 1996, the Treasury Department introduced a new reporting form for financial institutions to report activities of clients, one that did not require the filing of CTRs or other formal reports on monetary instrument usage but that alerted the institution to possible illegal activity. The Suspicious Activity Report (replacing the earlier Criminal Referral Form) now allows banks to demonstrate alertness to possible money laundering activity and likewise protects banks from recrimination by clients whose records may be provided to law enforcement agencies. The new report thus refines the requirement for reporting such activities in the Annunzio–Wylie Act of 1992. The FinCEN was designated as the federal agency responsible for receiving and analyzing these reports, as with the CTRs.

GEOGRAPHIC TARGETING ORDERS (GTOs)

As part of the anti-money laundering arsenal, U.S. enforcement agencies have been given the right to target specific, limited geographic areas for defined, short periods of time and to demand that banks and other reporting institutions provide more detailed information than what is required in the BSA and other broad legislation. The geographic targeting orders (GTO) have been used to target banks in Miami, jewelry stores in Los Angeles, and money transmitters in New York and Texas, among other applications. In the summer of 1996, for example, a GTO called for 12 money transmitters and 1,600 agents in metropolitan New York to report all cash transfers over $750 to Colombia. This order was initially imposed for 60 days and was renewed six times. It was estimated to have cut the flow of drug trafficking cash shipped to Colombia by one-third and to have caused 900 of the money transmitters to cease operation.[7]

INTERNATIONAL COOPERATION

One major difficulty in the U.S. government's effort to combat money laundering during the past two decades has been the lack of parallel legislation in other countries so that information that could be used to pursue money launderers was not possible to obtain from other governments. Significant cooperation was begun under the auspices of the Organization for Economic Cooperation and Development (OECD) in 1989, when the Group of 7 (G-7) industrial countries launched a major initiative to combat drug trafficking. The summit meeting of that year led to the creation of the Financial Action Task Force (FATF), which had grown to 26 member countries by 1997.

The FATF initially worked to define a set of recommendations for dealing with the problem of drug-related money laundering. It produced 40 specific recommendations in a 1990 document and recommended that all member countries pursue efforts to implement all of the points. These points ranged from mutual adoption of the United Nations 1988 Convention against Illicit Traffic in Narcotic Drugs and Psychotropic Substances to the adoption of legislation in each country to criminalize money laundering. (The 40 points are reproduced in the Appendix at the end of this book.)

The "FATF recommendations" included a number of points that have subsequently been adopted as U.S. policy. For example:

- the application of anti-money laundering rules to non-bank financial institutions such as exchange houses
- the establishment of "know-your-customer" rules
- the need to report "suspicious activities" that may not be specifically identified in reporting rules but that may indicate money laundering activity
- the collection (and sharing) of information about cash flows through the banking system, so that money laundering activities may be identified
- the coordination of money laundering investigations between government agencies and countries, and the sharing of assets that may be confiscated

These recommendations have been fairly widely adopted among the industrial member countries of the FATF and also in many of the less developed member countries.

The FATF, in its 1997 annual report, nevertheless pointed out that the level of commitment to anti-money laundering efforts was low among the member countries, and that the problem had not been resolved or even reduced noticeably.

NOTES

1. See General Accounting Office, "Bank Secrecy Act Reporting Requirements Have Not Yet Met Expectations, Suggesting Need for Amendment," July 23, 1981 (GGD-81-80). Also, according to the President's Commission on Organized Crime, "The Department of the Treasury took several years to implement the Act [BSA] by establishing a system of reporting and analysis to facilitate the detection and investigation of money laundering." *The Cash Connection: Organized Crime, Financial Institutions, and Money Laundering.* (Washington, D.C.: President's Commission on Organized Crime, October 1984), p. 18.

2. Ibid., p. 26.

3. Operation Greenback is described in Robert Powis, *The Money Launderers* (Chicago: Probus, 1992), ch. 2.

4. This point is made in Charles Thelen Plombeck, "Confidentiality and Disclosure: The Money Laundering Control Act of 1986 and Banking Secrecy," *The International Lawyer* (Spring 1988), pp. 69–98.

5. See, for example, Sarah N. Welling, "Smurfs, Money Laundering, and the Federal Criminal Law: The Crime of Structuring Transactions," *Florida Law Review* 41 (1989), pp. 287–339.

6. There has been quite a bit of criticism of the FinCEN since its inception, largely due to the agency's inability to make rapid decisions or even to demonstrate its value through any high-profile success in uncovering a major money laundering venture. It took five years to design and gain approval for the Suspicious Activity Report, and the rules on Know Your Customer, as of mid-1998, had not been implemented.

7. This incident was reported in the Financial Action Task Force's *1997–1998 Report on Money Laundering Typologies* (Paris: FATF, February 12, 1998), p. 5.

Part II

How to Launder Millions

Chapter 5

Early Cases, 1970s and Early 1980s

Before entering into a detailed discussion about major drug money laundering schemes, a few examples from the 1970s and early 1980s will help illustrate the way in which launderers operated during that period.

The best known early drug money launderer during the 1970s was Steven Kalish, who began as a marijuana smuggler in the 1960s and then expanded into cocaine smuggling and money laundering in the 1970s. Kalish was both a smuggler and a launderer; in those days, the two activities had not yet become as specialized as they developed in the 1980s.

Kalish began his drug-running career in his hometown near Houston, Texas, in the mid-1960s. He dealt in marijuana, which was the drug of choice for college students at the time. As his income rose from buying and selling marijuana, he began to develop mechanisms for getting large quantities of cash into the banking system. At the time, there was no particular effort by banks to question the source of large or small cash deposits, so Kalish was able to funnel huge amounts of cash into Houston-area banks without attracting the attention of law enforcement agencies.

When his business reached the level of hundreds of millions of dollars of marijuana, and increasingly, cocaine, he significantly diversified his channels of money laundering. In addition to making large cash deposits in local banks, he shipped millions of dollars to the Cayman Islands for deposit in numerous accounts there. He also set up accounts in Panama, taking advantage of the lax concern about money laundering and drug trafficking there in the early 1980s.

Because of the opportunity available in Panama, Kalish built up an enormous cash shipment business there in the early 1980s. He found that by bribing General Noriega and other members of the Panama Defense Forces, he was able to obtain privileged access to the Panama City airport, where he repeatedly brought in millions of dollars of cash from his U.S. marijuana and cocaine sales. Since the banking law in Panama at the time did not restrict or even require an investigation of massive cash deposits, the task was simple to transfer the sachels and suitcases of cash into bank deposits and then to transfer the funds to any number of target bank accounts or investments in almost any country, including the United States.

Once this system was established, Kalish provided the same service to members of the Colombian cocaine cartels, charging a 6–8 percent fee for taking the money from the streets of New York, Los Angeles, and many cities in between and turning it into bank deposits in Panama. The drug barons then were able to move the funds to other accounts and countries, just as Kalish himself did.

The downfall of Steven Kalish occurred when he was in Tampa during July 1984, involved in the operation of his smuggling organization. He was arrested at the airport as he attempted to board his Lear jet for a trip to Panama. After spending several years in jail, he subsequently became a key witness for the U.S. government in its attempt to convict General Noriega of Panama for narcotics trafficking and conspiring to assist the Colombian cartels in narcotics trafficking.

Another early entrant into the narcotics money laundering business at the time was Isaac Kattan. Kattan was a Syrian national whose family had moved to Cali, Colombia—home of the future Cali cartel—in the mid-1950s. His father had operated a money exchange business in Syria, and he set up a similar business in Colombia. At that time, Kattan was in his early 20s, and he joined his father's money exchange business in Cali.

This activity was ideal as a complement to the narcotics trafficking business. As described in Chapter 3, peso/dollar exchange in Colombia took place to a certain extent in the legal market through commercial banks. However, due to the strict exchange controls in place from 1966 through 1990, businesspeople frequently resorted to the foreign exchange black market to buy dollars. Likewise, exporters who wanted to make the most of their foreign currency earnings would try to leave as much as possible of those funds outside of Colombia. This would enable the exporters to avoid having to sell their dollars to the Colombian Central Bank at the official exchange rate. By holding onto the dollars in, say, New York, the exporters could then bring them back to Colombia through the (unreported) foreign exchange black market and receive 10–50 percent more pesos in the exchange.

The classic foreign exchange black market dealer was an exchange house that did some business buying dollars from tourists and others who brought them in from abroad and then selling the dollars to the Central Bank, as required under Colombian law. This business in the front office was used to hide the much more profitable back office business of buying dollars from all kinds of people and selling them at a much higher price to Colombian businesspeople, savers, and so on who wanted their money in dollars, and often outside of Colombia.

The Kattans fit perfectly into this mold, offering to buy dollars from tourists, exporters, and other holders of dollars while selling cash dollars to those who wanted that service. On the dollar-buying side were mainly Colombians who wanted to save their wealth in dollars to protect its value and hide that wealth, plus importers who needed dollars, but due to exchange controls, they were not able to obtain them easily. This business in cash alone was a profitable but an illegal one.

As the money exchange business grew, the Kattans encountered increasing demand for putting the money overseas rather than buying cash dollars in Colombia. Isaac traveled to the United States, Panama, Nassau, and other places to look for ways to channel funds into bank accounts there. He established bank accounts in Miami, Panama, Nassau, and other cities and began to receive funds from Colombian exporters and from Colombians living abroad who wanted to obtain pesos back in Colombia. The Kattans offered these dollar deposits in the United States to clients in Colombia who wanted that additional service and who would pay in pesos—obviously at a higher fee than for a simple cash exchange.

Another business that was permitted to deal in dollars in Colombia at the time were travel agencies. These firms were permitted to receive dollars from tourists for the purchase of travel packages, airline tickets, and so on. The travel agencies had to report the amount of dollars received and turn in those dollars to the Central Bank, as was required of exporters. However, a travel agency could report some level of legal activity in dollars to the government while carrying out unlimited, unreported dollar exchange in the back room.

Isaac Kattan opened a travel agency in Bogotá in the early 1960s and thus matched up new sources of dollars (i.e., tourists) with his existing customers who wanted to buy the dollars (i.e., Colombian businesspeople and savers). Viajes Pacifico grew to be a very successful travel agency.

Although there are certainly no published records of the prosperity of the money exchange and travel agency businesses—other than the miniscule amounts reported to the Colombian government for tax purposes—it is clear from the Kattans' lifestyle that they were prospering.

By the mid-1970s, Colombia had become a major marijuana exporter to the United States. The drug runners in this business found the same needs that their successors with cocaine faced, namely large incomes in dollars in the United States and a need to bring some of the profits back to Colombia to pay bills, to buy consumer goods as well as business-related purchases, and to generally use an underground means of carrying out the transfer. The Kattans and other black market money exchangers once again fit the bill perfectly.

Isaac Kattan began to buy dollars from the marijuana traffickers in 1976, according to law enforcement records. This additional source of dollars enabled him to better serve the Colombian customers who wanted to buy dollars, especially those who wanted to hold dollars overseas. In 1977, he connected with Jaime Escobar, a money manager for some Medellin cocaine traffickers. This turned out to be a huge boost for his business, since cocaine use was sweeping the United States at the time, and drug income for these traffickers required them to find multiple money launderers to handle the volume of cash produced. Isaac Kattan was able to build the business of buying drug dollars and selling them to Colombian businessmen and savers to the point where, in the years 1977–81, he was estimated to be exchanging approximately $100 million a year.

At this time in the late 1970s, there were no rules prohibiting the deposit of huge quantities of cash, unless of course it was proven that the money was directly earned from drug sales. When Kattan or one of his assistants arrived at a bank with boxes and bags of cash, they simply had to provide the information necessary for filing CTRs, and then the deposits were made. One bank Kattan used heavily was the Bank of Miami, which took in millions of dollars in cash deposits, plus a large volume of bank drafts from Deak–Perera currency exchange company in New York. Kattan was buying bank drafts with large quantities of drug dollars collected in New York at Deak–Perera there. In addition, he was bringing in dollars from Colombia to New York and laundering them through Deak–Perera. Kattan consistently claimed that he was bringing dollars into the United States from his Colombian money exchange business— even though most of his dollars were in fact drug dollars collected in U.S. cities.

Kattan was investigated over a period of more than a year during 1983–84, and law enforcement officials were initially halted by the fact that money laundering was not a crime and that they needed to demonstrate a link to narcotics trafficking. This evidence was not long in coming, and in February 1981, Kattan was arrested with two drug traffickers and eventually convicted of cocaine possession and money laundering (i.e., CTR violations).[1]

SMURFING

The use of multiple small-time helpers to deposit small sums of money into bank accounts or to buy money orders or cashier's checks was another part of the money laundering chain that characterized early times before the "structuring" of cash deposits and the purchasing of monetary instruments were made illegal by the 1986 Money Laundering Control Act. Although this activity still continues today, it is a less common laundering technique, since structuring has specifically been made illegal.

Alberto Barrera (Papa Smurf) was the leader of the largest smurfing operation that was discovered and dismantled by law enforcement in the early 1980s. His Miami-based smurfing team included a dozen people who took cash delivered by drug traffickers and placed it into hundreds of banks in cities across the United States. His scheme was fairly complicated and expensive to operate, but it avoided the problem of depositing large amounts of cash in the location of the drug sales.

Barrera put together a smurfing team of a dozen Colombian nationals who received cash from him and traveled to various cities around the United States to buy money orders and cashier's checks in amounts less than $10,000. Once the checks and money orders were purchased, the smurfs delivered them to Barrera, who arranged deposits of multiple checks and money orders into bank accounts that he controlled for further transfer to accounts in Panama, Colombia, and elsewhere.

According to law enforcement records from the operation that dismantled Barrera's money laundering network, he received large deliveries of cash in Miami during 1983 and 1984. Once a delivery of, say, $200,000 was received, Barrera would divide it up among his team, sending groups of two or three people on airline trips to other cities such as Phoenix, San Francisco, Omaha, and Portland, where they would systematically visit a dozen or so banks each, buying either money orders or cashier's checks for about $5,000 each. In this way, the team of three people could launder the whole $200,000 in a day or two and then return to Miami with the new instruments.

Barrera did not have a good system for disposing of the money orders and cashier's checks. His deliveries of packages of these instruments to Miami banks drew the attention of bankers when he deposited them, which turned out to be part of the reason for his downfall. Still, since depositing cash and structuring deposits to evade the CTR requirement were not illegal at the time, he was safe from prosecution on those grounds. Law enforcement agents gained a clear picture of the Barrera smurfing operation from watching his activities and following his smurfs around the country as they transformed the cash into other financial instruments.

It turned out that Barrera and his smurfs were not the only clever people in this picture. Law enforcement agents figured out that they could pursue the Barrera group as a *conspiracy* to evade CTR reporting requirements, which was illegal. However, it required some very detailed evidence that Barrera was controlling the operation, that the smurfs were conspiring to buy the cashier's checks and money orders in order to evade the CTR requirement, and that there was enough interaction among the members of the team to prove that they really were operating as an organization.

Internal Revenue Service (IRS) agents chased Barrera's smurfs around the country, following them into banks and obtaining testimony from bank tellers about the purchases of checks and money orders, digging up receipts for the transactions from trash cans, and tracing telephone calls from Barrera to his subordinates in the traveling show. Local law enforcement agents were called in to help when the IRS agents could not keep up with the smurfs' flights to all of the different cities. In all, the law enforcement venture was an enormous undertaking, just like Barrera's operation.

Among other evidence, IRS agents found bookkeeping records that showed $4 million of checks deposited at Security Pacific Bank in California, with subsequent wire transfers of the funds to Banco de Occidente in Panama. From the total evidence collected in the case, it appears that his organization laundered about $12 million during the year of government pursuit, and probably much more that was not discovered. The organization was prosecuted by U.S. au-

thorities; Papa Smurf escaped to Colombia along with half of the team, while
the others were put in jail for terms of one to two years each.[2]

UNITED STATES V. ONE SINGLE FAMILY RESIDENCE AT
6960 MIRAFLORES AVENUE, CORAL GABLES

An interesting example of the operation of money laundering law in pursuing
illegal banking activities before the Money Laundering Control Act of 1986 is
the case of Republic National Bank of Miami and a loan to cocaine trafficker
Indalecio Iglesias. Iglesias had bought a house at 6960 Miraflores Avenue in
the exclusive Coco Plum neighborhood of Coral Gables, Florida, in 1983. He
was said to have paid for the $1.2 million house, and subsequent extensive
remodeling, in cash. When federal drug investigators questioned a friend of
Iglesias' about his activities in 1987, Iglesias began to close out his local affairs
and then fled to Switzerland.

As part of his efforts to get his assets out of the hands of federal investigators,
he arranged an $800,000 loan on the Miraflores house, through accomplice Ra-
mon Puentes, who was a long-time customer of Republic National Bank. The
loan was, in fact, taken out by a Panamanian corporation, Thule Holding, and
no credit check or loan committee approval was obtained by Republic. The
owner of Thule Holding was another individual unknown to the bank. The
bank's president, Fred De la Mata, circumvented the normal lending procedures
and approved the loan. The $800,000 was immediately wire transferred to Ig-
lesias' Swiss bank account, and he withdrew it from the bank.

In 1988, the government filed a civil forfeiture case to obtain the property,
which was claimed to be purchased with the proceeds of narcotics trafficking,
and subsequently filed a criminal money laundering case against the bank's
president. The government demonstrated that the bank had failed to follow normal procedures for making the loan, had carried out no title search, and so on.
The borrower also was shown to have made an apparent bribe, an expensive
wedding gift to De la Mata's son. The civil forfeiture case brought against the
house wound through the court system with some conflicting rulings, until in
1993, the 11th Circuit Court of Appeals ruled that the house would be forfeited
as proceeds of narcotics trafficking. The related criminal case resulted in an
acquittal for De la Mata.

In a separate case resolved at about the same time, De la Mata and two other
Republic National Bank officers were convicted of bank fraud and criminal
conspiracy and sentenced to prison. These charges and convictions were the
result of a pattern of criminal behavior in which the Miraflores house transaction
was just one example.

Obviously, this transaction was dubious, but at the time the U.S. law was not
100 percent clear on the bank's responsibility to "know your client," much less
to deal with "suspicious activity." The only clear rule was that a bank could not
knowingly carry out transactions with narcotics traffickers or with proceeds of

narcotics trafficking. The idea of willfully ignoring the available evidence in order to avoid knowing about drug trafficking was not clearly defined.[3]

CONCLUDING THOUGHTS ABOUT THE EARLY DAYS

The situation in the cocaine cowboy days was really amazing as far as money laundering was concerned. Government authorities had not yet focused their attention on the fight to catch the money, even if they could not catch the drug traffickers. Things have changed, and with the attack on both drugs and money, it is estimated that more than one-third of cocaine traffic was interdicted in the late 1990s.

However, in the late 1970s and early 1980s, the drug runners themselves and some more specialized money launderers had almost free rein to get their funds into banks and to move them around the world. By the time the Money Laundering Control Act was passed in 1986, the business had gotten more sophisticated and specialized, so that the Colombian drug traffickers had moved almost completely to using contracted money laundering services from unrelated organizations. This remains the situation today.

While the money laundering schemes discussed in the next eight chapters tend to be more sophisticated than those in the present chapter, there is still plenty of smurfing of cash into accounts, structuring of deposits to avoid exceeding the $10,000 limit before mandatory reporting comes into play, and other fairly simple techniques. One thing is certain: as the number of drug traffickers expands, and likewise for the laundering organizations, the schemes that have worked in the past will be tried again and again.

NOTES

1. This section on Isaac Kattan is largely based on Robert Powis, *The Money Launderers* (Chicago: Probus, 1992), ch. 2.

2. This section on Papa Smurf is largely based on Powis, *The Money Launderers*, ch. 3.

3. This section on Republic National Bank is largely based on court documents from the case *United States v. One Single Family Residence at 6960 Miraflores Avenue, Coral Gables* (88-0349-CIV-Scott, S.D. Fla.).

Chapter 6

La Mina, 1985–88

La Mina was the largest cocaine money laundering scheme uncovered to date. This laundry was operated principally for the Medellin cartel (Pablo Escobar, Jorge and Fabio Ochoa, Gerardo Moncada, Jose Rodriguez-Gacha, et al.) during the period 1985–88. La Mina laundered more than $U.S. 1 billion during its four-year operation, and in the related Operation Polar Cap, U.S. authorities laundered more than $U.S. 300 million, capturing and successfully forfeiting about $U.S. 50 million. The related Operation C-Chase produced the forfeiture of another $U.S. 14 million. In the Los Angeles prosecution of La Mina, 35 people were arrested and 292 kilos of cocaine were seized, along with the money.[1]

La Mina operated as a gold mine for the Medellin cartel—using gold exports and fake exports from Latin America as well as gold trading in the United States to hide the source of the dollars being laundered. The scheme began in 1985, when Argentine gold refiner Raul Vivas found that he could earn large profits from shipping gold-plated lead to the United States and remit drug dollars in apparent payment for the shipments. The idea was presented to him by Eduardo Martinez, sometimes called the chief money manager for the Medellin cartel. Vivas was asked to arrange for gold sales that would justify large payments of cash in the United States, and then to pass the money on to cartel bank accounts while keeping the gold. Vivas was able to use his regular business of selling gold to hide the source of the money involved.

To operate this venture, he opened an exchange house in Montevideo, Uruguay, called Cambio Italia, and he used it to receive the funds transfers. Uruguay often is called the Switzerland of South America, and its banking system has been largely open to international transactions, even during the periods of exchange controls in neighboring Argentina and Brazil. Exchange houses and international banks abound there, operating in a highly competitive environment.

The process began at one end with a gold refinery in Uruguay. Before entering the money laundering scheme, Vivas' company operated a business that would buy gold from mines, refine it, and sell it to jewelers locally and overseas. He then encountered this opportunity to sell gold to the cocaine traffickers, in which no gold was really needed except to shield the source of the dollars involved. That is, the narcotics traffickers had no direct interest in the gold, except that they could pay cash for it and thus bring cash dollars into the legal financial system as apparent payment for gold. The drug traffickers then would have the gold exchanged for dollars in bank accounts, thus completing the laundry process.

In the process of money laundering, Vivas figured out that he could send *lead* plated with gold to the United States, where it was received and declared as pure gold at U.S. Customs. This gave an enormous value to the shipments, which were then transported to Los Angeles. Thus the gold-plated lead was used as the basis for depositing millions of dollars into commercial banks in Los Angeles and New York for the supposed "sale" of gold to jewelers in the United States. The gold plating was removed from the lead and either sold or recycled to Uruguay for the next round of fake gold shipments. Vivas passed the dollars on to Medellin cartel accounts, keeping a fee of about 5 percent, which after his expenses left about 1 percent of the money for himself.

After a few months of this business, Vivas realized that there was really no need to ship gold, fake or real, from Uruguay. The precious metal transactions could be limited to the United States, thereby time and expense could be cut from the laundering process. In the next phase of the scheme, Vivas set up an office in Los Angeles, where he used drug proceeds in cash to buy pure gold from local precious metals vendors. This gold was then physically transported to New York and sold to banks, and the resulting funds were wire transferred to cartel-controlled accounts in Panama, principally at Banco de Occidente. Figure 6.1 shows this phase of La Mina's operation.

On the drugs side, the Medellin cartel sold cocaine in Los Angeles and arranged to have money collected and delivered to Vivas or his employees. Eduardo Martinez managed the financial business for the cartel, receiving instructions from the cartel about cash to be picked up and accounts into which it should be deposited. Martinez then gave instructions to the cartel about where to deliver the cash payments, and he arranged his own subordinates as cash handlers. Among others, he then used La Mina as a major channel for getting the cash into banks. Once instructed that cash would be delivered, Vivas counted and bundled the money for deposit into banks as purported revenues from the gold business. He followed up by depositing the funds in major banks. Then Martinez gave him instructions for wire transferring the funds to Panamanian accounts, or accounts elsewhere.

Figure 6.1
La Mina: Los Angeles Laundry

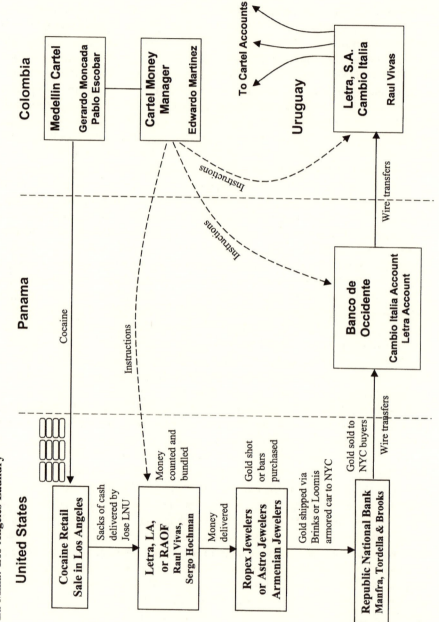

On the money side, retail drug sales produced cash that was counted and bundled at the offices of Letra, Inc., or RAOF, maintained by Vivas in Los Angeles. This cash was then delivered to Ropex jewelers or Astro Jewelers, Armenian-owned gold and jewelry stores that dealt in gold bars and gold shot as well as gold-based jewelry. The jewelers then could deposit the cash into banks, in the guise of payments for their gold, without creating problems for the money launderers.

Once the gold was purchased, it was shipped via armored car to New York, where Vivas sold it to major gold wholesalers such as Manfra, Tordella & Brooks. Payment for the gold sales was then wire transferred to a Letra account at Banco de Occidente in Panama. Funds from accounts maintained at Banco de Occidente were then wire transferred to Vivas in Uruguay and subsequently distributed to cartel accounts, as instructed by Martinez.

Within a few months, the operation was expanded to New York, where Sergio Hochman, working for Vivas, opened a company called S&H Imports. This front company was used to receive cash from retail drug sales. Hochman would count, bundle, and ship the cash to gold refiners, including Ross Refining and Orosimo in New York. As with the Los Angeles operation, La Mina (Hochman, in this instance) would receive instructions from Martinez about which cartel member owned the money so each member could be credited properly for the cocaine sales. La Mina then kept track of the money and ultimately transferred it to accounts belonging to the proper owner, as instructed by Martinez.

Sometimes the cash was shipped all the way to Los Angeles, to Ropex Refining, for the purchase of gold. The gold from both New York and Los Angeles was shipped via armored car to the Fort Lauderdale refinery of Ronel Refining Corporation, a large gold refiner and trader. Ronel would pay to buy the gold and place funds into its own New York account to be paid to Letra or Omensal, both accounts used by Vivas. Typically, Vivas would then wire transfer the money to one of his accounts in Uruguay for subsequent disbursement to cartel accounts, as instructed by Martinez.

The New York laundry enabled La Mina to avoid shipping gold from Los Angeles to New York, since it was accompanied by the opening of business with New York gold vendors to absorb the New York drug dollars and the Los Angeles gold refiner/trader Ropex to take in the Los Angeles drug dollars. Figure 6.2 shows the New York laundry arrangement.

In this structure, the main sale of gold was arranged through the Fort Lauderdale company, Ronel, which required shipping the gold to Florida from either New York or Los Angeles. The shipments in the original scheme from Los Angeles to New York were eliminated, but gold still had to be transported all the way to Fort Lauderdale from either place of purchase. This cost time— usually about five days—and money to pay for the shipments. While it surely was an imperfect scheme, this arrangement was used for more than a year before being replaced by alternative structures and using different banks and bank accounts.

Figure 6.2
La Mina: New York Laundry

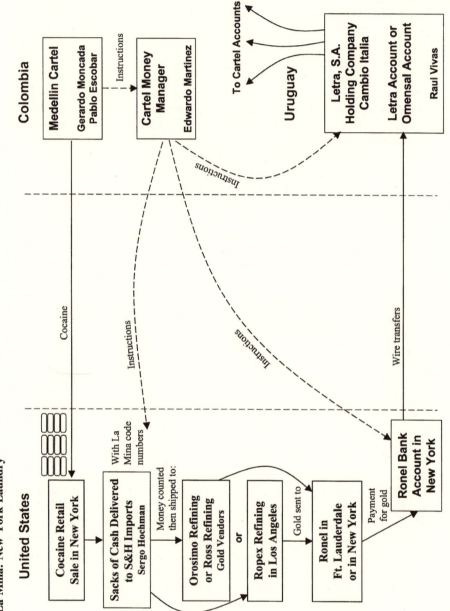

In fact, during the four-year life of La Mina, even the processes for laundering money that worked efficiently were replaced from time to time, primarily to avoid detection by government agencies such as the Drug Enforcement Admin- istration (DEA) and U.S. Customs, which were constantly looking for drug money laundering activity. Bank accounts were changed, one jeweler or precious metals dealer was replaced by another, and so on.

At one point in 1988 the money counting office in New York was investigated by police officers—and the La Mina staff took off, leaving more than $2 million laying on a table in the office. This was a typical response to the problem of encounters with law enforcement. If the people involved with the laundry were able to avoid capture, they would readily abandon the money. Without the money, they were not tied to any illegal activity, so they could easily escape prosecution and move on to new locations or activities.

On quite a few occasions, the money couriers who were used to transport cash from retail cocaine dealers were suspected to have been discovered by law enforcement agencies. These people were then dropped as couriers or sent back to Colombia if they were Colombians, often to be assigned elsewhere for the same function. Even if they were caught by the police, the DEA, or another agency, the money couriers basically had no information, except that they were instructed to pick up a bag (of cash) from "Jorge" and deliver it to "Pedro" for a commission. The couriers did not count cash or even necessarily see it in the containers that they transported. No links at all were evident to the rest of the laundering chain other than the pickup and delivery points. This kind of sepa- ration of each stage of processing—on the cocaine side as well as on the money side—is standard for money laundering processes.

In its never-ending quest to simplify the laundering process, and to avoid detection by law enforcement, La Mina created an additional means of operation. One of these methods was to use gold sellers and buyers in the same city. This way, drug cash could be exchanged for gold and gold resold to refiners or dealers without shipping it around the country. This worked well for awhile in 1987, but by early 1988, the volume of cash to be laundered had become so large that the physical gold available for trading could not support the laundry.

At this point, the La Mina operators decided to set up yet another method of laundering money that would skip the use of gold entirely. They arranged with A-Mark gold dealers to have paperwork created to fake gold purchases and sales, and thus to receive lots of cash and to transfer out funds via wire transfer to cartel accounts (this method is shown in Figure 6.3).

Here the structure is the same as for the original Los Angeles laundry, except that the gold purchased at A-Mark was never taken into possession by La Mina. A-Mark was simply instructed to accept the cash delivered by the Andonian Brothers Jewelers and to use that cash to buy gold. The gold purchase was then credited to Ronel's account at A-Mark. The next day, Ronel would sell the gold back to A-Mark, and A-Mark would place funds into Ronel's account at a bank in New York. No real gold was needed to complete this loop. As long as

Figure 6.3
La Mina: The "No Gold" Laundry

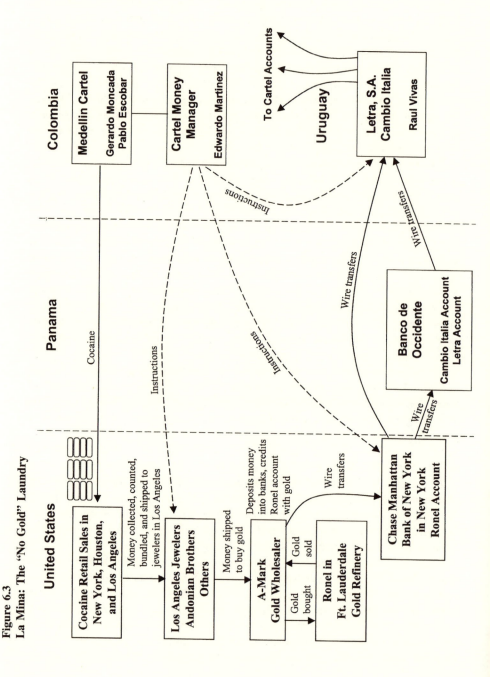

A-Mark was willing to file false documentation, the laundry could operate indefinitely without the need for shipping and handling actual gold.

As you might imagine, the only problem with this scheme was that it was quite transparent to an observer that no gold sales were actually taking place. So, if law enforcement agents were to stumble onto the scheme, it would be difficult, to say the least, to justify the activity as legitimate business. This was, of course, considered by the people at Ronel and A-Mark. In the case of Ronel, the company was apparently in very weak financial condition, and the La Mina business helped keep it afloat. In the case of A-Mark, the La Mina business became so profitable that it was too attractive to drop. People from A-Mark estimated that they earned more than $U.S. 1,000,000 during 1987–88 with the La Mina activity.

The business also was obviously not legitimate, because Letra was losing money at every turn. Letra paid Andonian Brothers Jewelers $260 per kilo of gold for taking cash and using it to buy gold from A-Mark. Letra paid A-Mark the London gold price, plus a premium of about $1.25 per ounce ($41 per kilo) to buy the gold, and then sold it back to A-Mark for the London gold price minus $0.60 per ounce ($20 per kilo). At the time, gold was selling for about $400 per ounce, or $13,200 per kilo. If all of the charges are added together, by the time the money arrived at Letra's account at Banco de Occidente in Panama, or its account in Uruguay, La Mina had lost about 7 percent of the value of the cocaine sales in transactions costs.

This venture fell apart in 1989, when U.S. law enforcement agents penetrated La Mina and arrested Raul Vivas plus the principals in Ronel, A-Mark, Andonian Brothers Jewelers, Ropex, and several other participating firms and individuals. Eduardo Martinez was arrested in Colombia and extradited to the United States, where he was imprisoned. La Mina was spectacular in its meteoric rise to a billion-dollar business, but rather mundane in its demise in the confiscation of more than $100 million, plus cocaine.

POLAR CAP

The DEA-based operation that penetrated La Mina was called Polar Cap, since it was intended to freeze large amounts of Medellin cartel money. It was initiated and built up (i.e., laundering Medellin cocaine cash) before the La Mina money laundering scheme was closed down. Once the DEA agents came to understand the functioning of La Mina, they were able both to set the stage for dismantling it and to pursue additional cocaine traffickers and drug runners. As part of the enforcement effort, U.S. government agents opened their own money laundering business and attracted some of the La Mina participants—particularly Eduardo Martinez—to use their services similar to Raul Vivas'.

This operation offered money laundering services to the cartel parallel to La Mina. In fact, Eduardo Martinez was a main target of this sting, and he was attracted to try out the new laundering operation just as he used other organizations such as La Mina. Martinez operated as more or less a broker for cartel cash receipts in the United States, constantly looking for organizations that could help him get the funds into banks. Because of the huge volume of funds involved, he needed much more than just La Mina to deal with the drug revenues. After testing the reliability of the Polar Cap system, he began to use their services extensively. As with La Mina, this system used individuals (undercover agents) who would receive cash pickups from retail cocaine sales and deposit the funds into bank accounts in the United States. Then, on cartel instructions through Martinez, the funds were wire transferred to offshore accounts, typically at Banco de Occidente in Panama. When La Mina was intervened and many of the participants arrested, Martinez shifted an enormous amount of his business to Polar Cap's scheme.

You can imagine his surprise when the Polar Cap venture was ended with numerous arrests and money confiscations. The government agents used this operation to net numerous money couriers, cartel bank accounts at Banco de Occidente, and other accounts into which drug-generated funds were transferred. Martinez himself was indicted, though he had fled to Colombia. In one of the few instances of this kind of transnational cooperation, Martinez was extradited to the United States and jailed for several years.[2]

This effort led to a number of positive results for law enforcement, namely, the criminal arrests of more than two dozen people and the forfeiture of more than $50 million. But it also produced one black eye for the government, when more than 700 bank accounts were frozen because they had received proceeds of the drug money transferred from Banco de Occidente. The black eye occurred because the government could not prove that all of the recipients of the drug dollars knew that they were receiving drug proceeds. And, because many of the account holders successfully demonstrated that they were "innocent owners" of the funds, they were allowed to keep that money. Among the account holders were literally hundreds of Colombian businesspeople who had purchased dollars in the foreign exchange black market, as well as a number of major multinational companies and even the Chicago Board of Trade, which had a trading account frozen. In each case, these were entities whose clients had paid bills using the black market, thus had transferred drug proceeds through those payments.

Although the use of the foreign exchange black market was illegal in Colombia at the time, the U.S. government would not consider that that activity constituted "specified unlawful activity" that permits the U.S. forfeiture of laundered funds. Therefore, many of the account holders who had received drug money into their accounts were not forced to give up the money, and the law enforcement agencies were stung with criticism for their overzealousness.

In all, the La Mina money laundering operation was a monumental scheme, transacting hundreds of millions of dollars of drug cash per year and demonstrating to U.S. law enforcement the extent of the problem. If this were just one of the money laundering organizations, then how much additional laundering must have been going on? This glimpse of the mechanics of the money laundering and the creativity of the launderers served as a model for further efforts to penetrate the narcotraffickers' money dealings.

NOTES

1. The content of this chapter comes largely from public documents generated in the government's prosecution of La Mina participants under Operation Polar Cap and Operation C-Chase, for example, Criminal Case #89-086-A in the Northern District of Georgia, *USA v. Pablo Escobar et al.* Additional information comes from numerous sources, including, Robert Powis, *The Money Launderers* (Chicago: Probus, 1992), ch. 2, and Jeffrey Robinson, *The Laundrymen* (New York: Arcade, 1996), ch. 16.

2. Actually, Martinez spent relatively little time in prison. It turned out that he had worked with Manuel Noriega in Panama in laundering Medellin cartel money there. When Noriega was tried in Miami for drug trafficking, Martinez was enlisted as a prosecution witness, and for this service he was freed to return to Colombia in 1990.

Chapter 7

General Noriega and Panama, 1981–89

Probably the single largest center for money laundering in the Western Hemisphere, outside of the United States, is Panama. This fact has arisen from the history of Panama's offshore banking center, which has been one of the country's main sources of economic development during the second half of the twentieth century, the Panama Canal, which opened in 1914, and the spending of U.S. military forces in the Canal Zone.

Just after taking power through a military coup in 1968, General Omar Torrijos supported banking legislation that opened Panama to foreign banks and established a high degree of bank secrecy and anonymity of depositors. Interest income is tax free, and bank accounts may be established in corporate and nonpersonal forms. As in Switzerland, Panama has offered users of the financial system a wide scope for secrecy and an ease for moving funds. This combination, along with the dollarization of the Panamanian financial system since 1904, produced a booming financial center, with over $U.S. 36 billion of assets (mainly loans) and $U.S. 37 billion of deposits at the end of 1998. More than 100 international banks (84 of them based in other countries) operate in Panama, almost all of which operate in the offshore sector, taking deposits and making loans to non-residents.

The small and relatively weak Central American countries make an excellent base for money laundering of U.S. currency and other financial instruments. The countries are geographically close to the United States, and dollars are widely used in all of them. For transportation of goods between South America and the United States, again, the Central American countries are located in a desirable intermediate point (see Figure 7.1)

Panama is especially well situated, for several reasons. First and foremost, historically, it is the country through which the Canal permits shipping from the

Figure 7.1
Central America and the Caribbean Islands

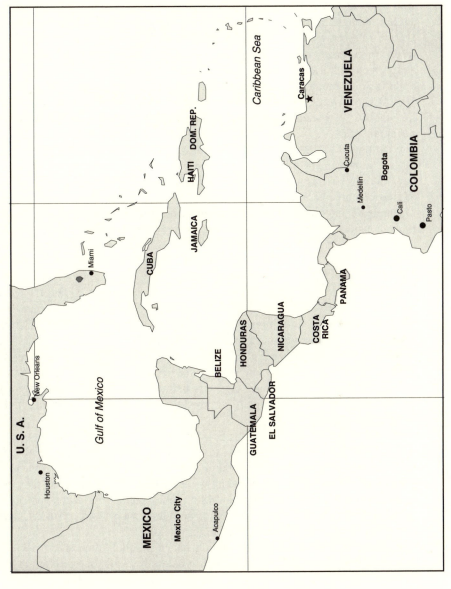

Atlantic (through the Caribbean) to the Pacific, and vice versa. For this reason alone, billions of dollars of dollar-denominated business pass through Panama every year. Second, Panama is the second least troubled Central American country (after Costa Rica) with civil and inter-country conflicts. Guatemala and El Salvador have experienced more years of armed conflict since World War II than years of peace. Honduras has likewise faced continuing civil strife, as well as war with El Salvador. Nicaragua went through the Sandinista revolt and chaotic rule from 1979–89 and still remains extremely weak economically as a result. In contrast, Panama has been at peace for many years and has economically been quite stable with revenues from the Canal and with a completely dollarized economy. Perhaps even more important, the presence of more than 10,000 U.S. troops in the Canal Zone has provided both income and support for stability in Panama (until the Canal Zone was placed under Panamanian governance in 1997). A third feature of Panama's attractive environment is the international banking center, which has resulted from enabling legislation in 1970, along with strict bank secrecy that has kept U.S. enforcement agencies at bay. Eurodollar business in Panama dwarfs that activity anywhere else in the Western Hemisphere.

Panama's international banking center possesses almost all of the finance-related characteristics that make a location attractive for money laundering. Panama's legal system does not differentiate between domestic and foreign bank depositors; both are free to bring money in and take it out of the country, tax-free. The rules on bank secrecy, incorporation and taxation, and financial transfers were established decades ago and remain unchanged. Overall, the country has been very stable economically, resulting in the lowest "country risk" premium for Panamanian borrowers in international capital markets relative to all other Latin American and Caribbean borrowers.

Panama also functions as a tax haven. All foreign income is tax free, as is all locally earned interest income on bank deposits and securities and capital gains on securities. Stock shares can be issued in bearer form, so ultimate owners are not identified. Confidentiality is protected by law in both banking and securities investments.

Finally, Panama's economy has been extremely stable over the past two decades. Inflation has remained similar to U.S. inflation, and not surprisingly, since the currency in use is the U.S. dollar and the essentially free trade environment permits the entry of foreign products without limit. All of these characteristics have favored Panama's development as a money laundering center, not just for drug traffickers but for any number of activities such as tax evasion, capital flight, and funds from other contraband trafficking.

Panama's use as a money laundering haven parallels the career of General Manuel Noriega to some extent, though it certainly began before Noriega's rise to power, and it continues after his ouster by U.S. forces in 1989. When marijuana became a very popular narcotic in the United States in the 1960s and 1970s, Latin American growing sites such as Colombia and Mexico became significant sources of the drug. Particularly for the Colombian traffickers, Panama was a useful target both for staging deliveries of large quantities of marijuana for U.S. destinations and for placing the large amounts of cash generated by the business. Also, for U.S. traffickers, Panama presented an excellent location for placing drug proceeds outside of the reach of U.S. authorities and into accounts that were almost impenetrable due to bank secrecy legislation.

THE NORIEGA SAGA

Manuel Noriega came to power in the Panamanian National Guard under military dictator Omar Torrijos in 1968. When General Torrijos took control of the Panamanian government in a bloodless military coup in November of that year, he named his protégé Noriega as head of Intelligence and second in command of the National Guard. Torrijos and Noriega had worked together for more than a decade of assignments in the National Guard, culminating with Torrijos' overthrow of the elected government of Arnulfo Arias and the establishment of a military dictatorship.

Even before his rise to national power, Noriega had been recruited by the U.S. Central Intelligence Agency (CIA) as a supplier of information about political conditions in Panama, military and economic affairs in Cuba, and similar information in other Central American countries. Additionally, he consorted regularly with the FBI, the DEA, the Defense Intelligence Agency, and many foreign governments, such as those of Israel, Libya, Cuba, and others. As an officer of the Panamanian National Guard, Noriega had significant access to information, and his ambition to gain power and wealth led him to build a relationship in trading information with the United States as well as with other countries. One senior U.S. official in 1981 said something to the effect that "you can't buy Noriega, but you can rent him!"

Noriega had found a solid niche for himself as Torrijos' Intelligence chief during the 1960s, as both were rising through the ranks.[1] This role enabled Noriega to obtain superb access to information and connections with other powerful members of the Panamanian military over the years. It was only when Torrijos took power and Noriega became head of Intelligence for the country that he began to gain access to large quantities of money paid by businesspeople and other governments seeking favors from Noriega himself or from the Panamanian government in general.

Noriega apparently became involved in narcotics trafficking in the early 1970s, when the opportunity arose for him to offer protection to marijuana, heroin, and cocaine smugglers. As head of Intelligence for the National Guard, he was positioned to find out about drug smuggling through the country. In addition to pursuing drug traffickers, he was able to deal with some of the smugglers secretly to receive bribes in exchange for allowing them to continue their activities. In several instances discovered by the U.S. Bureau of Narcotics and Dangerous Drugs (the predecessor of the DEA), Noriega was named by traffickers either caught or under investigation for shipping drugs into the United States as the Panamanian official whom they paid off for their use of Panamanian locations for their business. At that time the U.S. Justice Department chose not to indict him, because it was viewed as a futile pursuit to go after a government leader in a friendly country.

In fact, the DEA was quite happy with Noriega, since he led them to some spectacular seizures of both cocaine and money in Panama after he took over in 1983. (He probably was turning in his competitors in those pursuits, but this is not known for sure.) Even when the U.S. government began to distance itself from Noriega in 1986, after a couple of highly critical *New York Times* articles but prior to the indictment, the DEA was reluctant to drop him as a useful ally.

In any event, after the initial episodes in 1970–72, no further drug smuggling activity was tied to Noriega by U.S. investigators until the beginning of the next decade, when Noriega became involved in the State Department's secret effort to finance the Contra movement in Nicaragua and to overthrow the Sandinista government that had toppled pro-U.S. dictator Anastasio Somoza in 1979. In fact, the most complicated problem for the United States in dealing with the drug running and money laundering carried out or facilitated by Noriega was his many relationships to U.S. authorities. Since arriving at the national level of power in Panama, Noriega had provided the CIA, FBI, and Defense Intelligence Agency with intelligence about his own country and about other countries' military and espionage activities in Panama. From the perspective of the intelligence agencies, Noriega was a valuable asset in Panama in support of U.S. national interests, despite his failings on other fronts.

During the years of the Contra effort against the Sandinistas, internal conditions in Panama changed markedly. In July 1981, President/Dictator Omar Torrijos was killed in a plane crash, which was apparently an accident and not the result of Panama Defense Force (PDF) officers' scheming to overthrow him. A three-way struggle ensued among the highest-ranking PDF officers—Noriega, Ruben Dario Paredes, and Roberto Diaz Herrera. Over a period of more than a year, Noriega and Diaz Herrera maneuvered to push Paredes out of power, and then Noriega subsequently was able to position himself as a PDF leader. In August 1983, Noriega finally consolidated his power and was named head of the PDF and the de facto leader of Panama.

While his drug trafficking participation may have had its ebbs and flows, Noriega was involved in money laundering from the days of his first ventures to bribe taking in the early 1970s. Although his laundering activities were not well documented at that time, once he turned to the BCCI for personal banking services, his trail of suitcases of cash and other financial instruments picked up dramatically. It is known that Noriega held accounts at a dozen or more international banks; the only detailed records that have surfaced thus far come from his dealings with the BCCI. Records obtained from the BCCI in that criminal case showed that Noriega maintained an account averaging more than $U.S. 20 million in the name of the PDF, but with only himself as signator and with no records passed to anyone else.

Amjad Awan, Noriega's personal banker at the BCCI, told fascinating stories about providing banking and personal services to Noriega, from receiving bags of drug cash from couriers all the way to providing credit cards and cash to Noriega, his wife, his mistress, and others on shopping trips to the United States.[2]

Awan described how the BCCI received large quantities of cash from drug traffickers such as Steven Kalish (a major marijuana smuggler) and participants in the Medellin cartel during the 1980s for deposit into Noriega's account. General Noriega's activities became so large that Awan advised him to place the bulk of the funds in London, away from Panamanian eyes and into accounts and real estate that would better hide the nature and source of the money. Among many transactions, Noriega bought a chateau in France with several million of the dollars, and he transferred more than half a million dollars through First American Bank in Washington, D.C., on its way to London. This was interesting, since First American Bank was purportedly owned by independent investors but actually was owned and controlled by the BCCI, despite the Federal Reserve's refusal to allow the bank to buy or establish a full-service financial institution in the United States. When the BCCI was prosecuted in 1990, Clark Clifford and Robert Altman, president and chairman of the board of directors of First American Bank, ultimately had to explain how this fraud had been achieved without their knowledge.[3]

Noriega was indicted for drug trafficking and conspiracy on February 4, 1988, in separate indictments in Miami and Tampa. This explosive set of charges led to no immediate change in the situation but touched off an almost two-year effort by U.S. authorities to force Noriega out of office. Once the charges had been leveled, Noriega moved much of his wealth out of Panama and the Americas and into Europe. This step was once again accomplished with the help of Amjad Awan and the BCCI. More than $23 million were moved into BCCI accounts in London, then transferred to Luxembourg. Then half of that money was moved to a BCCI account in Germany and the other half to an account in Switzerland. Later in the year, the whole amount was wire transferred to the Middle East Bank in London, and then to an account in New York at Capcom, a company formed and owned by BCCI executives.

These funds were ultimately frozen when General Noriega was captured by U.S. forces in 1989. As with the drug money laundering activities of the Colombian traffickers, it is almost certain that Noriega has many additional millions of dollars hidden elsewhere, and that only a small portion of his laundered wealth has been recovered.

LESSONS FROM THE PANAMA/NORIEGA STORY

There is little doubt that the use of Panama as a money laundering center has nothing to do with Manuel Noriega. That is, the attractiveness of Panama for this purpose predates his rise to power and continues after his exit. On the other hand, the fall of General Noriega has everything to do with his being in the right place at the right time to aid drug traffickers moving narcotics to the United States and funds back out of the United States and to aid U.S. authorities in their efforts to deal with revolutions and other problems in Central American countries.

As long as transportation and banking realities continue to favor Panama as an intermediary location, these activites are likely to continue. With bank secrecy becoming less complete as countries, including Panama, try to crack down on money laundering, this activity may decline somewhat. As drug trafficking becomes easier tracked to sites in Panama, the traffickers will look to other locations (such as Mexico) to move their products on the way to the market in the United States. Even with these tendencies, there is no reason to believe that Panama will lose its status as the leading money laundering center in the Western Hemisphere (outside of the United States) for some years to come.

NOTES

This chapter is based on several accounts of the Noriega affair, including: John Dinges, *Our Man in Panama* (New York: Random House, 1990); Frederick Kempe, *Noriega: Toda la Verdad* (Mexico City: Grijalbo, 1990); and testimony in the Polar Cap cases related to the La Mina affair and the government's parallel undercover operation.

1. For a more detailed discussion of this period and the mutual rise of Torrijos and Noriega, see Dinges, *Our Man in Panama*, chs. 2 and 3.

2. Awan became especially cooperative in relating this information about General Noriega's activities when he (Awan) was indicted in the BCCI case for his own participation in laundering millions of dollars for drug traffickers and for Noriega. By providing this testimony that helped convict Noriega, Awan was able to reduce his own jail sentence.

3. This fascinating story was told in several journalistic presentations during the 1990s. See, for example, James Ring Adams and Douglas Frantz, *A Full Service Bank: How BCCI Stole Billions* (New York: Pocket Books, 1992).

Chapter 8

The Bank of Crooks
and Criminals, Inc., 1988–90

The Bank of Credit and Commerce International (BCCI) was born in 1972 in
Abu Dhabi at the beginning of the Middle East's oil-based boom in wealth and
power, and it was put to rest in London and New York on July 5, 1991, after
the bank pled guilty to 11 counts of money laundering in a $U.S. 15 million
Miami court case (in 1990) and was on the verge of indictment in New York
in a $U.S. 30 million case alleging fraud, money laundering, and criminal con-
spiracy. The bank had been founded by a Pakistani businessman, was owned
by a number of Arab businesspeople (see Figure 8.1), and grew to employ more
than 14,000 people in 73 countries around the world. This entire story has been
told several times,[1] thus the discussion here focuses on the money laundering
activity that was led by the bank's officers in Tampa, Miami, and Panama.

BCCI entered the United States in 1978 by opening an agency in New York.
This legal form allowed the bank to make loans to domestic and foreign clients,
but could only take deposits from non-residents. Additional agencies were set
up in Miami and Los Angeles in 1982.

This presence was not adequate for the expansion intended by the bank's
founder, Agha Hasan Abedi, so an attempt was made to purchase a bank in
New York. This attempt was not permitted by U.S. federal regulators, who were
not satisfied with the adequacy of regulation on the bank's parent firm, which
was (legally) headquartered jointly in Luxembourg and the Cayman Islands.

BCCI moved ahead covertly in 1982 by purchasing Financial General Bankshares (later, First American Bankshares) in Washington, D.C., through several
wealthy Arab investors acting as intermediaries. This investment became the
centerpiece of a major governmental investigation, since the BCCI claimed not
to be involved in the venture but subsequently was proven to be the beneficial
owner and controller.[2] In fact, the closure of the bank in July 1991 was tied to

Figure 8.1
The Global Structure of the BCCI Group: Bank of Credit and Commerce International Shareholders (1978)

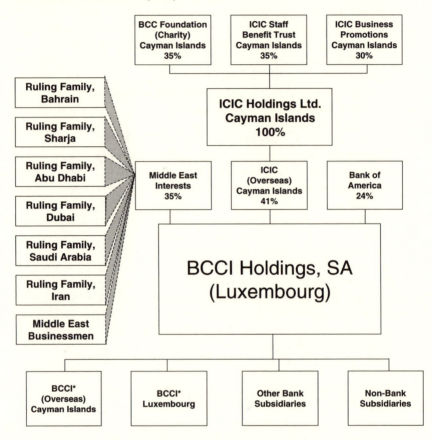

*The Cayman Islands subsidiary established agency offices in Miami, Tampa, and Boca Raton, Florida, during the 1980s. The Luxembourg subsidiary established agency offices in New York, San Francisco, and Los Angeles during the 1980s.

this fraudulent purchase as well as to fraudulent misstatement of BCCI's financial condition and to a series of illegal activities in multiple countries.

The bank generally used its Florida offices as bases for receiving deposits from foreign individuals and companies as well as lending to firms controlled by those individuals and for trade financing in general. The bank was known from the outset of its U.S. activity as an institution that was bent on building its deposit base and assets at a rapid rate. Within the Florida banking community, there was some resistance to BCCI, since the bank was building its business aggressively and taking some customers away from competitors by offering better loan pricing and/or superior service.

BCCI was especially adept at arranging deposits and financing for Arab-country clients and, more generally, clients from less developed countries.[3] This was a particularly important role in the 1980s, when the less developed country (LDC) debt crisis led many governments to impose or to make more strict exchange controls. Such controls typically forbade residents of a (less developed) country from taking funds out of the country or holding dollars or other foreign currency. BCCI, as well as many other banks, often arranged for deposits in less restrictive environments such as tax havens (e.g., Panama, the Cayman Islands) or industrial countries (especially the United States and the United Kingdom).[4]

According to the rules at the time in the United States, banks were to ignore the source-country exchange control rules and only follow U.S. rules on banking activity when dealing with such deposits.[5] This policy allowed foreign nationals to move money into U.S. bank deposits legally in the United States, as long as they declared cash if importing it into the United States, or if they wire transferred funds into the United States from locations where such transfers were legal, such as Panama or Nassau. BCCI became particularly known for its willingness to carry out this type of business, as well as for making loans back to depositors based on the value of their deposits minus a small percentage to cover interest charges. That is, BCCI made "cash collateral loans" in which a deposit was used for collateral to back a loan, thus funds were disbursed in a legal loan after those funds were deposited, often through means that evaded Colombian or other source-country foreign exchange laws.

THE MONEY LAUNDERING CASE IN TAMPA

In late 1988, BCCI was indicted, along with five of its officers, in U.S. federal court in Tampa on 33 counts[6] of money laundering, conspiracy to launder cocaine-derived funds, and conspiracy to traffic in marijuana and cocaine during the period 1983–1988. This was one of the major money laundering cases in the United States during the 1980s, and it began the downfall of BCCI. The specific activity of primary focus in the case was the use of cash-collateral loans by BCCI orchestrated by offices in Florida to serve non-resident depositors, who turned out to be money launderers for narcotics traffickers.

The events leading up to this prosecution appear to be taken directly from the annals of detective fiction of the 1980s. An undercover U.S. Customs agent had offered to deposit drug money into the bank if the bank could transfer that money offshore and make it available for disbursement to various recipients. BCCI bankers suggested that the business be structured as deposits in BCCI offices that would then be exchanged for loans that would effectively launder the money and allow the depositor access to the cleaned funds through loan

Figure 8.2
A Cash-Collateral Loan

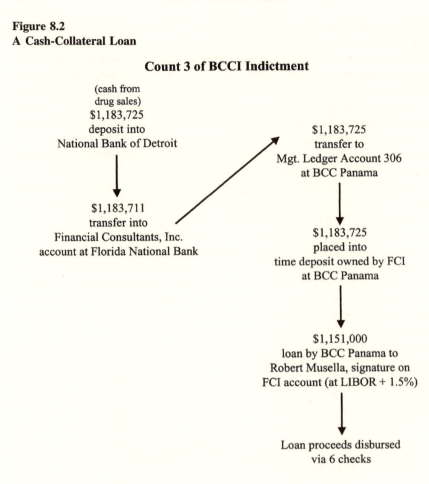

Count 3 of BCCI Indictment

(cash from
drug sales)
$1,183,725
deposit into
National Bank of Detroit

$1,183,711
transfer into
Financial Consultants, Inc.
account at Florida National Bank

$1,183,725
transfer to
Mgt. Ledger Account 306
at BCC Panama

$1,183,725
placed into
time deposit owned by FCI
at BCC Panama

$1,151,000
loan by BCC Panama to
Robert Musella, signature on
FCI account (at LIBOR + 1.5%)

Loan proceeds disbursed
via 6 checks

proceeds that could be disbursed anywhere. The cash-collateral loan process is shown in Figure 8.2.

This set of transactions constituted the third count in the indictment of this case. On December 8, 1987, two money carriers in Detroit, Jaime Giraldo and Norberto Giraldo, delivered $U.S. 1,183,725 in cash to undercover U.S. Customs operatives, who deposited it in the National Bank of Detroit. The next day, BCCI Manager Syed Aftab Hussain opened a bank account at the BCCI in Panama on behalf of Financial Consultants Inc. (FCI), owned by Robert Musella (an undercover U.S. Customs agent). Hussain then arranged to have the funds from Detroit wire transferred to Musella's FCI account at Florida National Bank. The funds were then transferred to the new FCI account in Panama. Several days later, Musella arranged a loan of $U.S. 1,151,000 from the FCI account in Panama. The loan proceeds were disbursed in six checks to Colombian cocaine distributors (through Gonzalo Mora, Jr.). The loan was never repaid, and BCCI simply took possession of the deposit to satisfy the loan payment at maturity.

In general, cash was brought into various banks' offices around the United States and then concentrated via wire transfer in single accounts.[7] BCCI offices in Tampa and Panama then received large wire transfers of funds, and the bank's officers paid no attention to the sources. Within a few days of the deposits being booked, the depositor would take out the funds in the form of a loan for slightly less than the amount of the deposit. The intent, discovered by investigators after the fact, was to take out the funds permanently and to use the deposit to pay off the loan when it came due. This simple method was used to launder $U.S. 15 million in the specific counts in this legal case; it was estimated that more than $U.S. 200 million was laundered by BCCI through these offices during the late 1980s.

The broad strategy of BCCI appears to have been to build up a deposit base without paying much attention to the quality of the clients involved. It was never proven that the bank was involved directly in cocaine trafficking, but there was extensive evidence that BCCI bankers in many locations were willing to turn a blind eye to the sources of money coming into deposits and the uses of those funds when disbursed.[8] The bank became involved with Medellin cocaine traffickers in this case, apparently without purposeful interest in this business.

BRIEF HISTORY OF EVENTS

In the late 1980s, U.S. DEA, Customs, and Treasury agents in many parts of the country were looking for ways to challenge the Colombian cocaine traffickers, whose exports supplied a large part of the U.S. narcotics trade and whose money movements laundered millions of dollars through the U.S. financial system. Since the drug traffickers and money launderers were not interested in making their activities known to law enforcement, tracing those activities was generally a tremendously difficult task.

The Money Laundering Control Act of 1986 gave federal enforcement agencies greater ability to deal with these activities by allowing them to pursue the money involved. For the first time, money laundering itself became a crime rather than just a tool that could be used to demonstrate participation in an illegal activity such as drug trafficking. Now money launderers and even banks could be prosecuted for evading currency reporting laws and for moving funds derived from criminal activity.

One of the mechanisms employed by U.S. enforcement agencies to discover and penetrate these webs of illegal activity was to send agents posing as drug traffickers or money launderers into the "market" to look for business. As they were able to find receptive participants in the shipping of drugs or the movement of money, they would build cases based on the illegal activity and would try to bring the participants to justice. This strategy sometimes led to successful and occasionally spectacular cases being brought, but other times produced insufficient evidence to use in prosecutions.

In one instance where BCCI became involved, the situation evolved from a U.S. Customs operation trying to snare Colombian cocaine traffickers and their related money launderers in Florida. A U.S. Customs agent, Robert Musella, presented himself to a suspected money launderer and offered to provide the service of receiving U.S. dollars in cash at various locations within the United States and then converting them into bank deposits to be used for transferring the money to the drug traffickers. Musella began the episode by trying to do business with Gonzalo Mora, Jr., a Medellin-based export-import company owner who was suspected of being involved in money laundering activity in several U.S. cities. The goal of the sting was to capture Gonzalo Mora delivering cocaine-related money to government agents for supposed laundering and to see where the trail would lead from Mora to other money launderers, and perhaps to cocaine traffickers.

Musella arranged for cooperation with several banks in Florida, Detroit, Los Angeles, and New York. During the development of his relations with Mora, the Colombian asked Musella to arrange an account in Florida with a bank that had an office in Panama, since Mora wanted to use that location for moving some of his money. Musella responded by opening an account at BCCI in Tampa, the city in which he had launched the relationship with Mora.[9] BCCI had not previously been involved in the operation, but Musella picked it as a bank that would make the link with Panama.

The U.S. Customs agents were surprised to find that BCCI managers were more than willing to take on new business to build up deposits and to move funds through the financial system for rapid payout to unknown recipients. That is, BCCI executives in Tampa, and also in Miami and Panama, welcomed Musella with open arms into a business that would produce occasional large wire transfers of funds into BCCI offices, occasional transfers to offshore BCCI offices, and then distribution of the funds within days. In fact, BCCI managers recommended to Musella the use of the cash-collateral loan, in which the loan would actually be used to withdraw the funds, and the deposit would be used ultimately to pay off the loan (with fees charged by BCCI, of course, for carrying out the transactions).

The dealings with Mora began in 1986, and by early 1987, he had requested the arrangement of a funds transfer through Panama. The first transaction with the BCCI took place in 1987, and arrangements such as the one pictured in Figure 8.2 became common. In fact, the transactions sometimes became more complicated, as when General Noriega of Panama was accused by the United States in February, 1988 of being involved in protecting drug traffickers, and when some funds transfers from Panama were frozen. Mora's concern with this problem led to arrangements to pass the funds through BCCI offices in France, Luxembourg, and other European locations instead of in Panama, as depicted in Figure 8.3. Figure 8.3 also brings into the picture the cocaine trade, which was being facilitated through this money laundering process.

This figure depicts one of the many cash-collateral loans in the BCCI scheme, but it is fairly representative of the others as well. Cocaine was shipped from Colombia by pilots contracted by drug traffickers, in this case, members of the Medellin cartel. The cocaine was received in U.S. locations, often in Florida, and then shipped on for retail sales. The cocaine involved in the BCCI scheme was sold in Detroit, Los Angeles, New York, and Miami. The drug traffickers' employees would receive cash from retail sales in these various cities and arrange to place it in bank deposits. The particular transaction in the figure shows over $2 million in drug money delivered in New York City, which was then wire transferred to Miami and on to Luxembourg and Nassau. A loan was taken out based on that deposit, and four checks were used to pay out about 90 percent of the amount, leaving the rest to pay off the bank for the services rendered.

The whole process of getting the millions of dollars of drug cash into the banking system is a story told elsewhere (see Chapter 1). Once funds were entered into a bank account, they could then be shuffled to different locations and disbursed as chosen by the bank account owner. Musella arranged to have the cash deposited into cooperating banks in each of the cities, and then he made transfers as agreed upon with money launderers. In this case, he had funds wire transferred first to an account at Florida National Bank in Miami and then to BCCI offices, from which Gonzalo Mora withdrew them to pay cocaine traffickers.

The money movements were numerous, enormous, and quite varied as to accounts and bank locations used, up to the final point of paying out funds to cartel-related individuals or accounts. In Count 11 of the indictment, for example, drug cash of $U.S. 1,384,810 was picked up in Houston and deposited in Interfirst Southwest Bank there. These funds were wire transferred to an account at Florida National Bank per instructions from Gonzalo Mora. Of this total, $1,287,873 was wire transferred to the Lamont Maxwell account at BCCI in Panama. These funds were then divided into $1 million, which was wire transferred to Algemene Bank Nederland in Amsterdam. This $1 million was subsequently wire transferred to a new account in the BCCI office in Paris. The remaining $287,873 was wire transferred to New York and then on to Banco Occidente in Montserrat. The transfers out of Panama were to avoid the political problems in Panama. The funds were subsequently retransferred to Panama after several months and then disbursed to cocaine traffickers through checks drawn on the Panama account.

After almost two years of these activities, the U.S. government issued the indictment of BCCI and its officers. The bank officers were arrested in Tampa and held until trial. Once convicted, they all began serving prison sentences ranging from 3 to 12 years. The bank paid a $U.S. 15 million fine and agreed to close its offices in Florida.

Figure 8.3
The Full BCCI Cocaine Trafficking–Money Laundering Cycle (Indictment Count 13)

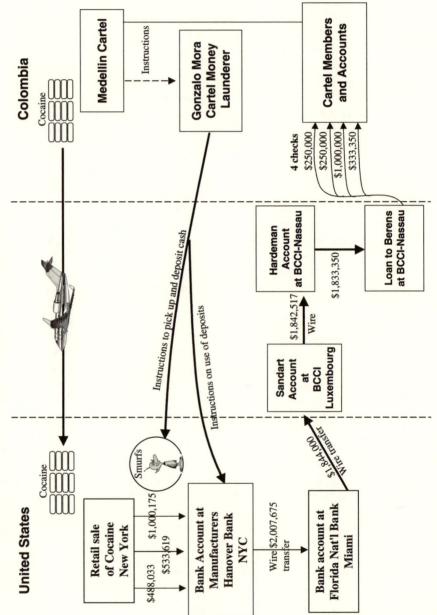

RESPONSES BY U.S. AUTHORITIES

How did the U.S. authorities deal with the money laundering problems raised by this case? With respect to the specific bank officers involved, the response was rapid and relatively harsh—jail sentences for all involved. With respect to BCCI, the penalty was a fine of $15 million and an admittance to guilt of money laundering but not conspiracy to distribute cocaine. The broader involvement of the bank in laundering money around the world was not fully detected, and the activity that was detected was not prosecuted until further events placed BCCI under scrutiny once again.

U.S. government agencies demonstrated a continued failure to communicate among themselves and to cooperate when communications did occur. The findings of corrupt behavior and pervasive money laundering uncovered by the U.S. Customs agent in the Tampa case were shelved by the Justice Department, which did not carry out further prosecution until massive evidence had surfaced about BCCI's covert ownership of First American Bankshares in Washington, D.C. Likewise, evidence that the bank was involved in drug-related dealing with General Noriega was presented by the CIA in a report in 1985, but this was never used by enforcement agencies to pursue the bank.[10]

The specific money laundering activity of BCCI and its officers, as uncovered in the U.S. Customs operation and prosecuted in the Tampa case, probably demonstrates a reasonable response by the U.S. government. The subsequent huge outcry against the bank and against the government's slow reaction had much more to do with its fraudulent activities and its non-U.S. dealings with corrupt politicians and with the terrorist Abu Nidal. Under the money laundering laws in place at the time and even in 1999, this prosecution was as far as the government could go in dealing with BCCI.

LESSONS FOR BANKERS

The fact that the U.S. government followed this trail to a reasonable conclusion, and the fact that the bank in question was itself corrupt, does not protect other banks from falling into similar problems of money laundering. Even one rogue manager can conceivably portray a proposed client in a sufficiently positive light so that the bank accepts that client. Then wire transfer activity such as the cash-collateral loan structure can be used to hide underlying illegal business of the client. No individual bank in the chain of the laundry process would have reason to know the additional movements of funds that are shown in Figures 8.2 and 8.3.

The first key lesson here is that a bank should require sufficient information on a client so that one bank officer cannot control the entire information process seen by the rest of the bank. Not only does the bank need to follow a careful "know your customer" policy, it also needs to ensure that the policy is implemented by more than one person in every instance.

Second, the bank needs to identify types of activity such as the cash-collateral loan that may be used to hide drug money laundering. This may be devilishly difficult to deal with in contexts such as the situation in Florida during the Latin American debt crisis of the 1980s. At that time, many Latin American clients brought in deposits that contravened exchange control laws in their own countries. U.S. (Treasury) policy was to turn a blind eye to those foreign laws and to accept deposits if clients were involved in otherwise legitimate business activities. Thus discerning which additional activities of clients are legal and which are not may appear to be a rather silly step for bankers to take—but the money laundering prosecutions of the late 1980s and 1990s demonstrate that this is anything but silly. Bankers need to identify and codify the kinds of transactions that become known as money laundering vehicles and then need to establish bank policies that weed out such activities.

The lesson of the BCCI experience that brought down the bank is not applicable to other banks, unless they too are operated as criminal enterprises. In a normal, competently regulated, legally and prudently managed bank, the problems are more likely to be the unwitting assistance to money launderers of money deposit and transfer through the bank. These problems can be dealt with as suggested above.

NOTES

1. See, for example, James Ring Adams and Douglas Frantz, *A Full Service Bank: How BCCI Stole Billions* (New York: Pocket Books, 1992). See also Peter Truell and Larry Gurwin, *False Profits* (Boston: Houghton Mifflin, 1992).

2. Truell and Gurwin, *False Profits*, pp. 58–70.

3. Adams and Frantz, *A Full Service Bank*, p. 92.

4. During the 1980s, the BCCI was prosecuted by the Colombian government for operating a business for transferring Colombians' wealth overseas in contravention of the country's foreign exchange laws. See Adams and Frantz, *A Full Service Bank*, p. 93; Truell and Gurwin, *False Profits*, pp. 168–169.

5. The U.S. Treasury perspective was that deposits from foreign country nationals that may have broken those countries' exchange control laws were to be accepted in the United States, because they enabled flight capital that would move anyway to move in a way that is visible and manageable by U.S. authorities. Also, the U.S. Treasury viewed such flight capital as "open market" funds flows, which should help force the home countries to open up their capital markets as the U.S. government desired.

This perspective conflicted with the U.S. Justice Department's; the latter was interested in stopping the flow of narcotics-related funds through the U.S. financial system. It became well known in the United States and in Colombia in the late 1980s and early 1990s that drug money was being laundered through this mechanism. The Treasury Department view prevailed, and drug money prosecutions were forced to trace drug-related funds explicitly rather than stop them because of their transfer in evasion of Colombian foreign exchange laws.

6. The case was filed in U.S. District Court for the Middle District of Florida (Case #88-330-CR-T-13 (B)).

7. It is interesting to note that the conversion of drug dollars (cash) into bank accounts took place outside of the BCCI. If the drug money had not been traced to the banks in Detroit, Miami, and elsewhere, the whole process of undercover work that implicated the BCCI might never have unfolded.

8. The story is incredibly more extensive than this involvement with Colombian cocaine traffickers. The BCCI was found to have operated an illegal, multimillion-dollar account for General Noriega in Panama, into which bribes and stolen Panamanian government funds were deposited and then used by Noriega. The BCCI was found to have operated an account for terrorist Abu Nidal through which millions of dollars were transferred to buy and sell weapons and to support terrorist activities. In addition, the BCCI was found to have operated many other accounts that were used by Arab officials to move money for personal use and for numerous third-world businesspeople to evade exchange control laws in their home countries. See Adams and Frantz, *A Full Service Bank*, or Truell and Gurwin, *False Profits*, for details.

9. The federal enforcement operation described here was called Operation C-Chase, named after the Tampa apartment complex, Calibre Chase, where U.S. Customs agents began their plan to capture Mora.

10. This point is documented by Adams and Frantz, *A Full Service Bank*, p. 134.

Chapter 9

The Santacruz-Londoño
Organization, 1988–90

The story of this cartel would require a book in itself, and the full range of money laundering activity likewise would be quite a tale. The activities described here are ones that were uncovered by law enforcement and traced carefully through the details—but certainly hundreds of times this amount of money laundering also was carried out by the Santacruz-Londoño organization and has not met the light of day. The money laundering venture that was uncovered led to the seizure and eventual forfeiture of about $U.S. 58 million in bank accounts around the world.

Jose Santacruz-Londoño was known as one of the leaders of the Cali-based cocaine cartel, beginning as early as 1979 and ending "officially" with his arrest and imprisonment in 1995. His colleagues as leaders in the Cali cartel included the Rodriguez brothers, Miguel and Gilberto Rodriguez Orajuela. Santacruz was first indicted by U.S. authorities for cocaine distribution in New York in 1985 and was subsequently indicted in other cases. He remains a fugitive from U.S. authorities to the present, although he is currently imprisoned in Colombia.

In 1989 and 1990, his organization became involved in a money laundering scheme that authorities were able to penetrate, and it is this scheme that makes up the heart of this chapter. In addition to the complex web of money movements that constitutes this laundering venture, it is an interesting example of the use of wire transfers to try to convert cocaine revenues into legitimate, or at least laundered, forms in far-flung locations.

The cast of characters in this story is fairly extensive, from the cocaine kingpin and his family to smurfs moving street-sale revenues into bank accounts in the United States. The main participants in the scheme include Jose Santacruz-Londoño, his father-in-law Heriberto Castro-Mesa, his wife Amparo Castro de Santacruz, and his daughter Ana Milena Santacruz. These family members helped with the business by opening bank accounts in their names and moving funds to various destinations around the world. A second set of main characters includes three Colombian money launderers in Europe: Jose Franklin Jurado, Edgar Garcia, and Ricardo Mahecha, who traveled to numerous cities in Europe opening bank accounts and transferring funds out of accounts in the United States and in Panama into and among the European accounts. And a third and final set of main participants in this money laundering venture are the cambistas in Colombia, who arranged to obtain and deposit dollars in overseas accounts for Colombian businesspeople and to receive Colombian pesos from them for credit to Cali cartel beneficiaries. These people include Jaime Vargas, Gonzalo Velez, Manuel Mora, Jairo Carrascal, and others.

The scheme was uncovered serendipitously in 1989, when the neighbor of a Colombian national living in Luxembourg complained to police that a person was living in a luxury apartment and receiving and sending phone messages and faxes late into the night. That irritation, plus the fact that the person in question, Jose Franklin Jurado, had no evident job or other means of support, led to the complaint that in turn led police to discover that Jurado was indeed involved in some suspicious activity.

A local police investigation led to the discovery that one fax transmission had gone to Miguel Rodriguez Orajuela, one of the leaders of the Cali cartel. The Luxembourg police, the Sureté Publique, conferred with the U.S. DEA to see if they had encountered any information about Jurado in money laundering or cocaine trafficking investigations. A routine investigation by both agencies then turned up an increasingly complex web of Jurado's movements and transactions in Europe and connections to Santacruz, in particular in Colombia.

Jurado was found to be operating with two other Colombian nationals, Edgar Alberto Garcia and Ricardo Mahecha. Together and individually, the three were traveling through Western Europe in 1989 and 1990, opening bank accounts in the names of family members and associates of Jose Santacruz and depositing checks and wire transfers in huge amounts.

In one such transaction, the three deposited about $U.S. 170,000 into an account at Banca Nazionale del Lavoro in Bologna, Italy. The account was in the name of Heriberto Castro-Mesa, father-in-law of Jose Santacruz. Castro-Mesa also was the assistant manager of at least three companies owned by Santacruz. These funds were in the form of a check drawn on the account of the Siracusa Trading Company at a Costa Rican bank in Panama. This transaction is sketched in Figure 9.1.

The Siracusa Trading Company proved to be a front company, established to launder cocaine proceeds. Its owners were listed as Jose Santacruz, Heriberto Castro-Mesa, and Amparo Castro de Santacruz. The funds arrived at Siracusa from the United States and were then transferred via check to the account in Italy.

A few days later, Mahecha and Jurado were observed making deposits of $U.S. 150,000 each into four different banks in Copenhagen, Denmark. These

Figure 9.1
The Siracusa Laundry

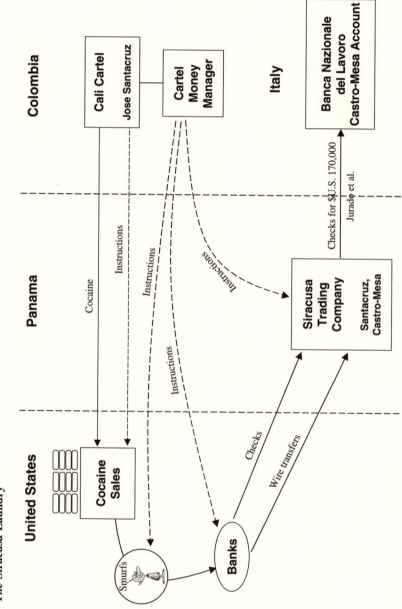

deposits also were made by check, and in at least two instances, they were drawn on the same Siracusa Trading Company account in Panama.

Two weeks later, Jurado and Garcia were arrested in Luxembourg on money laundering charges. Jurado claimed that he was working for Garcia and that he controlled $U.S. 28 million of accounts throughout Europe in this money handling business.

Where did this money come from, and where was it going? While the record is not complete on the hundreds of millions of dollars that appear to have been laundered through this scheme, more than $U.S. 58 million has been carefully traced through its path from cocaine sales in the United States to bank deposits in Panama and transfers elsewhere throughout the Americas and Europe.

The process began with the sale of cocaine imported by the Santacruz organization into New York City. The drugs were shipped from Colombia and sold in New York. Retail sales produced millions of dollars of cash, which were systematically smurfed into the banking system by dozens of individuals. Some of the cash was taken physically from the United States and shipped to Panama for deposit in various banks there as well. This process is common to most of the money laundering ventures described here.

In the context of the $U.S. 20 million that was followed through the U.S.-Panama-Colombia part of the laundry, about $U.S. 3.5 million was concentrated in the account of the Siracusa Trading Company in Panama. The money arrived there through various wire transfers, checks, and cash moved from the U.S. points of initial receipt of the funds from cocaine sales. Figure 9.2 shows this initial stage of the laundering process.

From the Siracusa account, among others, funds were moved into European accounts. These transfers were done by check and wire transfer, including the transactions described earlier. Jurado, Garcia, and Mahecha appear to have been the main money movers at this stage of the process. The movement of funds to Europe was done through accounts in the names of Cali cartel individuals, but the actual transfers were carried out by these money men. While the transfers of money out of Panama may have been simply to diversify the holdings into several banks, they probably were done to get the money out of Panama, which had become highly visible and scrutinized as a money laundering haven as a result of the overthrow of General Manuel Noriega there and his subsequent trial in Miami in 1990.

The money did not rest for long in European accounts. The ultimate goal for most of these funds was their remittance to Colombia and conversion into pesos for Santacruz and his associates. There the money would be used to pay expenses, make purchases, and invest in financial instruments and real estate. Another step or two was needed to accomplish that result.

While Jurado and others were moving money from Panama into Europe, the laundry also was operating in Colombia. The final step of converting the money into pesos and delivering it to cartel accounts in Colombia required finding providers of pesos. This was easy to do, since many Colombians wanted to take

Figure 9.2
The Jurado et al. Laundry

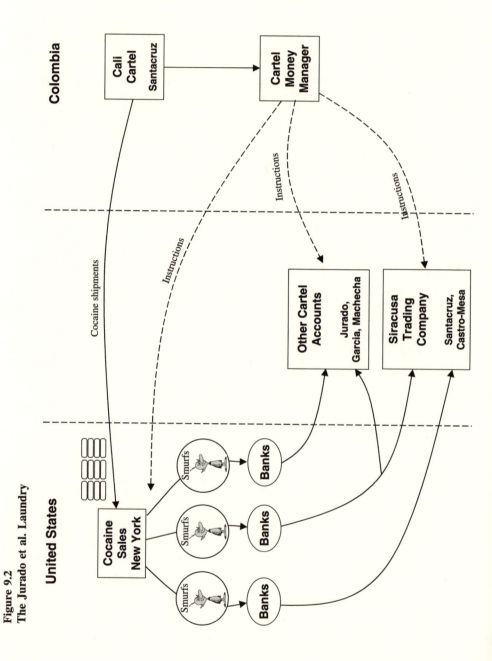

some of their wealth out of the country and put it into safe havens such as the United States and safe currencies such as the U.S. dollar. The match of interests was obvious, but the mechanism for putting the two sides together required additional subterfuge.

At the time of this series of events, Colombian residents were prohibited from holding overseas bank accounts, except by obtaining permission from the government for purposes such as paying for approved imports, paying for overseas medical treatment, paying for overseas student expenses, and other selected uses. The net result was that many Colombians who wanted to hold funds overseas chose to use the foreign exchange black market to do so.

One way for them to do this was to buy dollars in cash from cambistas in Colombia in exchange for pesos. This would give the person dollars, which he or she then had to take physically out of the country to deposit somewhere, such as in Panama, Miami, Nassau, New York, or any other presumably safe destination. This was an effective way to place wealth outside of Colombia, but it certainly was complicated by the need to travel overseas, to carry bulky currency, and to deal directly with a financial institution there. An easier way to accomplish the same goal was to hire someone else to carry out the transfer—for example, the cambista who was selling the dollars in the first place. The cambista would buy pesos from the individual and in return would arrange the transfer of dollars into a bank account in that person's name (or company name, etc.) in the United States or elsewhere.

Presto! A beautiful match for the drug runners. If a Colombian businessman wanted dollars on deposit in the United States, and if a drug runner wanted pesos in Colombia, then a cambista could receive cash dollars from drug sales in the United States and could deposit them in a U.S. bank account while accepting pesos from the businessman in Colombia and depositing them in the drug runner's account. No money needed to cross national borders—no plane trips, no bulky cash to transport. The only inconvenience was the fee charged by the cambista, which would take a bite out of both the businessman's and the drug runner's funds. At the time, this bite was about 6–8 percent of the value being transferred, charged to each side.

In sum, then, the last step needed by cartel associates in order to repatriate their earnings from U.S. drug sales was a source of pesos in Colombia to exchange for those dollars. The cambistas[1] offered just this service.

In reality, the cambistas generally were independent operators, not direct employees of the cartels. So the cartel managers would search for willing and reliable cambistas to help with their funds deposits and transfers. The cartel money managers would shop around among cambistas to obtain better (lower) rates for receiving, depositing, and transferring the money, and they also would diversify their use of cambistas to avoid overdependence on any one of them. The result of this set of considerations was that cartel money managers dealt extensively with bids for services, instructions for money pickups and transfers, and bank account information, but the actual laundry process was carried out largely by independent cambistas.

THE BARRANQUILLA SCHEME

In the present situation, the cartel money managers included Roberto Juri and Edgar Garcia, both in Cali. The cambistas were several, but a few in particular were used intensively. They included Jaime Vargas, Manuel Mora, and Jairo Carrascal.

Some of the dollars earned from street sales of cocaine in New York were transferred to cartel accounts in Panama. These funds arrived as wire transfers from U.S. banks, where smurfing operations had gotten them into the banking system and sometimes in cash shipped physically from New York. In a fairly direct manner, millions of dollars that had been concentrated in cartel accounts in Panama and managed by Edgar Garcia and others were transferred through New York banks to Colombia. These transfers were made through correspondent accounts of the Banco de Caldas and the Banco del Estado, both Colombian commercial banks, at the New York offices of banks such as Manufacturers Hanover and the Bank of New York.

The funds were then wired on to the Banco de Colombia, Colombia's Central Bank, which converted the money into pesos and passed it on to the Banco de Caldas or the Banco del Estado. These banks in turn credited the accounts of individuals specified by cambistas such as Carrascal and Mora. The individuals were generally Colombian businessmen based in Barranquilla, who had claimed to be exporting clothing and who thus were receiving the funds as payment for their exports. In fact, these businessmen were operating front companies that did little or no clothes exporting,[2] and they received fees for allowing their businesses to be used for receiving the pesos from the Central Bank. They passed the bulk of the money on to cartel associates in exchange for keeping a percentage as a commission.

The arrangement was even more lucrative for the Colombian businessmen in this instance, due to Colombia's tax system. A rebate of 12 percent of export sales was offered to clothing exporters to stimulate the production and export of this non-traditional product. By creating false invoices for clothing exports, the businessmen were able to justify bringing in large amounts of dollars through the legal banking system, keeping a small percentage of the funds for themselves before passing the bulk on to the cartel. At the same time, they received 12 percent of the value of the feigned exports directly from the Colombian government in subsidy payments. Needless to say, this was a very profitable racket! Figure 9.3 depicts the complicated path of the money in this part of the laundry. Even this picture fails to capture the full complexity of the scheme, since more than one cambista was used to arrange money deposits and transfers, and almost two dozen fake clothing exporters were involved as participants.

The clothing exports were themselves quite a creative activity. Some of the

Figure 9.3
The Clothing Export Scam

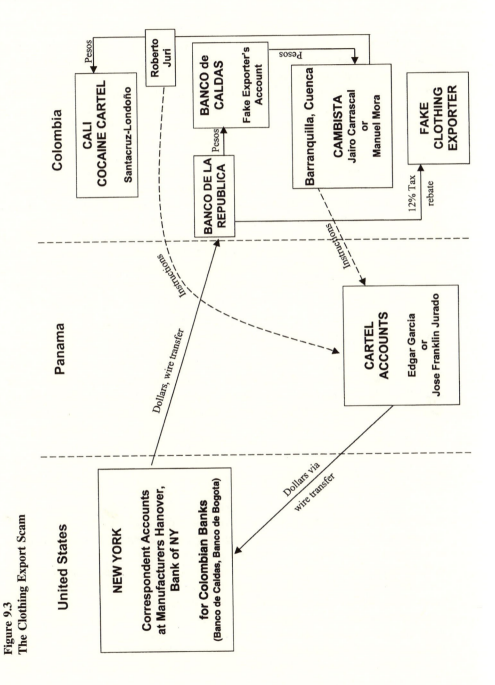

exporters actually shipped some clothes, generally to a "purchaser" in Panama. The company in Panama did not sell the clothes but repackaged them and sent them on a return voyage through the Caribbean that apparently returned to Colombia. The clothes were then sold in the underground market of San Andresitos—unregistered vendors of imported products who sometimes brought the products into Colombia through the free trade zone on the island of San Andres. Most of the clothing exports were completely fictitious and existed only as falsified documents that were used to claim the drug dollars repatriated from U.S. accounts and the 12 percent tax rebate from the Colombian government.

As with other money laundering schemes, this one did not continue in the form shown for very long. Fear of pursuit by law enforcement (a very well-founded concern in this instance!) and difficulty in assuring the continued reliability of the smurfs, fake exporters, bankers, and other participants led to the use of this structure on a temporary basis, before moving on to other arrangements. The Panamanian connection was particularly unsettled, since the initial indictment of General Noriega in 1988 by U.S. law enforcement led to a crackdown on drug running and money laundering there for more than a year. Subsequently, it appears that business has returned to more or less normal, but in 1990, when General Noriega was captured by U.S. law enforcement, Panama again was subject to intensive drug and money laundering enforcement efforts.

ANOTHER PIECE OF THE BUSINESS—MONEY ORDERS, CASHIER'S CHECKS, AND STRUCTURED DEPOSITS

Another link in the chain of laundering drug proceeds for the Santacruz organization by Jose Franklin Jurado was a New Jersey-based scheme operated by Paulina de Quintero and Julio Montes. This part of the overall set of mechanisms used by the Jurado organization specialized in the use of money orders and cashier's checks to convert street dollars from drug sales ultimately into bank deposits. The operation processed mainly dollars from New York drug sales, and the laundry was operated from a duplex at 225–227 Woolworth Street in South Plainfield, New Jersey.

The origin of the scheme, operated by Montes and de Quintero, was their link to Jurado, who agreed to have drug cash delivered to them in exchange for returning those funds (minus a commission) through wire transfers out of bank accounts that Montes and de Quintero managed. The scheme operated essentially as a subcontracted extension of Jurado's activities.

The Montes/de Quintero organization used money orders and cashier's checks extensively as part of the scheme to get drug dollars into bank accounts without filing CTRs. Enforcement agencies discovered that, during 1989, the organization had routinely used smurfs to make numerous cash deposits of less than $U.S. 10,000 per transaction in New Jersey banks. In addition, and sometimes in the same visits to banks, they bought cashier's checks and money orders, also in amounts less than $U.S. 10,000 per transaction, to convert drug cash into other monetary instruments. In each of the two methods, the launderers were structuring transactions to avoid CTR filing requirements. If the total number of cash deposits and/or money order purchases for an individual smurf was counted for any given date, the sums generally were far more than $10,000. In fact, law enforcement agents found several dates on which more than $U.S. 100,000 had been converted from cash into checks and money orders and sent together to recipients in Miami. The checks and money orders were routinely shipped via courier service to Miami or New York for deposit into accounts controlled by de Quintero or Montes.

Some of the checks and money orders were deposited into the accounts of third-party individuals. These people were discovered to have purchased the checks and money orders through the Colombian foreign exchange black market. They were not generally aware of how the funds got into their accounts, since these individuals simply delivered pesos to foreign exchange black market dealers (cambistas) in Colombia and then expected to receive dollars in their U.S. accounts. This wrinkle and the entire scheme operated by de Quintero and Montes are depicted in Figure 9.4.

One of the recipient accounts of the structured cashier's checks and money orders was in the name of the Friko Corporation. It was discovered that this company was headed by Johnny Daccarett, a Colombian national living in Barranquilla. Daccarett was the same person whose Manufacturas JD company was falsely claiming to export clothing from Barranquilla and had received several million dollars in drug proceeds in that previous instance. Interestingly, Daccarett was unable to pursue his claim on the seized funds because he was a convicted cocaine trafficker and money launderer fugitive from U.S. law enforcement. As with the Manufacturas JD account, the Friko account was at Merrill Lynch in New York.

The Montes/de Quintero organization was quite consistent in never depositing $U.S. 10,000 or more at a time or buying money orders for values in excess of that amount. In this way they avoided the CTR filings that otherwise would have been required at the banks that were used. Unfortunately for them, the Money Laundering Control Act of 1986 also made the structuring of cash transactions to avoid detection a crime—and obviously these activities constituted the structuring of cash deposits to launder the drug money. The 20 or so lead participants in the scheme were apprehended and jailed in 1989, although Paulina de Quintero remained a fugitive in Colombia after safely escaping the crackdown.

The Cali cartel was gravely hurt by the 1995 arrests of its three known leaders—Jose Santacruz-Londoño, and Miguel and Gilberto Rodriguez Orajuela. This turn of events caused a large drop-off in the drug shipments owned and distributed by the organizations of the three leaders, but they were quickly replaced by other entrepreneurs. Even the annual narcotics shipment estimates for 1995 and 1996 show no appreciable decline in Colombian overall drug activity. The money laundering scheme that has just been described no longer functions,

Figure 9.4
The Montes/de Quintero Structuring Scheme

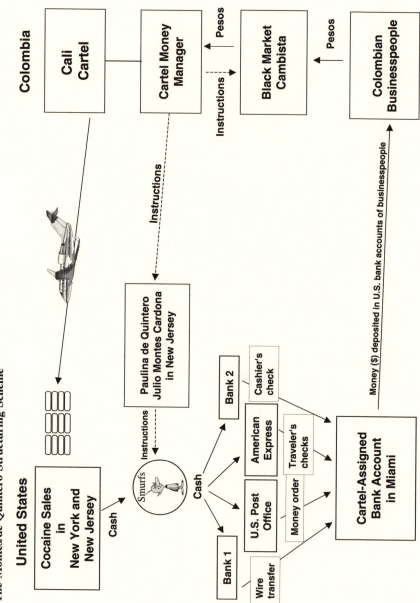

but hundreds of millions of dollars that were not caught in the law enforcement effort remain in the hands of the cartel associates.

NOTES

This chapter is largely based on information obtained from the legal proceedings in four legal cases, including: *U.S. v. Jose Franklin Jurado and Edgar Alberto Garcia* (CR-94-547, Eastern District of New York); *U.S. v. All Funds at Merrill Lynch et al.* (CV-90-2510, Eastern District of New York); *U.S. v. Monies deposited in Lloyd's Bank et al.* (CV-90-2269, Southern District of New York); and *U.S. v. Julio Montes Cardona, Myriam Marchena, Paulina DeQuintero et al.* (CR-90-0069-01, District of New Jersey).

1. It should be noted that cambistas are merely money exchangers, common throughout Latin America and elsewhere in the world as well. By no means were all cambistas linked directly to cocaine distributors in Colombia. Probably relatively few of them were at the time, however, the cambistas traded funds among themselves to be able to service the market efficiently, and so the dollars delivered by any cambista ran the risk of being drug dollars, either directly or secondhand.

2. In some cases, a small amount of clothing was actually exported to Panama, where it was repackaged and reshipped back to Colombia. The clothing was then sold in the underground market, and the sales were not reported to the government.

Chapter 10

Stephen Saccoccia, 1988–91

A money laundering venture that rivaled La Mina was built by Stephen Saccoccia just after the downfall of the Raul Vivas/Eduardo Martinez laundry. In the late 1980s, Saccoccia began to operate a money laundering business through his gold and precious metals company, Trend Precious Metals, near Providence, Rhode Island. This business grew to the point in 1990 that it was able to take in over $150 million in drug cash during the year from three major Colombian drug traffickers and to move it into bank accounts and then out again into overseas accounts.

The precious metals business has proven to be an excellent cover activity for money laundering schemes because of the large dollar volume that can be involved in precious metals transactions and the apparent legitimacy of numerous transactions as one "plays the market." In other words, a precious metals dealer may buy and sell hundreds of millions of dollars worth of gold in a year in numerous transactions, show a minimal profit, produce limited business records that appear legitimate, and not raise suspicion.

Saccoccia had built a precious metals business in Rhode Island during the 1980s. This business was engaged mainly in the buying and selling of gold, coins, and precious metals such as silver and platinum. He and his wife, Donna, operated the business in the suburbs of Providence, while they began to build up an underground activity on the side.

Beginning in 1987, as far as law enforcement could determine, the business began to change to reflect the entry of a new type of client. This new client would deliver large quantities of cash in bills of a small denomination, in return for which Saccoccia's companies would deposit the funds into bank accounts and transfer the bank account balances to other accounts in various U.S. cities and abroad in Colombia, Panama, and Switzerland. Saccoccia's firms would retain a small percentage of the deposits as a commission for the processing, and the rest was sent to the ultimate Colombian owners of the money, who were members of the Medellin cartel.

Just as with La Mina, the amounts of money laundered were staggering—over $U.S. 100 million, at least in 1990 and 1991. If these cases combined represent perhaps 1 percent of the total drug money laundering, as is probably the reality, then the overall laundering business must have been approximately in the tens or hundreds of billions of dollars in these years.

As far as law enforcement agencies have found, beginning in 1986, Saccoccia began to launder money through his precious metals business. One particular arrangement that was uncovered began in 1987, when he arranged for drug cash received from Duvan Arboleda, a Medellin cartel money manager, to be delivered to Barry Slomovitz, another money launderer in New York City. Slomovitz used the cash to covertly purchase gold, which he resold on the open market. The amounts realized from those sales were then wired to bank accounts maintained by two of Saccoccia's corporations, Trend Precious Metals in Cranston, Rhode Island, and International Metal Marketing (IMM) in Los Angeles. In order to create the appearance that the funds transferred were derived from legitimate business transactions, the Saccoccias had phony invoices issued to Slomovitz, falsely indicating that the amounts wired to Trend and IMM were payments for gold purchases.

Another arrangement early in Saccoccia's money laundering career involved cash delivered to him in Rhode Island, cash that he would receive at Trend's offices at 129 Fletcher Avenue in Cranston, Rhode Island. He would then have couriers deposit the money typically in the Heritage Loan and Investment Company but also in several other financial institutions. The cash would be taken by armored car—contracted with Brinks or Loomis—and presented to the banks as the proceeds of gold and jewelry sales.

Some of the money was used to buy checks from these banks. The checks were made payable to various companies controlled by Stephen Saccoccia, such as Trend Precious Metals, International Chain Sales, and Gold Enterprises Refinery. The couriers would then take large numbers of checks—each written for an amount under $U.S. 10,000—and deposit them in the accounts of the payees. Subsequently, the accounts were debited and the funds were transferred to the Trend Precious Metals account at Citizens Trust Bank in Providence, Rhode Island.

The representative of the drug trafficker, either Fernando Dueñas or Raul Escobar, would send him instructions by fax to distribute the funds after laundering the cash. Sometimes the instructions were passed through Duvan Arboleda in Miami for disposition of the funds. Once the funds were concentrated at the Trend account in Rhode Island, Saccoccia would transfer them according to those instructions to banks in New York, Panama, Colombia, and elsewhere. This initial phase of the laundry is described in Figure 10.1.

This process worked well enough to encourage Saccoccia and his drug traf-

Figure 10.1
Saccoccia: Initial Rhode Island Laundry

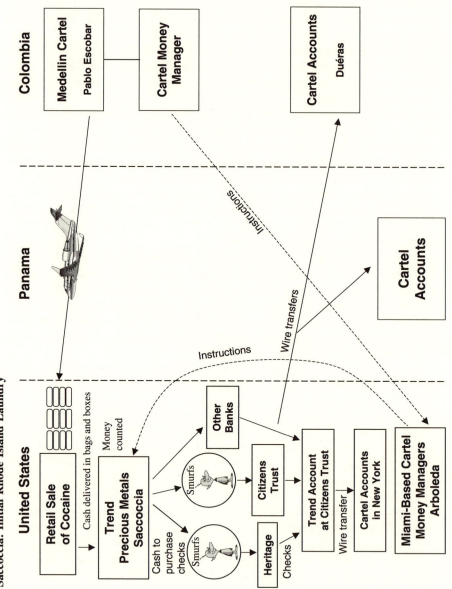

ficking clients to increase their level of activity in 1990 and 1991. During those two years, the laundry was expanded to operate on Fifth Avenue in New York (under the Trend Precious Metals name). At 580 Fifth Avenue and at 42 West 48th Street, Saccoccia's team received much greater amounts of street cash from drug sales. At these locations, money couriers sent by the drug traffickers would deliver bags and boxes of cash on a daily basis. According to law enforcement records, the laundry was receiving almost $U.S. 400,000 a day in New York!

This money was transported to one of two Rhode Island locations, where almost a dozen people were employed to count the cash in automatic money machines and bundle it for further transport to banks. They used coded conversations to discuss the cash, talking about "ounces" of their product (referring to thousands of dollars) and "karats" of purity (referring to denominations of the bills, e.g., 20 karats or 10 karats), as well as "low grade" or "high grade" for talking about small or large denominations of bills. This code might sound fairly plausible, except that gold is not traded in purity levels of 10 or 20 karats, but rather in pure (24 karats) or grades of 12 karats, 14 karats, or 18 karats.

The Saccoccias would receive instructions by fax from Arboleda or Dueñas concerning the places to send the money. It was up to them to get the money into the banking system and to then transfer it to accounts designated by these Colombian cartel money managers.

In addition to the use of armored cars to ship money to Rhode Island, Saccoccia also purchased gold bars in New York and paid with the drug cash. He obtained the gold bars from various gold dealers, including other money launderers, and sold them at a loss in the open market to obtain funds in the form of checks or bank deposits. These checks were then deposited in the account of Trend Precious Metals in Rhode Island, or bank deposits were wire transferred to that account.[1]

By this time, Saccoccia had diversified his operation to include money pickups in Los Angeles, under the name of International Metal Marketing, on South Hill Street. Cash received from drug money couriers was delivered to this location, where Saccoccia's associates then counted it and smurfed it into bank accounts in that city. The funds were then wire transferred to Rhode Island or directly to Colombian cartel accounts, as instructed. Some of the cash was shipped to Rhode Island for counting and placement into the banking system, but this arrangement was more costly and risky with the long distance movement of the cash.

In just the transactions that were captured by law enforcement agents during 1990 and early 1991 in Rhode Island, Saccoccia's group bought more than 400 checks in amounts over $U.S. 10,000, for a total value of $U.S. 26 million that was deposited into the Trend account at Citizens Trust Bank. Checks for under $10,000 were even more numerous and accounted for several million more. Another $U.S. 100 million was wired into the Trend account from International Metal Marketing in Los Angeles and from accounts in New York. Some additional money was smurfed directly into the banks, often into Heritage Loan and Investment Company, Citizens Savings Bank, Citizens Trust Company, Old Stone Bank, Fleet Bank, Attleboro-Pawtucket Savings Bank, and Rhode Island Hospital Trust National Bank.

A similar pattern existed in Los Angeles, where Saccoccia's group would receive bags of cash at the South Hill Street office of International Metal Marketing and deposit them into banks in structured transactions to avoid the reporting requirement for deposits of more than \$U.S. 10,000 a transaction. The money deposited by International Metal Marketing in Los Angeles was then wire transferred to the Trend Precious Metals account at Citizens Trust in Rhode Island.

Saccoccia explained to one of the money couriers involved with International Metal Marketing that he placed bids with Colombian drug traffickers to launder money by offering a specific commission and by guaranteeing the return of the laundered funds within a given period of time (for example, within five days). This is exactly analogous to the La Mina organization, which competed with Saccoccia and other laundering organizations to get the business. In fact, the drug traffickers often worked with several laundering organizations at the same time to move more money than any one of them could handle and also to spread the risk of detection among various intermediaries.

It turned out that La Mina and Raul Vivas worked more with Eduardo Martinez, whose clients included the Ochoa family and Pablo Escobar, while Saccoccia worked more with Duvan Arboleda, Mauricio Mejia, and Carlos Dueñas, whose clients included Guillermo Moncada, Pablo Escobar, and the Ochoa family. Obviously, there was extensive overlap among the laundering organizations and their ultimate clients. Also, when La Mina was intervened by law enforcement in February 1989, its leading participants jailed and the laundry dismantled, it appeared that much of the business then shifted to Saccoccia's organization by the end of 1989.

In the Los Angeles business of International Metal Marketing, Saccoccia himself, on some occasions, received drug cash from couriers and brought it to the IMM offices. The cash received in Los Angeles was used to buy gold from various metals dealers, and then the gold was sold for personal, business, or cashier's checks. These checks then were deposited into various bank accounts, as instructed by Saccoccia. He in turn received instructions from Arboleda or Dueñas to transfer the funds to Medellin cartel accounts in Colombia, Panama, or elsewhere. Figure 10.2 summarizes the operation that Saccoccia ran in Los Angeles in 1990–91.

Notice that the process is somewhat similar to La Mina, but Saccoccia used checks much more often, and his laundry sold gold in Miami and Rhode Island rather than in Los Angeles. Saccoccia also largely used a single account at Bank of America to concentrate his funds, whereas La Mina operators used multiple accounts for holding, consolidating, and transferring funds.

Figure 10.2
Saccoccia: Los Angeles Laundry

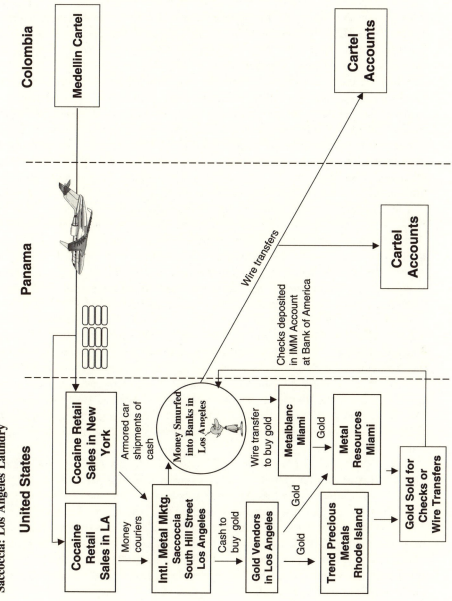

The Rhode Island money laundering scheme was uncovered by law enforcement agencies when several of the banks used by Saccoccia filed suspicious transaction reports with the Internal Revenue Service. These reports noted that Saccoccia, his wife, Anthony DeMarco, and several other people were purchasing numerous cashier's checks, both under and over $10,000 each, on a regular basis. The cash used to pay for the checks was usually in small denominations, bundled into $U.S. 1,000 quantities. Some of the cash was tested by authorities for drug traces. Basko, the drug dog, reacted positively to drugs on all of the money tested from these transactions.

When the quantities of cash offered by the drug traffickers proved too large for Saccoccia to handle quickly, he often would invite other money launderers to participate in the process. This arrangement of "laying off" funds was common in all of the laundries described here. Saccoccia would receive a fax or phone call from a Colombian source asking him to receive a large quantity of cash, and he would agree to take some of it and have some of it delivered, for example, to Barry Slomovitz. Slomovitz used a company called Capital Refiners and an account at Republic National Bank in New York to launder the money.

The competition among money laundering organizations often was not intense. Saccoccia, Slomovitz, and several other launderers held weekly meetings during 1989 in New York to discuss the amounts of cash coming in and the ability of each to handle the laundering requirements. With the cash arriving at an average of more than a million dollars a day, none of the organizations could manage it all. The launderers also would sell each other gold from time to time to help maintain the appearance of a legitimate business activity.

On April 2, 1991, Citizens Trust Bank closed the Trend Precious Metals account, advising the client (Stephen Saccoccia) that the activity in the account was not the kind with which the bank wanted to be involved. Namely, the bank was not satisfied with the explanation given for the massive transfers of checks into the account and wire transfers to Colombia out of the account during the previous 12 months. Between January 1, 1990, and April 2, 1991, Stephen and Donna Saccoccia wired $136,344,231.86 from Trend's account at Citizens to various Colombian and other foreign bank accounts, designated by Arboleda or Dueñas.

Rather than alter the business significantly, Saccoccia simply switched the check and wire transfer activity to the account of International Metal Marketing at the Bank of America in Los Angeles. This account had been in existence for more than a year, and it was operated in the same way as the Trend account in Rhode Island. Essentially, the next day, Saccoccia's laundry reopened for business and merely shifted more transactions to California. This revised scheme continued to launder cartel money until September 1991, when the Saccoccia organization was intervened by law enforcement agents, and most of its principals were arrested and jailed.

PART OF THE FURTHER USE OF THE LAUNDERED
FUNDS—BUYING AIRPLANES

One of the ways in which Colombian cocaine traffickers use the money earned in their business is to buy equipment needed to operate that business. An excellent way to transport up to a ton of cocaine is in a small jet airplane such as a Cessna Caravan. This kind of plane retails for about $U.S. 1 million, and it can be configured to hold adequate fuel to fly from Colombia to U.S. destinations with large amounts of cocaine.

During the operation of the Saccoccia laundry, some of the money wired out of Trend Precious Metals and International Metal Marketing accounts (plus other Saccoccia accounts) was used for exactly this purpose. A Colombian airplane broker who turned out to be involved in numerous purchases for various narcotics traffickers created the following deal. The broker, Johnny Finkelstein, negotiated with a Denver-based airplane broker to buy the airplane. When the transaction took place, it was paid by wire transfers from Saccoccia accounts and by two checks drawn on bank accounts in Panama and New York in which funds had been placed by unknown depositors. Finkelstein claimed to be the owner of the accounts, but he could not prove the source of the money going into the accounts.

Perhaps the easiest way to visualize this fairly complicated set of transactions is with another flow chart. Figure 10.3 shows the various steps in the deal for the Cessna Caravan.

This arrangement is similar to other transactions undertaken by Finkelstein to buy aircraft for Colombian clients. On at least three occasions prior to this instance, the airplanes involved were later seized in Mexico, the United States, and elsewhere with large quantities of cocaine aboard. In 1990, a Super King Air 300 was sold by AMR-Combs to Finkelstein and was subsequently seized in Mexico with more than a ton of cocaine aboard. In 1991, a Convair 580 propeller plane was seized in Mexico, and it turned out to have been bought by Finkelstein for Avesca. Later, in 1991, a Beech King Air 300 was seized in Guatemala with 1.5 tons of cocaine aboard; it had been purchased for Avesca by Johnny Finkelstein and sold by AMR-Combs in Fort Lauderdale.

When U.S. authorities tried to establish the ultimate ownership of the planes, it was determined that the Colombian company, Avesca, was owned by several people, including Medellin cartel member Luis Carlos Lizcano.

Finkelstein had obtained the money from the cartel members by having funds transferred to AMR-Combs. The cocaine traffickers instructed Stephen Saccoccia's organization to wire transfer about half of it from his accounts in Los Angeles and New York. The traffickers also instructed Banco Agro Industrial in Panama to wire transfer half a million dollars from an account and to send a check for that amount to AMR-Combs. A small amount also was sent by check from a cartel-controlled account at Bank Hapoalim in New York.

The net result was to create a complex set of funds transfers to the airplane

Figure 10.3
Using Drug Money to Buy Airplanes

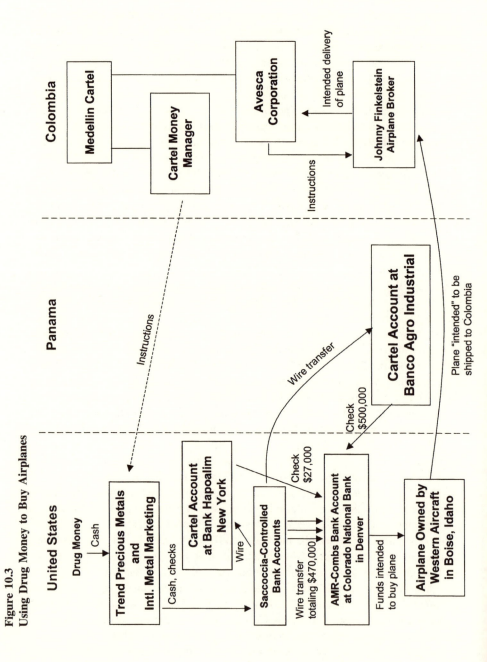

seller to pay for the plane and to hide the ultimate owner and user of the plane. The transfers were not in cash but rather used already laundered funds from the banking system. Interestingly, the reason the transactions were discovered came from both directions—the money was partially traced to drug dealing in the United States, and the airplane purchase was traced from a person involved in repeated airplane purchases where the planes later turned up in drug transporting schemes.

NOTES

This chapter draws heavily on documents from the legal case *U.S. v. Stephen Saccoccia et al.* (CR-91-115T, District of Rhode Island).

1. By the end of 1988, Saccoccia decided that he did not need the gold to disguise his activities, and he began contracting with local money launderers in New York to receive cash and to create wire transfers of the money to his account in Miami, or sometimes to Latin American accounts.

Chapter 11

Retail Money Laundries, 1990–95

This chapter describes a number of retail-level money laundering ventures in the United States. The point is to demonstrate the many kinds of schemes used to carry out the laundering process of the initial cash generated by street sales of cocaine and other drugs. More than anything else, the set of examples offered here points out the wide variety of businesses used to launder drug money and the ways in which they relate to the banking system, through which most of the drug proceeds ultimately pass.

THE EXPORT/IMPORT COMPANY[1]

In 1990, a small export/import company near the Miami airport was investigated because government agents had tailed couriers carrying large quantities of drug cash to this destination. The situation was obviously suspicious for this reason, and it was especially interesting as a case in which the company was participating in the Colombian black market in foreign exchange.

The company, MAC Imports, run by Patricia Saucedo, was receiving hundreds of thousands of dollars in cash on at least a weekly basis, and it was using some of these funds to pay for export shipments to Colombian clients. MAC Imports would arrange with Colombian businesspeople to buy goods such as machine parts, tractors, motors, and other equipment. The businesspeople would pay via black market transactions in which they delivered pesos to black market dealers in Colombia, and the black market dealers arranged to have dollars delivered to MAC Imports in Miami. The Colombian businesspeople did not necessarily know that they were buying drug dollars, but they did know that they were illegally buying dollars outside of the government-controlled exchange system of Colombia.

This was not unusual at the time, since Colombia had operated a fairly rigid exchange control system since 1966, and many Colombians freely admitted that they used the black market to obtain dollars for everything from buying imports (as in this case) to investing their wealth overseas to paying for U.S. health care or education costs for their families. In any event, many Colombians used the black market at the time, thus dollars were often obtained in "non-traditional" ways. Instead of just using wire transfers or direct payments through a bank, the black market dealers arranged peso payments to their accounts in Colombia and dollar purchases from many sources in the United States.

The particular source of the dollars that caused problems in the current example was the sale of cocaine in Miami, which produced large quantities of small-denomination bills that needed to be placed into the banking system. MAC Imports simply agreed to receive hundreds of thousands of dollars in cash and to claim that its clients were paying for goods in cash rather than with more typical checks or wire transfers.

The scheme is depicted in Figure 11.1.

THE EXPORT/IMPORT LAUNDRY

This method of laundering the drug money was difficult to use in convincing authorities about the potential legitimacy of the funds involved. It was not common for export/import companies in the United States to deal with large quantities of cash payments in the 1990s.

The situation was a lot more complicated than just the receipt of drug cash and subsequent deposits into bank accounts. Patricia Saucedo was observed through surveillance receiving phone calls from Colombia, instructing her to expect cash deliveries on a regular basis. Conversations were in coded language (for example, discussing "yards of green" instead of thousands of dollars). The deliveries were carried out by couriers whose names she did not know, for amounts of money undetermined until counted, and for subsequent payments and account transfers to companies she did not know. She had a difficult time explaining how this was a normal business, and ultimately she was unsuccessful in doing so. Her laundry was shut down.

THE CAR DEALERS[2]

In this scheme, a number of New York area automobile dealerships were discovered to be taking in large quantities of drug cash and laundering it through the purchase of cars. The government mounted a sting operation and offered to buy cars from the half-dozen auto dealers, and discovered a general willingness on their parts to take in payments for cars in cash and to register the cars in unknown or fictitious third-party names. This example illustrates the ability of drug traffickers to find good businesses to use in laundering the large quantities

Figure 11.1
The Export/Import Laundry

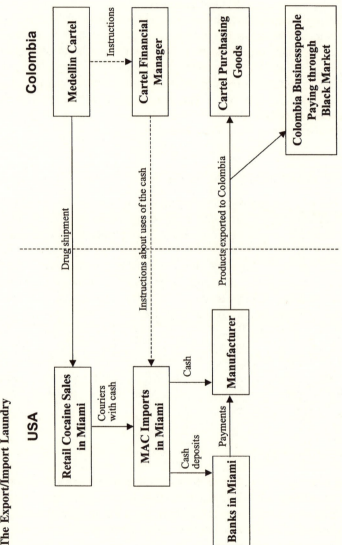

Colombia

Medellin Cartel

Instructions

Cartel Financial Manager

Cartel Purchasing Goods

Colombia Businesspeople Paying through Black Market

Products exported to Colombia

Instructions about uses of the cash

Drug shipment

USA

Retail Cocaine Sales in Miami

Couriers with cash

MAC Imports in Miami

Cash

Manufacturer

Cash deposits

Payments

Banks in Miami

Figure 11.2
The Auto Dealer Laundry

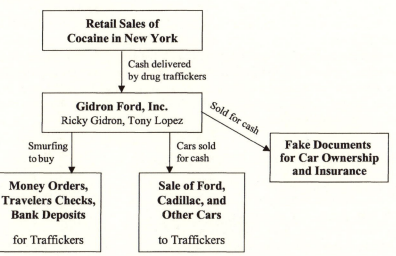

of money that their retail sales generate, though of course in this instance it did not work out well for them in the end.

Figure 11.2 shows an overview of the money laundering process that occurred through all of the dealerships involved.

AUTO DEALERS' LAUNDRY

This laundry involved the instruction of couriers by drug traffickers to deliver cash to car dealers, and then instructions to car dealers as to the names of (fictitious) car buyers to whom the vehicles were sold, for the ultimate benefit of drug dealers. In the sting operation undertaken to prove this money laundering, the dealerships each sold more than a dozen cars for what was represented to them as (and which was) drug cash during two months in 1990. In addition, each was observed in previous investigations to be carrying out the same activities with drug traffickers in the New York area.

The range of illegal activities being undertaken was quite impressive. In the case of Dick Gidron Ford, Inc., two of the firm's executives offered the services of taking in cash and converting it into money orders and traveler's checks, in addition to selling cars for cash. They also offered to find individuals whose drivers' licenses could be used to register the cars being purchased and agreed to register some of the cars in fictitious names. In addition, the Gidron executives offered to structure cash payments in sums of less than $10,000 to avoid the CTR reporting requirement. (This step backfired when the banks that accepted Gidron Ford cash deposits did file CTRs, thus the millions of dollars in cash coming into the dealerships were recorded at that level.) Finally, the Gidron executives offered to provide additional laundering services, such as the regular placement of $500,000 a week into bank deposits (presumably through false documentation of car sales) and even the purchase of real estate for cash in the New York area.

Although this activity was related through the law enforcement investigation to specific cocaine shipments from Colombia, the basic money laundering was completely a retail activity. That is, the car dealers had no dealings with drug cartels but with local cocaine dealers in the New York area who were buying cars for themselves, their friends, and their relatives.

THE STOCKBROKER ACCOUNT[3]

Another example from the early 1990s of creative money laundering was the use of a stockbroker account to launder drug cash. In this case, Edilberto Miranda was prosecuted for laundering drug money through various mechanisms and then depositing them into accounts at Prudential Bache Securities, as well as subsequently using those funds to purchase a house in Coral Gables, Florida.

This scheme was quite simple, operating initially in a manner similar to smurfing of cash into bank accounts. Miranda purchased cashier's checks in amounts of $9,500.00 (and occasionally other amounts, typically just under the limit of $10,000, above which CTRs would have been required to be filed). These were deposited into the stockbroker accounts at Prudential Bache Securities in Miami. After using this mechanism for several months, he switched to taking funds that had already been deposited into bank accounts and wire transferred them in large amounts into the Prudential Bache accounts. As far as law enforcement agencies were able to determine, the total of funds put into these accounts through the two mechanisms was almost $2 million (actually $1,936,818.71) during late 1990 and early 1991.

From these stockbroker accounts, which were seemingly outside of the banking system and thus likely to be investigated by law enforcement agencies, Miranda took $725,000 to purchase the house at 335 Costanera Road in Coral Gables, Florida. All of these assets—the stockbroker accounts and the house—were forfeited in the criminal proceedings against Miranda.

THE MONEY TRANSMITTER[4]

Another type of business that can be used by money launderers for both entering cash into the banking system and moving it offshore is the money transmitting business. This activity often crops up in immigrant communities when local immigrants look for ways to transfer funds back to their families in their home country. In the United States in the 1990s, this was quite common for Caribbean and Latin America nationals seeking to send money back to their families in Mexico, Jamaica, Honduras, and of course Colombia.

One instance when this kind of business was used in money laundering involved the South American Exchange (SAE) in Queens, New York, run by Henry Melo. This company took in funds from Colombians living in the New York area and transferred them to Colombia. During 1993–95, the SAE recorded $750 million of total transfers, about 90 percent to Colombian destinations.

The scope of the SAE's activities is sketched in Figure 11.3.

HENRY MELO'S MONEY TRANSMITTER LAUNDRY

The SAE's main business was to receive cash from Colombians in the New York area and elsewhere through the firm's 350 agents (288 of them in New York). This cash was then forwarded to beneficiaries designated by the senders, mostly in Colombia. The company's agents received the cash and either sent it via courier to the headquarters of the SAE or deposited it into bank accounts and then transferred the funds to the SAE's bank account. Figure 11.3 shows the basic outline of this process, including the use of the firm to launder drug money.

Through various local police and federal narcotics investigations, it was discovered that money transmitters in the New York area were involved in laundering Colombian cocaine revenues. Taking advantage of the ability to use Geographic Targeting Orders (GTOs), in mid-1996, the U.S. Treasury Department designated 22 money transmitters in New York and New Jersey as targets of investigation. The money transmitters were required to report on special forms much more detail about their clients and their transactions involving Colombia. As a result of this action, the amount of money transmitted through the SAE dropped from more than $40 million in the last quarter of 1995 to just over $800,000 in the last quarter of 1996, and the number of transactions from more than 11,000 to less than 400 for the same time period.

Interestingly enough, the records kept by the SAE were quite detailed, with CTRs filed with the U.S. Treasury as required and voluminous accounts of money receipts and transfers with the names and other information required about the senders and receivers. It took the confessions of a number of the firm's agents who were convicted of laundering narcotics proceeds to discover that the main method used to launder the drug money was simply false documentation. That is, when deliveries of hundreds of thousands of dollars in cash were received, Melo or his agents would divide the funds into quantities under $10,000 and make up names, phone numbers, and addresses of clients. Likewise, on the receiving end, the SAE used fictitious names of clients to send multiple amounts to the same destination, thus evading the filing requirements in the United States. Clearly, the firm was structuring its declared deposits and transfers to avoid having to explain the source of the large cash receipts.

The amounts of money being transferred were clearly not related to the number of potential Colombian customers in the New York area (estimated to be just over 100,000 people, legal and undocumented residents). With local family

Figure 11.3
The Money Transmitter Laundry

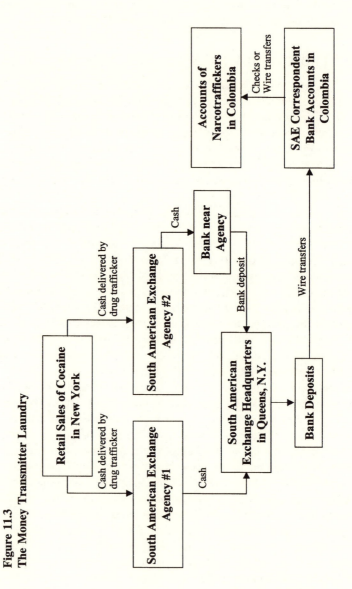

incomes around $27,000 in 1993, each family would have had to transmit $12,000 to relatives in Colombia in order to justify the total amount of funds that was being moved. Obviously, there was something else going on.

Henry Melo's laundry was shut down in 1996, and the money transmitter business in the New York area remained under the GTO. The use of money transmitters is logical for moving the drug money to Colombia as well as to other destinations, and it would not be at all surprising to see the fund simply transferred somewhere else before being ultimately shipped to Colombia as desired. If a location such as Panama were chosen, it would be easy to mix in the several hundred million dollars a year of transfers in this example, along with the billions of financial transfers that are already passing through.

THE INTERIOR DECORATORS[5]

During the period 1989–96, a firm of interior decorators in New York received more than $30 million of drug cash and other monetary instruments and transfers, all related to the activities of their client, Jose Santacruz-Londoño. The firm's principals, Alexander Blarek and Frank Pellecchia, then disbursed the funds to bank accounts in the United States and abroad to buy furnishings that were mostly sent to Colombia. Because Santacruz-Londoño was one of the three main leaders of the Cali cartel during this period, it is not surprising that these were narcodollars.

The interior decorating firm was able to operate relatively freely with its funds transfers and purchases, since it had a "legitimate" business of buying furniture, artwork, and other decorating materials. When the entire scheme was brought to light, it was truly impressive to see how many bank accounts the two men had established, from New York to San Francisco to Miami and many places in between, including Lake Tahoe, Nevada, and Milwaukee, Wisconsin.

The basic arrangement was to have drug cash deposited into a Blarek or Pellecchia account in New York or one of the other cities where they maintained bank accounts. One of the two men sometimes received the cash from drug money couriers and then made the deposit. The funds were typically deposited in numerous cash deposits of amounts in the $5,000–$15,000 range, sometimes triggering CTR filings and other times not. These funds were subsequently wire transferred to other Santacruz-Londoño-controlled accounts in the United States and abroad.

A second type of activity that was passed through this laundry mechanism was the purchase of artwork, furniture, and other interior decorating materials. On numerous occasions, Santacruz-Londoño wire transferred funds into a Blarek or Pellecchia account for the purpose of buying these materials, which were then shipped to him in Colombia. The whole picture is described in Figure 11.4.

Figure 11.4
The Interior Decorating Laundry

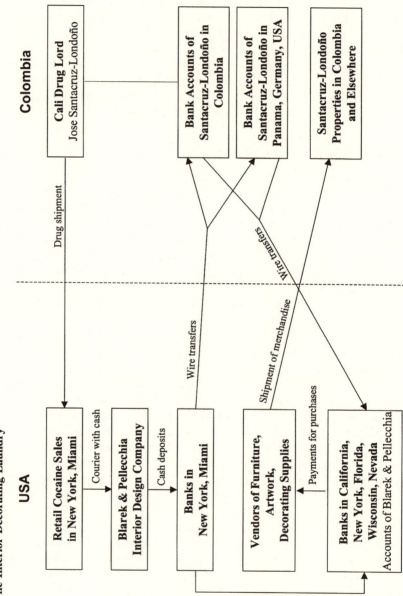

BLAREK & PELLECCHIA'S INTERIOR DECORATING LAUNDRY

This activity is interesting because not only did the laundry take care of drug cash depositing into banks in at least four U.S. cities, it also put drug funds into ultimate uses (integration) in the form of household decorating items and transportation to Colombia.

NOTES

This chapter has described a range of money laundering techniques that focuses on the retail end of the business and on the U.S. financial market. Whether the drug traffickers are U.S.-based or foreign nationals, the launderies described here enable them to get funds into the banking system through subterfuges that frequently escape detection— though not in the cases here, which were uncovered by law enforcement agents in every instance.

1. This case was listed as *USA v. $52,630* (Case #90-0843-CIV-Scott, Southern District of Florida). The commentary here is based on the complaint in the case and on a U.S. Customs service affidavit.

2. This section is based on the criminal complaints, *USA v. Richard Gidron, Jr., Anthony Lopez, Gidron Ford, Inc., and Allstate Insurance* (Case #90-MAG-1718, Southern District of New York); *USA v. Michael Miele, Glenn Peterson, Brad Schwartz, Bronx Acura* (Case #90-MAG-1739, Southern District of New York); *USA v. Lawrence Nash, Charles Luciano, Mercedes Benz Manhattan* (Case #90-MAG-1714, Southern District of New York); *USA v. Thomas Dunn et al., Manhattan Nissan, Manhattan Mazda* (Case #90-MAG-1730).

3. This case was registered as *USA v. Edilberto Miranda* (Case #95-482-CR-KING(s), Southern District of Florida).

4. This section is based on an indictment and an IRS affidavit in the case *USA v. Marcos Henry Melo and South American Exchange, Ltd.* (Case #97-942 (NG) in the Eastern District of New York).

5. This section is based on the criminal indictment *USA v. Antony Alexander Blarek II and Frank V. Pellecchia* (Case #97-CR-544 (JBW) in the Eastern District of New York).

Chapter 12

The Raul Salinas Saga, 1992–94

This chapter describes the strange case of Raul Salinas, the first brother of the president of Mexico, Carlos Salinas (whose term of office was from 1988–94). The story is incomplete because the full details of his activities are not yet confirmed. Even so, based on his own legal testimony and on additional evidence that has been compiled, it is reasonably clear that Raul Salinas moved more than $U.S. 120 million out of Mexico during 1992–94. It also is clear that he did so in a range of disguised methods to hide his ownership of the money.

At the same time Salinas was converting pesos into dollars and transferring them out of Mexico, it was also clear that Mexican drug lords were earning large sums of money in dollars, which they wanted to convert into pesos. The drug traffickers also were looking for protection against law enforcement, so they would be potential contributors to Salinas in their attempts to defuse or derail prosecution. It has come out during the legal proceedings against Salinas that he did indeed receive funds that turned out to be proceeds of narcotics trafficking, specifically from the so-called "Gulf Cartel," headed by Juan Garcia Abrego. According to prosecution statements in the Swiss case to forfeit Raul Salinas' money there, the funds were proceeds of narcotrafficking that originated with the cartel headed by Pablo Escobar in Colombia.

The case developed as follows. Raul Salinas, older brother of Mexico's ex-President Carlos Salinas, was imprisoned in Mexico in 1996 on charges of murder and "inexplicable enrichment." He was found to have amassed more than $U.S. 200 million of funds in accounts held in Switzerland and London, though his personal income and previous wealth would never have produced such an incredible amount. This story, which has not been concluded, follows the known and speculated path of the drugs and money that contributed to Salinas' unexplained bank accounts.

During the presidency of Carlos Salinas in Mexico, Raul Salinas undertook a large number of financial transactions that produced funds transfers out of Mexico totaling well over $U.S. 200 million. While the sources of all of this money are far from known, some actually seem fairly innocuous. For example, Salinas set up an investment fund with several business associates in 1992 and included the heads of several large Mexican firms in the group, which transferred money to him for the overseas investments.

In one specific instance, he was given $U.S. 50 million by Carlos Peralta, president of the large Mexican telecommunications company, Iusacell. This money was intended for overseas investment, according to both Peralta and Salinas. The exact means of transferring the money to Salinas was not remembered by either man, so that $U.S. 50 million may be traceable to this source— but only deductively, since Peralta has not identified the (presumably wire transfer) route that the money followed.

Three other businessmen who had received loans or investments from Raul Salinas in previous dealings agreed to place funds into this investment scheme as well. Adrian Sada Gonzalez, then-chairman of Grupo Financiero Serfin, admitted that he had transferred money (amount unspecified) to Salinas for the overseas investment fund. He likewise admitted to having previously received $U.S. 15 million from Salinas as part of a mutual investment project in Mexico. Jose Madariaga Lomelin had invested in the Mexican bus company, Masa, in 1989 with Salinas. In 1993, they sold their shares in the company for a gain of over $U.S. 30 million. And finally, Carlos Hank Rhon, owner of Grupo Financiero Interaccciones, transferred $U.S. 2 million from his Citibank account in Switzerland to a Salinas Citibank account in London. These transactions appeared to be wholly legal and reasonable business dealings between powerful Mexican businessmen in the early 1990s.

The picture became muddied in 1995, when Salinas was charged with involvement in the murder of his brother-in-law, Jose Francisco Ruiz Massieu, then vice chairman of the ruling Partido Revolucionario Institucional (PRI) political party. During the investigation of these charges, it was discovered that Salinas maintained bank accounts with Citibank and other banks in Switzerland and London. These accounts were recipients of funds derived from drug money, some of which was deposited in cash into accounts controlled by Salinas in Mexico City and in Houston, Texas, and then transferred to accounts in Europe.

In December 1995, Salinas testified that he had orchestrated a series of accounts and fictitious names through which to move and hold his growing wealth. He had opened bank accounts at Citibank Zurich, Banque Pictet, Julius Baer Bank, and Banque Edmond de Rothschild, all in Switzerland. He used false names, including Juan Guillermo Gomez Gutierrez and Juan Jose Gonzalez Cadena, and he even had a passport drawn up in the former name with his own picture. He claimed that Citibank executive Amy Elliot had suggested to him these account structures and methods for moving money from Mexico to European bank accounts.

This situation certainly reflects poorly on Citibank. Several of the bank's officers were involved with Salinas, and based on the evidence that has surfaced, they dealt with him in questionable practices. Elliot assisted Salinas in setting up accounts in the names of Cayman Islands corporations as well as with the fictitious names noted above. During the period 1992–93, while she was head of Citibank's Mexico team for international private banking, Elliot took responsibility for the bank's relationship with Salinas. The bank's senior officer in Switzerland at the time, Hubertus Rukavina, served as a member of the board of Confidas, one of the Swiss banks where Salinas held accounts in the name of Cayman Islands corporations. Rukavina also was Citibank's head of world-wide private banking at the time, with responsibilities over the Mexican private banking business, among others. It is not clear whether other Citibank senior executives were in a position to know about the bank's dealings with Raul Salinas, but obviously questions remain, since Salinas was the brother of the Mexican president and he was doing a very large volume of business with the bank.

One major channel of funds that characterizes Salinas' money laundering activity appears in Figure 12.1. The laundering described here shows the link between Raul Salinas and the ultimate source of the narcodollars, the Medellin cartel in Colombia. It has not been proven that Salinas knew anything about that ultimate source of the funds.

It appears that the more common and direct connection between Salinas and the drug money was through the Mexican cocaine trafficking organization of Juan Garcia Abrego. That is, Salinas apparently was paid for his help in ensuring the safe transit of cocaine through Mexico and into the United States.[1] The drugs came from Colombian traffickers, were handled by Mexican traffickers, and finally made their way to the United States. The money was then channeled as usual. Fees were paid to Salinas for his assistance as deposits into accounts at banks in Mexico City (especially Banca Cremi), from which transfers were made into Citibank in Mexico City. It is these fees that constitute his participation in drug money laundering. This activity has been documented in testimony to the Swiss court by prosecutors in the case there to forfeit the money in Raul Salinas' various Swiss bank accounts.[2] It was judged sufficiently compelling so that the funds were forfeited in Switzerland.

The case is sufficiently convoluted so that the Swiss prosecution, which led to the forfeiture of the money there, was followed up by attempts to bring court cases in Mexico and the United States. Federal prosecutors in the United States were not able to discover adequate information that they felt would produce a winning case against Salinas, so there has not been such a case brought to court. Likewise, there were no funds on deposit in U.S. financial institutions, so the money could not be prosecuted in the United States either. Prosecutors in Mexico did use the information presented in Switzerland and elsewhere in their case against Salinas. In Mexico, however, the case focused on his possible involvement in the assassination of Ruiz, and on his illegal, unexplained enrichment.

Figure 12.1
Raul Salinas' Venture in Money Laundering

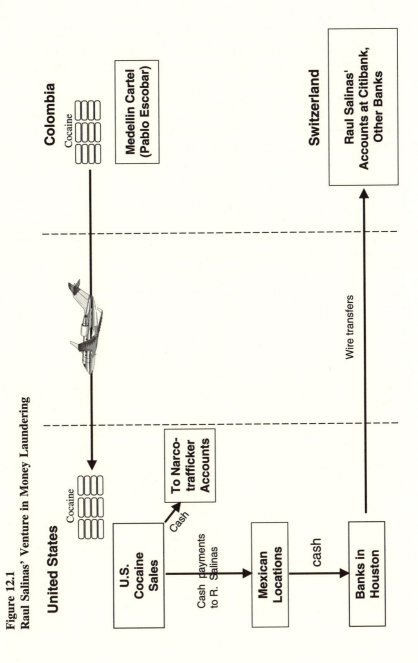

He was found guilty in Mexico and sentenced to a long prison term, which he is now serving.

This situation provides a truly fascinating look at the extent of money laundering, from high government officials to lowly crack dealers on the streets of U.S. cities, and at some of the problems in identifying and prosecuting it. The case of Raul Salinas was so high-profile that it almost assured a political (rather than an objective, legal) handling of the trial in Mexico. It also demonstrates the limits of the United States' ability to pursue drug money laundering when most of the activity occurs outside of the United States, even when a major U.S. financial institution is involved. In addition, it shows that Switzerland, a traditional bastion of bank secrecy, has moved into the fray to try to stop the use of its banks in criminal money laundering.

NOTES

1. This assertion was documented in the *Wall Street Journal*, April 23, 1997, p. A14.

2. *Money Laundering Alert* has an article in the April 1996 issue (p. 8), which asserts that Joseph Oberholzer at Union Bank of Switzerland was involved in Salinas' drug money laundering. This assertion was not publicly verified.

Chapter 13

The Mexican Connection: Operation Casablanca, 1995–99

Beginning in 1995 and continuing into 1998, the U.S. government ran a sting operation called Casablanca, offering to launder drug money in California for Colombian and Mexican narcotics traffickers. The sting captured a truly amazing collection of money launderers, drug traffickers, corrupt bankers,[1] and other assorted participants. This operation provides an up-to-date review of the common drug money laundering techniques used in the 1990s. It also shows the deep link between Colombian traffickers and their Mexican intermediaries when drugs are shipped through Mexico to the United States. Finally, the case points out some very real concerns about the money laundering problem in Mexico, where numerous bankers from various institutions were willingly involved in laundering money for the Juarez cocaine cartel, and where money launderers themselves were directly involved in cocaine trafficking.

Through ongoing law enforcement efforts in the early 1990s, U.S. anti-narcotics agents uncovered some of the activities of an enormous drug trafficking venture in Mexico—the so-called Juarez cartel, headed by Amado Carrillo-Fuentes.[2] While Carrillo-Fuentes was well known to the law enforcement community by 1995, he was still at large and had built probably the largest drug trafficking cartel in Mexico.

The activities of the Juarez cartel did not substitute for or necessarily compete with the Colombian cartels' activities. Rather, the Mexican cartels complemented the Colombians' drug trafficking by providing access to the U.S. market through Mexico. During the early 1990s, with a massive U.S. interdiction effort operating in the Florida Straits, the drug traffickers found Mexico a much more attractive trade route.

In addition to the physical shipments of cocaine, the Juarez cartel was able to arrange assistance to its Colombian clients in money laundering. This was especially helpful when shipments of cash could be made to Mexican cities from the United States for deposit in the less alert Mexican banks and then for subsequent transfer to accounts in the United States and elsewhere. The Alcala-Navarro money laundering organization in Mexico and the Oscar Saavedra money laundering organization in Cali, Colombia, were the main intermediaries on the money side in the Casablanca case. The overall structure of this cocaine trafficking, money laundering venture is sketched in Figure 13.1.

This picture looks fairly similar to those in the La Mina (Medellin cartel) scheme, described in Chapter 6 and the Cali cartel scheme with Jose Franklin Jurado, described in Chapter 9. The key difference here is that a different layer of intermediaries was superimposed on the traditionally Colombian-led venture.

In the newer, Mexico-linked drug running, money laundering venture, the physical distribution of cocaine in the United States and the subsequent initial movement of money into the banking system are being carried out by Mexican organizations. As shown in Figure 13.1, the cocaine shipments went from Colombia (or other processing sites controlled by the Cali traffickers) to Ciudad Juarez (or other locations in Mexico controlled by the Carrillo-Fuentes organization). Then the drugs were shipped into the United States across the Mexican border in trucks, cars, or through other transport methods. The money earned from sales of the cocaine was collected by Cali cartel agents in the United States and subsequently picked up by members of the Alcala-Navarro money laundering organization (under instructions from Saavedra in Colombia), either for deposit into U.S. bank accounts (shown here) or for shipment to Mexico and deposit into banks there.

The Mexican structure is somewhat different from the typical Colombian scheme, since the Mexican narcotics trafficking group also employed the money laundering team as part of its own organization. Victor Manuel Alcala-Navarro not only provided his money laundering service in the Mexican organization and to Saavedra in Colombia, he also sometimes participated in communicating instructions for the delivery of cocaine. In fact, he was present at least once during the operation of the scheme for the receipt of a major cocaine shipment from Colombia.

This is strikingly different from other schemes described in this book. In no other case since the 1970s were the drugs handled by the same people who dealt with the money. And in this case, just as in all of the others, the Colombian organizations that processed and sold cocaine did not manage the money process from the receipt of drug cash to deposit into banks and transfer to ultimate cartel-controlled destinations and uses. It seems that there is some reason in Mexico—either newness to the business or the structure of the criminal organizations—that the people who processed the money were willing to be involved in distributing the drugs. The risks are, of course, much higher in the drug activity, from jail sentences when caught to personal safety risk among traffickers.

Figure 13.1
The Mexican Connection: An Overview

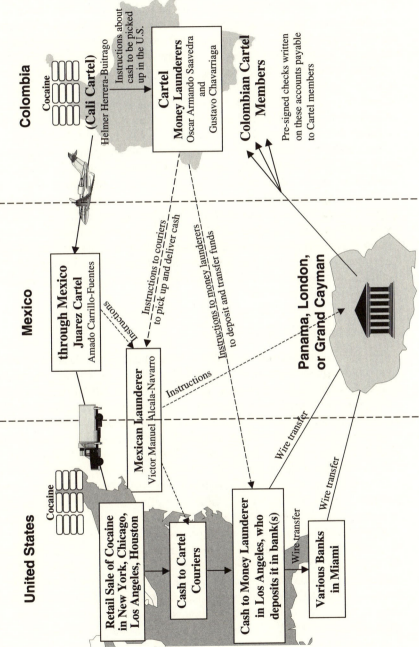
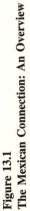

The overall picture in Oscar Saavedra's money laundering scheme included at least hundreds of millions of dollars of cocaine shipments by members of the Cali cartel to the United States during the 1990s. The drug sales were nation-wide, as were the money collections, initial bank deposits, and subsequent wire transfers, check writing, and other transfers of funds. In fact, the scheme is especially impressive because it covered the entire United States, with drug sales and money pickups from California to New York to Miami and many places in between, including Detroit, Houston, Chicago, and even Vancouver, British Columbia. Funds were wire transferred or paid through checks to accounts in Colombia but also to accounts in Atlanta, Chicago, Detroit, Los Angeles, Miami, New York, Washington, D.C., and several other U.S. cities. It is almost mind boggling to comprehend the full range of activities involved in this scheme.

To see things a bit more clearly, we can break down the activities into more manageable chunks—first the direct links to cocaine smuggling; then the place-ment of the drug cash into bank accounts, mostly in the United States but also in Mexico, Canada, and even Colombia; then the transfer of funds, typically through wire transfer, to target accounts, either controlled by cartel interests or by businesspeople in Colombia who wanted to get dollars into U.S. accounts (and who paid with pesos in Colombia); and finally the transfer of funds to Colombia, or the use of the funds to pay for purchases by the cartel in the United States, such as fees to the money launderers and purchases of products used by the traffickers.

THE COCAINE TRAFFICKING

The cocaine shipments that fed into Saavedra's money laundering organiza-tion originated with members of the Cali cartel in Colombia. The main drug trafficker who was identified as an owner of some of the cocaine that was shipped and in some cases confiscated in the sting was Helmer (Pacho) Herrera-Buitrago. In addition, Juan Upegui was identified as another one of the Cali traffickers involved. The Cali traffickers had dominated the Colombian cocaine trafficking business since the arrests or killings of all of the leaders of the Med-ellin cartel during the period 1989–92. When three of the Cali cartel's leaders were arrested in 1995, that group also lost a major base of its clout. Even so, many traffickers in both the Medellin and Cali cartels continue to operate, Her-rera and Upegui being two of them.

Shipments of cocaine went from processing sites in South America, mainly Colombia, to staging locations in Mexico, often Ciudad Juarez (across the border from El Paso, Texas), the home base of Amado Carrillo-Fuentes and his traf-ficking organization. Once the drugs were delivered by airplane to the Carrillo-Fuentes group, they were divided up and shipped to the United States, via truck, airplane, car, and other vehicles. Shipments of cocaine were traced to Los An-geles, Houston, New York, and other locations in the United States.

Retail sales of the cocaine were done by local traffickers, who paid the Colombian/Mexican traffickers the wholesale price for the shipments. Once a shipment was received by retail distributors, several days would pass and then payment was made to the wholesaler. These payments were the ones laundered by the Alcala-Navarro ring, either by depositing the cash in Los Angeles (through the sting operators) or taking it physically to Mexico and depositing it in banks there.

INITIAL CASH EARNINGS AND INFILTRATION INTO BANKS

Once the drugs were shipped to U.S. markets, Saavedra's organization instructed Alcala-Navarro whenever cash payments were made. Alcala-Navarro arranged to have cash picked up by local couriers for delivery to members of his money laundering ring. In some instances, this was done through the delivery of cash to the Los Angeles warehouse where the U.S. government agents were operating the sting. They then deposited the funds into a bank account in Los Angeles and subsequently wire transferred the funds as instructed by Alcala-Navarro. In other instances, Alcala-Navarro had the funds shipped to Mexican banks where he bribed bankers to take the massive quantities of dollars, to deposit them, and to wire transfer the proceeds to other banks in other countries.

In the first instance, getting the cash into banks was easy. The launderers had unwittingly contracted with U.S. agents to receive and deposit the money, thus U.S. agents had no problem receiving the drug cash, depositing it into their bank account in Los Angeles, and then transferring the proceeds as requested to accounts elsewhere. Of course, when the sting operation was closed, whatever funds that could be traced were frozen in banks in the United States, Nassau, Colombia, and Venezuela.

TRANSFERS OF FUNDS TO END USERS

When the cash was deposited into the U.S. agents' account in Los Angeles, the transfers of funds to end users were generally wire transfers to individuals and companies in the United States and in several Latin American and Caribbean countries. A large number of transfers were to bank accounts in Miami. These accounts in some cases belonged to the drug traffickers, while in other cases they belonged to Colombian businesspeople who wanted to hold deposits in the United States.

As in many similar situations, the Colombian businesspeople purchased dollars with pesos in the foreign exchange black market in Colombia, with the understanding that dollars would be placed into their accounts in the United States. And, as in many other cases, the money deposited into their accounts turned out to be drug money, which was claimed by the U.S. authorities as proceeds of illegal activity. Since the businesspeople had purchased the dollars illegally (that is, in the underground, unreported economy of Colombia), they had a difficult time claiming that they were "innocent owners" of the drug money, so in the sting operation, most of these funds were forfeited to the U.S. government. Of course, the sting only caught a percentage of the Alcala-Navarro money transfers, and many of the accounts were closed out or had reduced balances by the time they were frozen by the government, so certainly the majority of the money that was laundered escaped forfeiture.

One of the end users turned out to be the Bogotá office of Price Waterhouse. This firm bought about half a million dollars in the foreign exchange black market in Colombia, paying with 29 separate, sequentially numbered checks drawn on its peso account at Bance de Credito in Colombia. The dollars were wired transferred in four transactions into its account at Bank of Boston in New York. This is a curious turn of events, because multinational firms seldom venture into the foreign exchange black market in Colombia, nevertheless, it was swept up in the sting along with the others.

OPERATION CHECK MARK

A separate part of the investigation of Saavedra's and Alcala-Navarro's activities was called Operation Check Mark. In this section of the overall scheme, the Mexican money launderers were shipping cash from various U.S. cities to Los Angeles for deposit into banks there, just as in the rest of the scheme. But in this segment of the dealings, the funds were then sent to banks in Mexico, where bankers had been paid off to ignore the source and destinations of the wire transfers and checks being passed through their banks. Also, some of the funds were shipped as cash to Mexico for direct deposit into banks there. By bribing bank officials in Mexico, the launderers were able to get the funds into that banking system and then to transfer them to other countries without further complication.

This scheme is shown in Figure 13.2. Here the funds flow was not all that different from the previous examples, except that the banks in Mexico received wire transfers into and paid checks and wire transfers out of accounts without asking for an explanation for the unusual flow of funds. Additionally, the large cash deposits of hundreds of thousands or millions of dollars at a time were not questioned. In the previous examples in Casablanca, the cash was deposited into Los Angeles banks through the U.S. government's undercover operation. The wire transfer portion of this activity alone laundered about $64 million during 1997–98.

The Mexican banks that became ensnared in this scheme included all of the large domestic banks and several of the smaller ones as well. When the case was made public in 1998, it caused an enormous uproar, for several reasons. First, the Mexican authorities had not been informed about the operation, and they were understandably outraged at an undercover operation in their territory that had not been approved. Second, the major Mexican banks were indicted for criminal money laundering, which gave a big black eye to Mexico's banking

Figure 13.2
Operation Check Mark

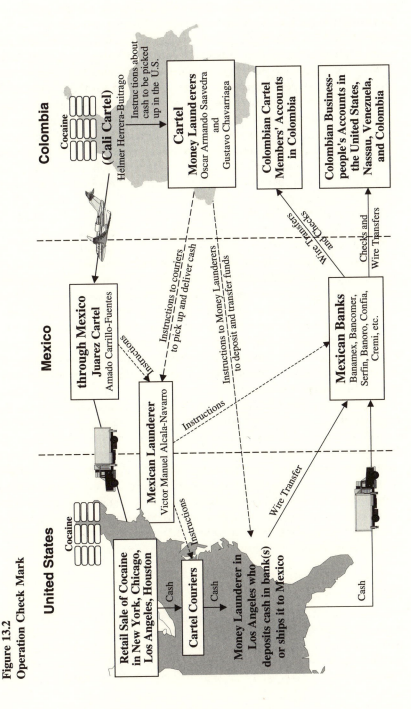

system, just as it was coming out of the tequila crisis and the Asian financial crisis, both of which had caused grave damage to the solvency of the banks. And third, if a bank was convicted of criminal money laundering, the U.S. law required the bank's charter to be reviewed and possibly revoked for operating in the United States, another potentially enormous blow to the Mexican banks.

When the uproar settled down, the facts demonstrated that, in each instance, one or a few bankers in each bank were responsible for the money laundering activity—and it was not proven that any of the banks was purposefully involved in money laundering as an approved practice. Nevertheless, under the law in the United States, the banks were liable for forfeiting the laundered money, for further financial penalties, and for the possible revocation of their U.S. charters. The Big 3 banks—Banamex, Bancomer, and Banca Serfin—pled guilty and paid large fines. Several medium-sized banks—Banca Cremi, Banco Internacional, and Banoro—also pled guilty and paid fines. One medium-sized bank, Banca Confia, agreed to forfeit the funds and pay a fine, but because the bank had been operating under government receivership for part of the period of time involved, a criminal conviction was dropped.[3] Several additional banks in Nassau, Venezuela, and Colombia also had funds forfeited and were fined.

This operation had the interesting side effect of increasing cooperation between the U.S. government and the governments of Mexico, Colombia, and the Bahamas in the prosecution of money laundering activities. In all of these cases, a major incentive for cooperation lay in the possibility of forfeiting large sums of money, millions or tens of millions of dollars. The three Latin American/Caribbean countries had recently established anti-money laundering statutes on the books, and this prosecution brought all of them the opportunity to utilize the law and to benefit from it.

Overall, Operation Casablanca and the related Operation Check Mark demonstrated the relatively new cooperation between Mexican and Colombian narcotraffickers and some new mechanisms for laundering the money they earned. The physical shipment of large quantities of U.S. dollars to Mexico was much easier than shipment to Colombia (by truck or car, rather than by airplane or boat), and the many bank offices in Mexico near the U.S. border provided a natural target for introducing narcodollars into the banking system. The money laundering organizations in Colombia and Mexico seemed to function smoothly, which of course posed a threat to law enforcement as the launderers built up additional schemes for escaping detection and prosecution.

NOTES

1. The sting involving the corrupt Mexican bankers was actually a related operation called Check Mark. In this action, the Saavedra-Alcala money laundering organization physically carried cash to Mexico for deposit in banks there, before subsequently sending the funds via wire transfer to other banks in the United States, Nassau, Venezuela, and elsewhere. See, for example, the affidavit of Stephen M. Perino (May 1998) as cited in

the Grand Jury indictment of Oscar Armando Saavedra, Victor Manuel Alcala-Navarro et al. (CR 98-509(A)-LGB, Central District of California).

2. Carrillo-Fuentes was considered one of the top narcotraffickers in Mexico in the early 1990s. He was under indictment in the United States beginning in 1988 for cocaine trafficking, ultimately for quantities amounting to several thousand kilos of the drug. He died in 1996 in an apparent effort to change his appearance through plastic surgery.

3. This situation became quite complicated, because Confia was in the middle of being acquired by Citibank of the United States. Confia had essentially fallen into a bankrupt condition after the tequila crisis in 1994–95, and the Mexican government had intervened managerially to prop it up in 1997. The government looked for a large multinational bank to rescue Confia and engineered an agreement with Citibank that was due to close in May 1998. When the Casablanca indictment was unveiled, one week before the agreed-upon takeover by Citibank, the agreement was thrown into chaos. It took more than a year to resolve the issues involved, up until July 1998, when the money laundering conviction was resolved, and Citibank disbursed the funds to make the acquisition. See Robert Grosse, "Global Corporate Strategy: Citibank's Acquisition of Confia in Mexico" (Glendale, AZ: Thunderbird Case Clearinghouse, 2000).

Part III

Economic Issues and Lessons

Chapter 14

Mexico's Black Market in Foreign Exchange and Its Relation to Narcotics Money Laundering

OVERVIEW

The Mexican foreign exchange market plays an important role in laundering the narcotics revenues of traffickers from that country and, to some extent, of traffickers from Colombia who ship through Mexico. This market is different from many other emerging foreign exchange market structures, because a legal, parallel market has existed for more than two decades. The black market, meaning unreported foreign exchange dealings, is relatively smaller (compared to the size of the economy) than in other Latin American countries, since businesspeople have broad access to dollars in the legal, parallel market.

Narcotics traffickers especially use the black market for cash transactions and the legal, parallel market and official bank market for moving narcotics proceeds into and out of Mexico, as well as into pesos and out of dollars. The laundering process includes cash transactions within Mexico, but more importantly, cross-border transactions in which narcodollars earned in the United States are laundered through Mexico in the form of wire transfers, checks and money orders, and other financial instruments.

In addition to the foreign exchange market, the financial market in Mexico is used directly for laundering narcotics money from the United States. That is, dollars are brought into Mexico from the United States by drug trafficking organizations, and this cash is deposited into Mexican banks for further laundering through wire transfers abroad and other means. Non-cash instruments such as money orders and checks are likewise used to bring dollar-denominated funds into Mexico for insertion into the banking system and transfer to destinations chosen by the traffickers.

INTRODUCTION

The focus of this chapter is on Mexico and the use of its foreign exchange market in the process of laundering narcotics funds. Mexico has long been a major exporter of both heroin and marijuana to the United States.[1] In the 1990s, as interdiction of Colombian cocaine was stepped up dramatically in the Florida Straits, a large volume of that drug was shipped through Mexico, with consequent money laundering involved as well. These narcotics activities contributed very importantly to the supply of U.S. dollars into the Mexican foreign exchange market, both the reported and unreported segments.

The laundering of the drug money could take place largely outside of Mexico, since the drug traffickers earn their main income from sales in the United States. Given Mexico's long border with the United States, it would be quite possible for drug traffickers to keep the vast majority of their income in the United States or to move it elsewhere through U.S. financial channels rather than bring any of it back to Mexico. Still, the Mexican growers of opium poppies and marijuana have to be paid for their crops, and the traffickers live in Mexico and spend much of their income there—so there must be a large amount of drug money that enters the Mexican economy, and certainly some of it leaves the country in the laundry process.

The aim of this chapter is to illuminate the ways in which funds generating from narcotics trafficking enter Mexico's financial markets and to estimate the possible amount of dollars transacted in those markets. An ultimate law enforcement aim would be to design intervention methods for dealing with these financial transactions. This chapter identifies the money laundering/drug trafficking details so that further steps may be taken in other contexts toward controlling this activity.

One major vehicle used to handle the narcotics proceeds is the foreign exchange underground market. Since the sales of drugs generally are in the United States, income is received in dollars. Since the traffickers begin in Mexico, with production costs and other expenses in pesos, some foreign exchange business must be generated from the narcotrafficking. Because the traffickers are not interested in publicizing their activities, they often resort to underground financial transactions that hide the source and ownership of the money, hence a foreign exchange black market. This market exists in any country as the unreported part of the foreign exchange market.

CHARACTERISTICS OF FOREIGN EXCHANGE BLACK MARKETS

A black market in foreign exchange is one that circumvents the local, legal financial system; it is the result of government intervention to restrict trade or capital flow, which forces the restricted users of foreign exchange to find alternative (non-official) means of carrying out their transactions. In most contexts, the black market operates as an illegal (but often broadly accepted) source of foreign currency, thus the cost of buying foreign exchange in this market is generally higher than in the official, legal market. That is, because of the excess demand for foreign exchange that spills over from the official exchange market, and because of the risk of government sanctions against participants in the black market, the buyer of foreign exchange will pay more local currency (e.g., pesos) for foreign currency than in the official market. Conversely, the suppliers of foreign exchange—often foreign tourists and local residents with holdings of foreign currency abroad—will receive more local currency for their money than in the official market.[2]

Examples of black markets in recent years demonstrate exchange rate premiums ranging from a few percentage points to more than 100 percent of the official market rate.[3] In Brazil, under the second cruzado plan at the end of 1986, the official rate was about 14.9 cruzados per dollar, while the black market rate was about 31.5 cruzados per dollar. In Peru, during late 1988, the official Inti traded for about 700 Intis per dollar, while the black market rate was approximately 2,000 Intis per dollar.[4] In India, through most of the 1980s, the black market rate maintained a premium on foreign exchange of about 25–35 percent over the official rate. In Venezuela, under the exchange controls imposed in 1994–96, the black market rate exceeded the official, controlled rate by as much as 50 percent. Some cases exist as well where the black market rate more closely approximates the official rate, as in Israel, where the black market sheqel has been valued at about 10 percent over (i.e., more sheqels per dollar) the official sheqel during most of the past decade. Colombia offers an especially striking example for its absence of such a premium; in fact, it shows an occasional *discount* on black market foreign exchange, including the 1999 rate.

THE MEXICAN CASE

In Mexico, the black market under discussion here has existed for many years, with ebbs and flows following cycles of foreign exchange availability in the legal market. Relative to most other Latin American countries (e.g., Argentina, Brazil, Colombia, Peru, and Venezuela), Mexico has had a relatively smaller black market. The government generally permitted the operation of a non-bank, legal, parallel market during the 1970s, 1980s, and 1990s. For example, during the 1970s, Mexico kept the peso linked to the U.S. dollar (thus floating relative to other currencies, once the dollar began to float in 1972). From the mid-1950s until 1976, the peso was fixed at 12.5 pesos per U.S. dollar. During that period, Mexico did not allow a free foreign exchange market,[5] so a black market existed and operated as elsewhere in the region.

Under intense speculative pressure due to Mexico's weak balance of payments and an anticipated likelihood of devaluation, on August 31, 1976, the peso was formally devalued and allowed to float relative to the U.S. dollar. At that time, the foreign exchange market was divided into a bank market for certain trans-

actions such as payment for exports, imports, foreign debt servicing, and remittances, which were transacted at the official (still variable) rate. All other
transactions were permitted to be transacted at banks or exchange houses at a
freely floating rate. This period of a dual rate system continued for many years,
with occasional controls and efforts by the government to influence the exchange
rate. As a basic principle, however, the market was open to transactions at the
free rate, so businesspeople who could not gain access to the preferential bank
rate (fewer pesos per dollar) still had easy access to dollars in the legal, parallel
market at exchange houses.

One aberration of the general rule that the government allowed the peso to
float occurred in 1988, when the peso was again fixed to the U.S. dollar. For
most of the year, the official rate was fixed at approximately 2,281 pesos per
dollar. The free market rate was allowed to vary, and it continued to drop
through the year until the fixed official rate was abandoned in December. This
experiment at stabilization through fixing the exchange rate did not succeed—
in contrast to the very successful policy in Argentina three years later, that
stabilized its currency for the entire decade of the 1990s.

During the early 1990s, the Mexican peso was allowed to float with some
degree of government intervention in the official market. On January 1, 1993,
the peso was redenominated, with 1,000 old pesos equal to one new peso. This
was not a devaluation but a renumbering of the currency to make it more manageable. The government's intervention to stabilize and maintain the peso value
was more intensive during the period 1992–94, until the decision of the Zedillo
government to allow devaluation in December 1994—triggering the so-called
tequila crisis, in which the peso dropped dramatically by about 50 percent (from
3.45 pesos per dollar to about 5.4 pesos per dollar) in one week, before recov-
ering a bit in mid-1995, and then dropping to more than 7 pesos per dollar by
the end of the year.

Throughout this entire period, the exchange market operated with the official
bank rate used by transactions that required or permitted it (especially import
purchases and overseas investments) and the free market rate for all other transactions. As seen in Figure 14.1, the rates were seldom very different. The only
exceptions to this rule were periods of time of major instability, such as late
1987 and 1988, after the October Wall Street crash, and the second half of 1994
(just before the tequila crisis). In the former case, the stabilization that accompanied the Brady Plan in March 1989 enabled the government to let the official
exchange rate drift, and it simply moved to a level near the parallel market rate.
In the latter case, the speculation was so intense that both rates dropped dramatically at the end of 1994.

The black market functions relative to the free-rate market, which in turn
functions relative to the official market in Mexico, as elsewhere. The official
market provides dollars and other foreign currency to importers for paying suppliers and to banks for satisfying their foreign debt commitments. Likewise,
foreign multinational firms must use the official market to buy dollars to remit

Figure 14.1
Mexican Official and Free Exchange Rate (pesos/U.S. dollars)

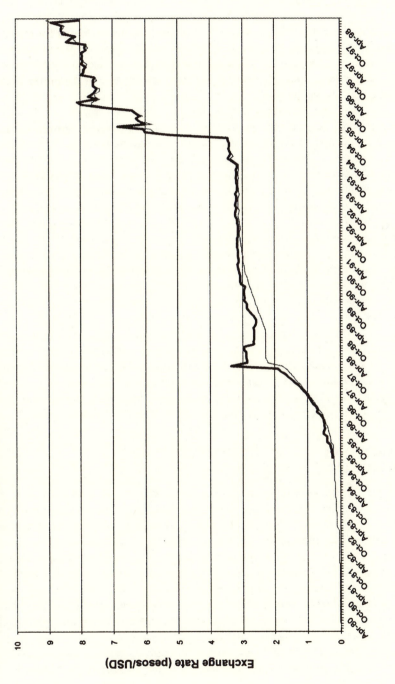

Exchange Rate (pesos/USD)

—— Official Exchange Rate   —— Black market rate (compatible)

profits to their parent companies. The official market is supplied largely by investors who bring dollars into Mexico for the purchase of financial instruments such as bank deposits, bonds, shares of stock, and even purchases of companies and real estate. In addition, exporters bring in foreign currency earnings that are transmitted to the Central Bank, which in turn provides the exporters with local currency, namely pesos. The legal, parallel market provides dollars to peso holders and pesos to dollar holders for any transactions not required to be transacted in the official market.

The black market then provides dollars to Mexican importers whose desired imports may be restricted by the government through high tariffs, quotas, and/ or red tape, and to importers who simply choose to evade government regulations (such as contraband importers). The black market also is used by Mexican investors who want to hold their wealth outside of the country but who do not wish to have this wealth known to the authorities or any others. The black market is supplied with dollars by exporters who choose not to follow the legal process of exporting (e.g., "contrabandistas" or "estucheros" selling Mexican products without paying taxes) by Mexicans living abroad ("braseros") who choose to remit some of their wealth to relatives in Mexico and, significantly, by drug traffickers. In all, the three foreign exchange markets serve similar purposes; the black market is the provider of foreign exchange service to those who are unable or unwilling to use the official bank market or the legal, parallel market.

And in Mexico in particular, the black market is important in the context of narcodollars, the earnings of Mexican narcotics traffickers. Casual observation shows very small differences between official and black market exchange rates over the past 15 years, which could be attributed to the supply of dollars to the market from narcotraffics exports,[6] initially marijuana and heroin and more recently cocaine. This point is considered in some detail below.

STRUCTURE AND FUNCTIONING OF THE BLACK MARKET

The black market in foreign exchange in Mexico has several layers of participants. On the demand side, they range from individuals seeking to convert $U.S. 10–20 equivalent of pesos into dollars to large companies buying millions of dollars with their pesos. On the supply side, they range from braceros living in the United States and trying to get dollars back to relatives in Mexico, to narcotraffickers seeking to convert millions of dollars they have earned from sales in the United States (and elsewhere). The intermediaries in most black market transactions are cambistas (foreign exchange dealers) who exist at both the retail and wholesale levels. Figure 14.2 depicts the various participants in the market and its geographic structure.

The simplest form of black market foreign exchange dealing occurs in the street market, in which a small-scale cambista buys dollars from foreign tourists

Figure 14.2
Map of Mexico Showing Key Narco/Money Laundering Locations

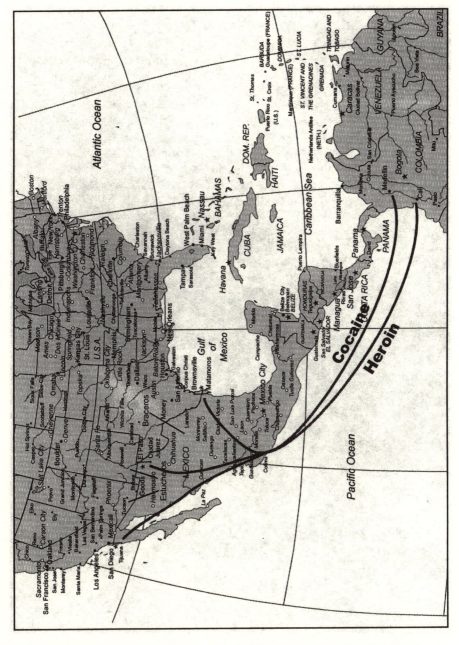

and sells them pesos, typically in quantities of $U.S. 10–100. Similar retail transactions occur in the underground economy throughout Mexico, where the entire set of business activities remains unreported.[7]

More complex transactions occur when the seller of dollars is a narcotics trafficker. In this case, a wide variety of means is used to deliver the dollars. One is to physically carry the dollars to Mexico, for example, from San Diego to Tijuana or from El Paso to Ciudad Juarez, for direct exchange for pesos in cash. Another is to convert the dollars into money orders or checks in the United States and then ship them to Mexico for sale in exchange for pesos. A third means of selling the dollars is to deposit them into bank accounts in the United States and to arrange for bank transfers into the accounts of the purchasers who reside in Mexico. In this instance, the dollar buyer specifies a bank account to receive the dollars and pays in pesos to the cambista in Mexico, typically with a personal check.[8] Many more processes have been devised to convert narco-dollars into pesos—just as the narcotraffickers have devised numerous means for holding and moving their dollar wealth outside of Mexico. A notable feature of these transactions is that most of the situations involve the delivery of dollars *outside* of Mexico in exchange for pesos delivered *in* Mexico.

Note that the narcotraffickers receive dollars for their sales of marijuana, heroin, or cocaine, and that they do not necessarily ever have to convert them into pesos. Since investment of earnings into U.S. financial instruments is very attractive, the dollars may simply stay in the United States. And since much of the consumption of the narcotraffickers includes imported products, these may be purchased in the United States with the dollars earned there, so only products come into Mexico, not funds. Finally, dollars are widely accepted as currency in Mexico (though not legal tender), so it is often not necessary to convert them into pesos, even for purchases in Mexico. Thus this entire part of the narcotraffic does not use any foreign exchange market, though it may use banks or exchange houses to transfer funds.

MONEY LAUNDERING ESTIMATES

While no precise measure of the volume of money transacted in the laundry of narcotics proceeds can be obtained, some estimates are available. The initial drug flow data are taken from reports by the National Narcotics Intelligence Consumers Committee (NNICC), a U.S. governmental interagency group that pools information from the law enforcement agencies that deal with narcotics trafficking. These data are certainly subject to question concerning their accuracy, but they provide a useful starting point for analysis.[9] Additional data on narcotics prices in the United States were obtained directly from the Drug Enforcement Administration (DEA).

Table 14.1 presents data from the 1990s on marijuana and heroin production in Mexico, along with wholesale prices in the United States. This data show huge amounts of revenues from the drug trade that could be involved in Mexican

Table 14.1
Marijuana and Heroin Production in Mexico

Year	Marijuana Quality (metric tons)	Marijuana Price ($/pound)*	Marijuana Total Value ($ million)	Opium Quantity (metric tons)	Heroin Price ($/kilo)	Heroin[#] Total Value ($ million)
1985	3,500			35		
1986	5,000			43		
1987	5,933			50		
1988	5,655			67		
1989	30,200			66		
1990	19,715			62		
1991	7,775			41		
1992	7,795	[700]	5,457	40	100,000	400
1993	6,280	700	4,396	49	112,000	549
1994	5,540	600	3,324	60	112,000	672
1995	3,650	600	2,190	53	112,000	594
1996	3,400	600	2,040	54	110,000	594
1997	2,500	[600]	1,500	46	112,000	515

* = dollars per pound commercial grade, in Houston or San Diego

= 10 tons of opium is estimated to produce one ton of heroin; Mexican heroin sells for less than Asian heroin because of its lower quality ("black-tar heroin")

Source: U.S. Department of State, International Narcotics Control Strategy Report (Washington, D.C.: U.S. GPO, 1989 and 1998); Drug Enforcement Administration.

financial markets. Unquestionably, much of the money produced by drug sales in the United States never goes to Mexico, so some fraction of the total would be the maximum possible to be laundered in Mexico. However, at the same time it must be recognized that money laundering in Mexico is really a multi-national phenomenon, and that the delivery of dollars may take place in Mexico, in the United States, or elsewhere, such as Panama or Nassau. This data show a total value of about $2 billion to $4 billion per year as revenues to the Mexican marijuana and heroin traffickers in recent years, with a declining trend.

If the NNICC data are used with several additional adjustments reflecting factors such as narcotics seizures, crop eradication, money confiscations, and others, the money laundering value could be either smaller or larger. We will assume that crop eradication has been accounted for in the data produced by the NNICC so that no adjustment is needed. One key adjustment needs to be made for seizures of marijuana and heroin shipments from Mexico to the United States in these years. Estimates of cocaine seizures range from 10–30 percent of drug shipments to the United States being interdicted annually; with both heroin and marijuana, the figures are much lower. In 1997, it was estimated that less than 5 percent of heroin was interdicted (about 1.4 metric tons). This adjustment obviously would somewhat reduce the total value of revenues going to the traffickers.

Another key adjustment is needed to account for the fact that Mexican traffickers do not bring all of their earnings back to Mexico, so the amount of money laundering that occurs through Mexico must be less than their revenues. As with Colombian traffickers, and really as with *anyone* who held large wealth in the 1990s, the Mexican traffickers invested some of it in international financial instruments such as dollar-denominated deposits in the United States or in the Euromarkets, for example, in London, Panama, or Nassau. In the Colombian case, it was estimated that possibly three-fourths of the revenues were left outside of Colombia.[10]

The next important adjustment to be made in the data arises from the need to account for Colombian cocaine that was transshipped through Mexico during the 1990s. Due to major interdiction efforts by U.S. government agencies in the coastal waters off Florida beginning in 1990, Colombian traffickers shifted a significant part of their cocaine transportation through Mexico. While no careful estimates are available, enforcement agents in Florida, Texas, and California asserted that as much as half of Colombian drug trafficking during the 1990s passed through Mexico. Because the Mexican traffickers earned income from their assistance in that transport process, they earned more than from their own production of marijuana and heroin alone, which would have added significantly to their revenues, since some estimates showed their fees for this transshipment service at around 10–15 percent of the wholesale value shipped.[11]

The Mexican drug traffickers also may earn more income from distribution in the United States. In the case of Colombian traffickers, the bulk of earnings comes from wholesale-level sales of cocaine in the United States. The retail-level distribution is operated predominantly by North American groups. In the case of Mexican traffickers, there is some evidence that they have been able to move further downstream in the distribution process within the United States, thus earning higher incomes when they are able to move down the value-added chain toward the final consumers. This possibility is not explored here.

A final adjustment to the amount of narcodollars that could be available for laundering in Mexico relates to the non-Mexican traffickers who may use the Mexican financial market for money laundering. Given the lower level of enforcement of the drug trafficking and money laundering laws that exist in Mexico—not to mention the much greater problem of corruption of bankers and government officials there—it is entirely possible that U.S. drug traffickers and Colombian drug traffickers also may use Mexico as a point of entry for their drug cash into financial markets.

This last phenomenon has not been measured directly, but some indication of its importance could possibly be gleaned from cash flow data reported by banks and the Federal Reserve System with respect to Mexico. For example, CMIR (Cash and Monetary Instrument Report) filings from Mexico showed an average of about $U.S. 7 billion a month taken from the United States to Mexico (and about $U.S. 1 billion into the United States from Mexico) during 1995–97. FinCEN also collects data on U.S. Federal Reserve Bank receipts of cash from banks in Mexico. These data were not available to the author, but they could provide an additional corroboration of the large amounts of cash shipped, some of which may have been drug money being laundered.[12]

In sum, the amount of funds flowing to Mexican narcotics traffickers who could launder the money through Mexico plus funds received by non-Mexican traffickers who choose to launder the money through the Mexican financial system can be estimated in the following structure:

Funds possibly laundered through Mexican financial system =

Mexican narcotraffickers' production minus interdiction of heroin and marijuana × prices, adjusted for funds left outside of Mexico and funds interdicted +

Mexican narcotraffickers' income from cocaine transshipped for Colombian traffickers +

Colombian and U.S. narcotraffickers' revenues that they choose to launder through Mexico.

If we accept the NNICC and DEA data for 1996, we find possible marijuana and heroin revenues of about $U.S. 2.5 billion. Assuming that one-half of the revenues is brought back to Mexico, this leaves a value of $U.S. 1.25 billion that could be laundered there. The amount of interdiction of drug shipments was estimated at a maximum of 10 percent of the total, leaving a value of about $U.S. 1.125 billion. Mexican traffickers' income from helping Colombian traffickers move their cocaine into the United States could produce another $U.S.

325 million, based on an NNICC estimate of 1996 Colombian cocaine sales of $U.S. 9.75 billion, of which one-third may be shipped through Mexico, and an estimate that the Mexican traffickers earned 10 percent on the transshipments. This produces a total of $U.S. 1.45 billion for the year. The possible use of Mexico's financial system for laundering by U.S. and Colombian drug traffickers also could be very large, but no reliable data were available to estimate these amounts, thus the final result would be a figure above $U.S. 2 billion.[13]

DETERMINATION OF THE PARALLEL MARKET EXCHANGE RATE

A final validity check on the above analysis may be made through estimating a model of the parallel market exchange rate in Mexico. If the market really is used importantly to launder drug money, then the drug money estimates should have an impact on the exchange rate.

The exchange rate in a parallel market may be expected to reflect several important relationships. First, it will usually offer an exchange rate worse than the official rate to sellers of local currency, because of the excess demand for foreign exchange spilling over from the official market and because the legal parallel rate is determined by supply and demand. Second, it may show a relationship, between foreign and local currency that more closely reflects parity conditions between the two than the official exchange rate, since there are no restrictions on the parallel market other than its cost of operation. That is, participants on both the supply and demand sides of the market are free to buy and sell at mutually agreed-upon exchange rates, resulting in a basically free market (biased only by the transactions cost of paying an intermediary for the various risks and costs involved). Therefore, the parallel market rate can be expected to equilibrate supply and demand for the currency and thus to reflect an equilibrium in the market. These two points are not inconsistent, since the government's intervention in the official market leads to a non-parity condition, which is relieved in the freely determined parallel market.

In virtually all countries, the parallel (or black) market exchange rate has a higher value of local currency per unit of foreign exchange than the official market because of the foreign exchange scarcity that caused the market to develop.[14] The next section presents a model of the Mexican parallel market and seeks to explain the exchange rate there.

THE MODEL

This section offers a simple economic fundamentals model of determination of the parallel market exchange rate in Mexico during the 1990s. The main factors that can be expected to influence the exchange rate between pesos and U.S. dollars are monetary and balance of payments influences plus the narco-traffic.[15]

For most of the relevant variables, monthly data were available for this period. End-of-month exchange rates for the official market were obtained from the *Direction of Trade Yearbook*, and parallel market rates were obtained from the *World Currency Yearbook*.[16] The narcotraffic was only measured quarterly or annually (depending on the specific series), so a moving-average time series interpolation was employed.

The model tested was:

Black market exchange rate = a + b1 (price level Mexico vs. price level United States)
− b2 (interest rate differential, Mexico vs. United States)
− b3 (trade balance Mexico) − b4 (inflow of narcodollars)

This specification hypothesizes a positive relationship between the ratio of the aggregate price level in Mexico to that in the United States and the exchange rate defined as pesos per dollar. The greater the difference between Mexican and U.S. price levels (i.e., the relative rate of Mexican inflation), the greater the devaluation of the peso (i.e., more pesos per dollar). This is one measure of the purchasing parity argument.

In addition, the relative rate of return available to Mexican investors between instruments in pesos and in dollars is expected to affect the parallel market exchange rate. The greater the premium on peso-denominated investments (such as bank deposits), the lower the expected demand for dollars, hence the lower the exchange rate (pesos per dollar). Thus there should be a negative relationship between the parallel market rate and the interest differential (defined as the peso interest rate on three-month CDs (certificates of deposit) minus the actual devaluation for the period, minus the U.S. dollar interest rate for three-month CDs).

A third factor that could be expected to influence the exchange rate is the trade balance, which is a proxy for Mexico's ability to generate foreign exchange to supply the (official) market. In fact, a positive trade balance could be expected to generate foreign exchange that puts downward pressure on the peso/dollar rate (i.e., for the peso to revalue upward compared to the dollar) *and* to generate confidence in Mexico's ability to service its foreign debt—both of which lead to an expected negative relationship between the trade balance and the parallel market exchange rate. An alternative specification of this relationship could use the change in Mexico's official foreign exchange reserves to measure the pressure on the exchange rate. Since the official reserves balance records both trade imbalances *and* capital account imbalances, it is really the bottom line in the balance of payments that would be expected to affect the exchange rate. As official reserves decline, the peso is expected to devalue relative to the dollar, because the reserve outflow results in a greater scarcity of foreign exchange.

The fourth factor that is expected to influence the rate is the supply of narcodollars into the market. Clearly, if a large part of the market is supplied by narcotics proceeds, then the flow of funds in that traffic will have an important

Table 14.2

Determination of Mexico's Parallel Market Exchange Rate, 1992–97 (Dependent variable: parallel market exchange rate)

Independent Variables	MODEL 1 (OLS)	MODEL 2 (GLS)
Measure of Inflationary Pressure*		
Mexican Price Index / U.S. Price Index	123.73	257.72
	(.000)	(.000)
Measure of Interest Rate Differential	2.71	-128.99
	(.957)	(.005)
Measure of Dollar Availability[†]		
Trade Balance	0.06	0.01
	(.000)	(.115)
Measures of Narcotics Flows		
1. Marijuana Flow Measure	-13.70	-16.00
	(.000)	(.000)
2. Opium Flow Measure	-61.78	-65.49
	(.000)	(.000)
Adjusted R^2	0.97	0.99
F-Ratio of Regression	573.46	
	(.000)	
Durbin-Watson Value	0.95	1.99

*The relative growth of the money supply in Mexico vs. the United States was used in an alternative specification that produced similar results with a slightly weaker fit.

†It was not meaningful to run regressions using official reserve flows, since these flows were 99 percent correlated with the relative monetary growth variable.

Significance levels, ρ, in parentheses.

OLS = ordinary least squares; GLS = generalized least squares.

Source: World Currency Yearbook, January 1992 through December 1997.

impact on the supply side and hence on the price of foreign exchange in the parallel market. The greater the supply of narcodollars, the lower the value of the peso/dollar exchange rate expected in the parallel market.

The estimation of this equation using monthly data from 1992–97 resulted in the model shown in Table 14.2. Two separate specifications of the model appear in the table, each listed vertically in one column. The basic model (column 1) produced highly significant coefficients for three of the four independent variables as well as explained almost all of the variation in the parallel market exchange rate during the six-year period in the 1990s. The price level ratio between Mexico and the United States explained most of the variation in the parallel market exchange rate, as is generally found in analyses of exchange rates in less developed countries. That is, the main factor contributing to the devaluation of Mexico's peso relative to the U.S. dollar was the greater rate of growth of Mexico's aggregate price level. The devaluation trend of the parallel market peso followed the price level differential closely; in the model, the relative price variable explained about 70 percent of the variation in the parallel market rate.

The interest differential between short-term bank deposits in pesos and in (offshore) dollars by itself could explain about 30 percent of the peso's devaluation in the black market. This factor was not significant in the initial model specification, but it was correctly signed.

Narcotics traffic (as measured by the U.S. DEA) explained an additional part of the variation in the black market exchange rate. The two variables representing marijuana and heroin exports were highly significant (at the .01 level), and together they explained over half of the variation in the parallel market exchange rate.

The trade balance coefficient is incorrectly signed but significant (at the .01 level). By itself, this variable explains some 40 percent of the variation in the parallel market exchange rate. This outcome is surprising, but it may be due to a specification error in the model.

Next, the model was respecified to adjust for the high degree of autocorrelation of error terms over time. The resulting generalized least squares model (shown in column 2) produces results broadly in line with the original model, demonstrating that no important bias was caused by the autocorrelation problem. Even so, the corrected model produces highly significant results for the interest rate differential, with the opposite sign from what was expected, while the trade balance coefficient is now not very significant. The instability of these two variables across specifications leads one to question their importance in determining the Mexican parallel market rate.

In sum, the Mexican parallel market, peso/dollar exchange rate is highly positively correlated to the rate of inflation (Colombia vs. the United States) and highly negatively correlated to the inflow of narcotics dollars into the market. The former relationship supports the hypothesis that purchasing power parity tends to be the most significant driving force behind exchange rate adjustment in Latin American currency black markets. The latter relationship supports the hypothesis that the currency black market is a significant recipient of narcotics-related dollars, and thus it serves to facilitate the drug trafficking business.

CONCLUSIONS

This chapter has pursued two goals: first, to demonstrate how the foreign exchange parallel market in Mexico is used to facilitate narcotics trafficking; and second, to explain and estimate the main elements of narcotics money laundering that occur through Mexican financial markets.

The description of the parallel foreign exchange market, and its participants, is supported by the statistical model of the exchange rate, showing the important impact of narcotics revenues on the rate. This does not directly lead to estimates on the size of the money laundering phenomenon, but it lends support for the explanation of that activity that is presented elsewhere in this chapter.

The description of money laundering through Mexico is primarily based on efforts to understand the activities of Mexican narcotics money launderers. However, it was discovered, in pursuing the analysis through interviews of market participants and law enforcement agents in both countries, that the money laundering includes not only the revenues of Mexican producers of heroin and marijuana but also Mexican traffickers' deliveries of Colombian cocaine, U.S. and Colombian traffickers' use of Mexico for money laundering, and possibly Mexican traffickers' earnings from retail rather than only wholesale transactions in the United States. The amount of money laundered through Mexico's financial markets in 1996 was most likely more than $U.S. 2 billion, and potentially significantly more based on unmeasured laundering by U.S. narcotics retail sellers and Colombian traffickers.

This last conclusion really calls for an additional effort to collect information on an ongoing basis concerning the scope of and participants in narcotics trafficking through Mexico. It also suggests the need to look more carefully at the money laundering activities of groups other than the Mexican traffickers, since those other groups also may be using Mexico as a convenient target for placing narcotics revenues into the global financial system.

NOTES

This chapter draws heavily from an article by the same title published in the *Journal of Money Laundering Control*, Henry Stewart Publications (August 1999). I thank Fabian Pino and Michael Crowe for their excellent research assistance on this project.

1. The marijuana and opium/heroin production and export from Mexico to the United States have been estimated and reported annually in the U.S. government's publications, *National Narcotics Intelligence Consumers Committee* report and the *International Narcotics Control Strategy Report*. Each of these publications is available in an annual edition from the U.S. Department of State.

2. Legal sanctions such as fines, funds confiscation, and imprisonment should serve to create a premium on use of the black market for *both* buyers and sellers of foreign exchange. Thus, the sellers typically face a better deal in the black market due to excess demand for foreign currency in the official market—but this deal would have been even better if no sanctions existed.

3. The International Currency Analysis (formerly Pick's) *World Currency Yearbook* (New York: International Currency Analysis), published tri-annually, offers a succinct, very useful commentary on currency black markets around the world. Both exchange rate quotations in black and official markets and an analysis of the differences between the two markets are presented.

4. The Peruvian case offers an interesting contrast to the Colombian one, since this

country also is a recipient of large quantities of narcodollars. Nevertheless, the underlying "formal" economy and balance of payments situation were so weak during the 1980s that the excess demand for dollars spilling over from the official foreign exchange market far surpassed the narcotics proceeds that were brought into the country, resulting in a very large premium on dollars in the black market. See Robert Grosse, "Peru's Black Market in Foreign Exchange," *Journal of Interamerican Studies and Word Affairs* 33, no. 3 (Fall 1991), pp. 135–165.

5. That is, dollars had to be transacted at the 12.5 rate, so that an excess demand for dollars existed.

6. This is somewhat difficult to interpret, however, since no black market exchange rates are quoted. The black market rate is generally the free market rate, plus or minus some percentage, such as 5–8 percent. On the sell side for dollars, the author has encountered recent quotes of the free market rate minus a "commission" of 7 percent. That would mean when the peso is quoted at 10.15 pesos per dollar at casas de cambio, the seller of dollars would receive about 9.50 pesos for each dollar sold in the black market.

7. The size of Mexico's underground economy has been estimated to be as much as 50 percent of the total economy. While this estimate is probably very high, the underground or informal economy in Mexico is very large and transacts large volumes of peso and dollar business every day.

8. This process of laundering narcodollars is described in detail in the documents presented by parties in the so-called *Casablanca* legal case. Criminal Case #98-509(A)-LGB, *U.S. v. Oscar Armando Saavedra et al.*, Central District of California.

9. The marijuana data in particular show a huge increase in production from 1988 to 1989, which is then reduced in two years back to a similar trend. The extreme variation in the measures is unquestionably not due to dramatic shifts in production but rather to changes in data estimation. Unfortunately, the U.S. government has not produced revised data to resolve the inconsistency problem. In the modeling done here, the data are only used back to 1992, so this problem is avoided.

10. See Robert Grosse, "Colombia's Black Market in Foreign Exchange," *World Development* 20, no. 3 (1992), pp. 1193–1207.

11. In a conversation with a U.S. analyst from Texas, it was stated that Mexican traffickers recently have been charging Colombian traffickers as much as 35 percent of the cocaine in payment for the transshipment service, and taking payment in cocaine. This would again raise the earnings of the Mexican traffickers and leave those earnings in the United States, where the cocaine is sold. The 1997 NNICC report noted that some Mexican traffickers were charging 50 percent of the cocaine as a fee to the Colombian traffickers.

12. This data on cash movements would include money being laundered by Mexican drug traffickers, possibly Colombian and U.S. traffickers, and of course huge amounts of money being transferred between Mexican family members who live in the border states and northern Mexico. It is not possible to separate the non-Mexican narcotraffickers' funds in these flows.

13. A DEA report for the previous year estimated narcotics earnings for Mexican drug traffickers at approximately $U.S. 7 billion (report of October 10, 1996, cited at website: http://www1.nando.net/newsroom/nt/626launder.html).

14. A notable exception is Colombia's foreign exchange market, in which the parallel and black market rates have long shown a discount on buying dollars relative to the

official market, largely because of the huge inflow of narcodollars. See Grosse, "Colombia's Black Market in Foreign Exchange," pp. 1193–1207.

15. See Michael Connolly and Dean Taylor, "The Exact Timing of the Collapse of an Exchange Rate Regime and Its Impact on the Relative Price of Traded Goods," *Journal of Money, Credit, and Banking* 16, no. 2 (May 1984), pp. 194–207; Rudiger Dornbusch et al., "The Black Market for Dollars in Brazil," *Quarterly Journal of Economics* 98, no. 1 (February 1983), pp. 25–40; W. Patton Culbertson, "Empirical Regularities in Black Markets for Currency," *World Development* 17, no. 12 (December 1989), pp. 1907–1919.

16. International Monetary Fund (IMF), *Direction of Trade Yearbook 1990* (Washington, D.C.: IMF, 1990); Philip Cowitt, Carolyn Edwards, and Elliot Bryce (eds.), *World Currency Yearbook* (various editions) (Brooklyn, N.Y.: Currency Data & Intelligence, 1990, 1996).

Chapter 15

The Colombian Connection

One of the most difficult aspects of the narcotics money laundering problem is that the activity focuses a tremendous amount of attention on Colombia as the source of the narcotics and the home of the major money laundering rings. While it is certainly true that a huge amount of narcotics production, trafficking, and money laundering occurs in Colombia and by Colombians, still the net result is that many Americans view the drug problem as originating in Colombia.

Of course, this is an incorrect inference, since the drug problem exists due to consumption of the drugs in the United States, accompanied by the production and distribution of the drugs by Colombians (among others). The goal of this chapter is to clarify how Colombia and Colombians fit into the drug trafficking/ money laundering picture and to emphasize the problems Colombia faces as a society in relation to this situation.

The result of this commentary on Colombia will be to demonstrate that: (1) the country most negatively affected by the illegal narcotics trade in terms of crime and law enforcement is Colombia, not the United States; (2) the Colombian authorities have made enormous efforts to deal with the problems involved; (3) Colombian society largely rejects the narcotraffickers as criminals rather than as folk heroes; (4) U.S. policy toward Colombia with respect to the drug problem has been very misguided; and (5) there are a handful of clear and feasible steps that can be taken to improve the situation. Perhaps more than this direct demonstration is the implicit thrust of the chapter—to show that, contrary to much U.S. public opinion, not all Colombians are involved in drug trafficking, and that Americans should be looking for ways to help the Colombians deal with the consequences caused by this societal problem.

Probably the most important starting point is to recognize that the Colombian narcotraffickers did not invent cocaine (or marijuana), nor did they create the demand in the United States for these drugs. Nevertheless, once the market was developed, these traffickers unquestionably took advantage of it. If the market were to disappear for lack of consumer interest, so would the Colombian supply network. Having made this point, let us next look at the actual economic impact in Colombia.

DRUG TRAFFICKING: THE COLOMBIAN SIDE OF THE STORY

Drug trafficking in Colombia and by Colombians overseas has generated an estimated $U.S. 2–4 billion a year income (about 4% of the GDP in the mid-1990s) for the Colombian traffickers, at least one-quarter of whom was estimated to return to Colombia each year during the 1980s and 1990s. On the other hand, the number of Colombians killed each year in narcotics trafficking and related activities since 1980 is well over 1,000 people, including many law enforcement officials, and even politicians and Supreme Court justices.

To put into perspective the financial aspects of this situation, consider Figure 15.1.

This figure demonstrates that, while Colombian traffickers earn enormous profits from their illegal business, the vast majority of the earnings is generated at the retail level of drug sales in the United States. In a business estimated to produce about $U.S. 100 billion a year in revenues, more than 90 percent is earned by U.S. drug traffickers and money launderers, while, at most, Colombian participants are estimated to earn about $U.S. 4 billion and Peruvian and Bolivian coca farmers and traffickers about $U.S. 1 billion in each of those countries.

The drug money that is returned to Colombia by the traffickers is used for many purposes, from purchasing raw materials and hiring workers to investing in real estate to bribing public officials so that they do not interfere in the drug business. It is estimated that over 5 percent of Colombian real estate is currently owned by drug-related investors, including the traffickers and money launderers, as well as their employees. This is an enormous social problem, since it implies an economic power of these criminals that exceeds the power of most individuals and legally run businesses in the country.

The basic business of drug trafficking in Colombia involves purchasing and transporting the coca leaf and/or cocaine base from growing regions in Peru and Bolivia, as well as domestically, and manufacturing cocaine hydrochloride in Colombia (or in Brazil, or elsewhere). Increasingly, in the 1990s, the production process moved backward into coca growing as well. The process also involves operating the cocaine factories in the jungles of Colombia and shipping the final product principally to the United States and Europe. It involves as well laundering the earnings of this drug traffic both in the United States and in Colombia. As noted above, this business generates about $U.S. 2–4 billion a year of earnings for the Colombian traffickers, on top of which are the earnings of the money launderers for providing their services in both countries, and of course incomes

Figure 15.1
Income Generated in the Cocaine Trade

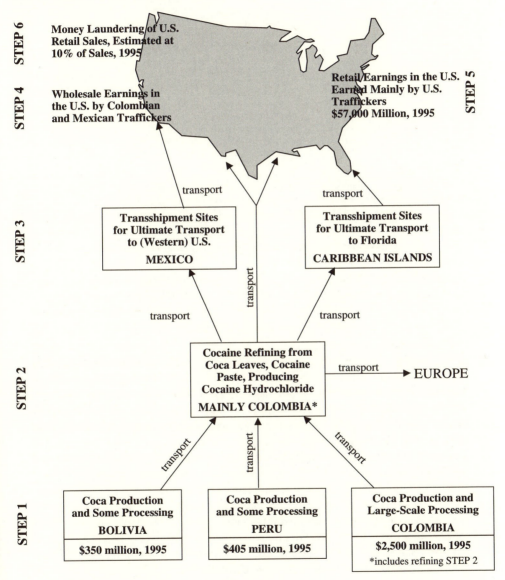

STEP 6 · Money Laundering of U.S. Retail Sales, Estimated at 10% of Sales, 1995

STEP 4 · Wholesale Earnings in the U.S. by Colombian and Mexican Traffickers

STEP 5 · Retail Earnings in the U.S. Earned Mainly by U.S. Traffickers $57,000 Million, 1995

STEP 3 · Transshipment Sites for Ultimate Transport to (Western) U.S. **MEXICO**

Transshipment Sites for Ultimate Transport to Florida **CARIBBEAN ISLANDS**

transport

STEP 2 · Cocaine Refining from Coca Leaves, Cocaine Paste, Producing Cocaine Hydrochloride **MAINLY COLOMBIA*** — transport → EUROPE

STEP 1 · Coca Production and Some Processing **BOLIVIA** · $350 million, 1995

Coca Production and Some Processing **PERU** · $405 million, 1995

Coca Production and Large-Scale Processing **COLOMBIA** · $2,500 million, 1995 · *includes refining STEP 2

Source: Data from U.S. Department of State, *International Narcotics Control Strategy Report* (Washington, D.C.: U.S. GPO, 1998); author's analysis.

Figure 15.2
Colombian Cocaine Industry

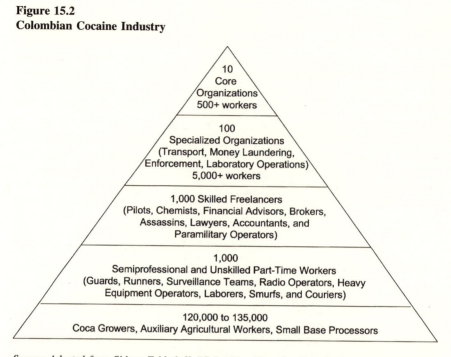

Source: Adapted from Sidney Zabludoff, "Colombian Narcotics Organizations as Business Enterprises." In U.S. Department of State, Bureau of Research and Intelligence and the Central Intelligence Agency, *Economics of the Narcotics Industry Conference Report* (Washington, D.C.: State Department and CIA, 1994).

produced for non-Colombians at various stages of the process. The potential direct impact on Colombia could come from the $U.S. 0.5–1.0 billion of earnings that may be brought back to Colombia each year. These earnings are spent on the consumption of goods and services and are invested into financial and real investments. Figure 15.2 depicts the structure of the Colombian cocaine industries in the context of the global scale of production and trade that includes the United States as a consuming country and Peru and Bolivia as key additional producers of the coca leaf.

The benefit of these earnings to the national economy is not straightforward. For example, often the earnings are brought back to the country through the foreign exchange black market, which is unrecorded by the financial authorities. These funds contribute to development of the underground economy in Colombia, so a significant part of the narcotraffic earnings does not directly affect the country's balance of payments or measured GDP.[1]

Another major economic impact of the drug trafficking results from the traffickers' links to guerillas, especially in remote areas of the country. During the 1980s, drug traffickers built up links to both of the main guerrilla movements in Colombia, the FARC (Fuerzas Armadas Revolucianarias de Colombia) and the ELN (Ejercito de la Liberacion Nacional).[2] In both cases, the traffickers offered money to the guerillas in exchange for protection against law enforcement or army intervention in their coca and marijuana growing, cocaine refining, and cocaine and marijuana transportation activities. The combination of these two interests has become a serious threat to civil order in Colombia. With these additional financial resources and the cooperation of the drug gangs, the guerillas have obtained de facto control of large parts of rural Colombia. Even the negotiations begun by the Samper government and continued under the current Pastrana government have recognized the guerillas' power to the extent of offering them legally sanctioned zones of the country that are not subject to government control (or military intervention). Once again, this impact of the narcotraffickers on the national economy is more to expand the size of the underground, unreported economy than to build the legally operating economy. And clearly, this impact is negative with respect to both the economic and social stability of the country.

A very difficult to measure but still significant economic impact of the drug trade on Colombia is the allocative effect on the structure of the national economy. That is, as people and resources are taken into the drug trade, they are taken away from other, presumably productive activities. This substitution of illegal for legal and negative value added in place of positively contributing activities constitutes another important negative contribution to Colombia's overall economy. The difficulties in measuring this impact are twofold. First, since many illegal activities are unrecorded, they cannot be directly measured for economic impact. Second, the participation of individuals in narcotics trafficking and related activities cannot be simply asserted to be the alternative to legal, productive activity. Given the large size of Colombia's (and Latin America's) underground economy, it is quite possible that a major part of the drug-related work done by people in the trade would be replaced by other unreported, underground business activity if they were to leave drug trafficking. And this underground activity does not contribute to Colombia's measured economy, plus it may detract from the effort to bring the country under a generalized rule of law, rather than being subject to guerilla-controlled regions, right-wing militias, and so on.

Thus, just as in the United States, drug trafficking and money laundering activities have a decidedly negative impact, although for different reasons. While in the United States, the key costs are health related (lost work, deaths, and health care costs, due mainly to drug addiction), in Colombia, the key costs are related to the violence involved with the drug trafficking and the impact of the traffickers' economic power on distorting the economy.

POLICY ALTERNATIVES

One of the first suggestions that tend to come up in discussions of this sort is to legalize cocaine and thus to decriminalize the production and trafficking business. The argument is, in oversimplified form, if people are going to consume drugs anyway, why not make it legal and put more effort into educating people about the harmful effects of drug consumption, plus offer greater health care support? This argument is a poor one for at least two reasons. First, the added cost of greater consumption, based on the comparison of legal and pro- hibited alcohol consumption in the United States, is much higher overall, par- ticularly in health care costs plus lost work. And second, the moral choice of not discouraging narcotics consumption would be a difficult decision at best. The former argument is pursued in greater detail in the final chapter of this book. In sum, the legalization of narcotics consumption would not be an attrac- tive policy alternative.

In terms of general policy guidelines, the logic should be to invest in anti- narcotics policies to the point where an additional dollar spent produces exactly one dollar's additional benefit in terms of reduced crime, reduced drug addiction cost, improved economic efficiency, and so on. This is a very reasonable frame- work to consider, but applying it is difficult because of the need to account for alternatives. If people stop trafficking in cocaine, what alternative business will they enter? If people stop consuming cocaine, what will they do instead? If one illegal activity is replaced by another, then the purported benefits of an anti- drug policy are not as clear. Our basic assertion is that reduced cocaine traf- ficking will largely push people into the legal, recorded economy, and it will therefore produce a positive impact overall.

Another area of great concern in Colombia, though much less so in the United States, is the "certification" process by which the United States rates its narcotics-producing trading partners and seeks to use this rating to support or to deny economic assistance to those countries.

This process began in 1987, with Colombia being certified initially but par- tially decertified in 1988–89, 1995, and 1998, and decertified in 1996–97. The idea of the certification process is admirable, in trying to push partner countries to make greater efforts toward staunching the flow of narcotics into the United States. However, the process is viewed in Colombia as a purely political gambit, in which the United States holds out economic incentives to the country if Colombia's government will follow U.S.-selected anti-drug policies. Sometimes this is possible; at other times it conflicts with various policy goals in Colombia (such as the peace process with guerilla groups or the effort to reduce drug cartel violence, in the context of U.S. demands for extraditing Colombian traf- fickers).

The process is especially flawed if one compares the treatment of Mexico, another major narcotics supplier to the United States, to Colombia. In 1995, the Mexican head of the federal police was arrested for participating in narcotraffic. The brother of former President Raul Salinas was arrested that year for having laundered more than $U.S. 100 million, including narcotics proceeds. Numerous other high-profile Mexican narcotics trafficking activities were in the news, and cocaine trafficking was shown by U.S. enforcement authorities to have shifted greatly away from the Florida Straits to Mexico for delivery into the United States. In that same year, Colombian authorities killed Pablo Escobar, jailed the Rodriguez Orajuela brothers (Cali cartel leaders), and subsequently began proceedings to extradite Jaime Orlando Lara for trial in the United States.[3] In addition, numerous trials of narcotraffickers and money launderers were carried out at great peril to the judges, attorneys, and witnesses in Colombia. And finally in that year, Mexico was certified as a partner in good standing in the drug war, while Colombia was partially decertified. This is one of the greatest hypocrisies ever perpetrated in inter-American relations, and even more so in the context of the drug war.

Table 15.1 lists the countries in the certification process and the ratings for the period 1987–99. The table demonstrates that all of the major drug producing and trafficking countries that supply U.S. consumers with illegal narcotics have at one time or another been at least partially decertified. The problem with the process is that it is politicized to some extent, leading to wildly unreasonable results such as the 1995 Mexico/Colombia ones, and it does not lead to consistent U.S. policy with the countries involved, since there are many other factors that intervene to sway the policy makers.

The simple policy response to this problem is to cease the certification process. The process has been proven to have limited relation to the partner country's efforts toward narcotics traffic reduction, and it has caused enormous harm to the U.S. image in Latin America, as well as some moderate harm to the countries that have been decertified. Alternatively, the process could be continued and used as an internal decision-making criterion within the U.S. government but not publicized as a muckraking tool in international relations. Either of these two alternatives would greatly improve on a process that is regionally (in the Americas) seen as unfair and domineering.

CONCLUSIONS

Colombia is unquestionably a pivotal player in the narcotics trafficking problem that affects the United States. There is little doubt that, if the amount of narcotics trafficking were to decline, the impact in the United States would be positive. However, it is quite likely that if Colombia were to succeed in drastically reducing or even eliminating the drug traffic, many U.S. consumers would find alternative suppliers or alternative drugs rather than simply reduce their drug habits. The way to reduce the trafficking would be much more direct if consumption were discouraged rather than limited to one source or channel of supply.

It should be recognized that the negative economic impact of the drug trade is not only in the United States but also in Colombia. This impact is largely overlooked in the United States due to lack of knowledge and also lack of interest. Policy makers need to be informed about the real costs Colombia incurs

Table 15.1
International Narcotics Control Certification Summary*

Country	1999			1998			1997			1996			1995			1994			1993
	Cert. with Expl.	Part. Cert.	Deny Cert.	Cert. with Expl.	Part. Cert.	Deny Cert.	Cert. with Expl.	Part. Cert.	Deny Cert.	Cert. with Expl.	Part. Cert.	Deny Cert.	Cert. with Expl.	Part. Cert.	Deny Cert.	Cert. with Expl.	Part. Cert.	Deny Cert.	Cert. with Expl.
1 Afghanistan			x			x			x			x			x		x		
2 Aruba ###	x			x			x			-	-	-	-	-	-	-	-	-	-
3 The Bahamas	x			x			x			x			x			x			x
4 Belize ****	x			x				x		x			-	-	-	x			x
5 Bolivia	x			x			x			x				x		x			x
6 Brazil	x			x			x			x			x			x			x
7 Burma			x			x			x			x	x				x		x
8 Cambodia ##		x			x		x					x	-	-	-		x		x
9 China **	x			x			x			x			x			x			x
10 Colombia	x			x					x			x	x			x			x
11 Dom. Rep #	x			x			x			x			x			x			-
12 Ecuador	x			x			x			x			x			x			x
13 Guatemala ***	x			x			x			x			x			x			x
14 Haiti #		x		x			x			x			x			x			-
15 Hong Kong	x			x			x			x			x			x			x
16 India	x			x			x			x			x			x			x
17 Iran #####	-	-	-			x			x			x			x			x	
18 Jamaica	x			x			x			x			x			x			x
19 Laos	x			x			x			x			x			x			x
# Lebanon ####	-	-	-	-	-	-		x			x			x				x	x
20 Malaysia #####	-	-	-	x			x			x			x			x			x
21 Mexico	x			x			x			x			x			x			x
# Morocco ****	-	-	-	-	-	-	-	-	-	-	-	-	-	-	-	-	-	-	x
22 Nigeria		x				x			x			x			x			x	x
23 Pakistan	x				x			x			x			x				x	x
24 Panama	x			x			x			x			x			x			x
25 Paraguay		x			x		x				x		x				x		x
26 Peru	x			x			x			x					x		x		x
# Syria ####	-	-	-	-	-	-			x			x			x			x	
27 Taiwan #	x			x			x			x			x					x	
28 Thailand	x			x			x			x			x			-	-	-	-
29 Venezuela **	x			x			x			x			x			x			x
30 Vietnam #	x			x			x			x			x			-	-	-	-

178

1992			1991			1990				1989				1988				1987				
Deny Cert.	Cert. with Expl.	Part. Cert.	Deny Cert.	Cert. with Expl.	Part. Cert.	Deny Cert.	Cert.	Cert. with Expl.	Part. Cert.	Deny Cert.	Cert.	Cert. with Expl.	Part. Cert.	Deny Cert.	Cert.	Cert. with Expl.	Part. Cert.	Deny Cert.	Cert.	Cert. with Expl.	Part. Cert.	Deny Cert.

*All Foreign Assistance Act of 1961. Section 481(h) certifications listed in this table were made on March 1 of the calendar year indicated. Some exceptions apply.

**Added in 1991.

***Added in 1990.

****Belize was removed from the major drug-producing country list in 1995, Morocco in 1994. Belize was added as a major drug transit country in February 1996.

#Added in 1995.

##Added in 1996.

###Added in 1997.

####Removed in 1997.

#####Removed in 1998.

as a result of this activity, as well as the real government efforts to try to deal with it.

NOTES

1. In 1999, the Colombian government announced its intention to include illegal narcotics trafficking in the national GDP. The argument was that this activity is important in size and impact, therefore it should be recorded as part of the national income. The argument has major holes in it, because the narcotraffic earnings do not necessarily enter the legal economy except after passing through one or more stages of the underground economy. Since the government cannot tax or regulate this activity, or offer social security to those participating in it, the idea of including it in the GDP is unsound. Clearly, it could be recorded (estimated) as part of the underground economy.

2. This phenomenon is described in more detail in Patrick Clawson and Rensselaer W. Lee III, *The Andean Cocaine Industry* (New York: St. Martin's Press, 1996), ch. 7.

3. Colombia only restarted its agreement to extradite drug traffickers sought by the United States in 1997, after six years of a constitutional ban on extradition. Lara was extradited in 1997.

Chapter 16

How Should Banks Deal with Money Laundering?

INTRODUCTION

After all of the changes in legislation since 1970, the main concerns of banks and other financial institutions in relation to money laundering are first to meet the reporting requirements of the Bank Secrecy Act (BSA) and second to make a careful effort to avoid allowing their banks to be used for money laundering.

The 1970 Bank Secrecy Act has been revised and updated several times in the past 30 years, but still the basic idea is that banks need to file appropriate reports on cash and monetary instrument transactions so that law enforcement agencies will be able to find records of activities that may turn out to be the laundering of proceeds from "specified unlawful activity." In our context, this unlawful activity would be related to narcotics trafficking, but it also applies to kidnapping, robbery, extortion, and fraud, among other crimes.

The 1986 Money Laundering Control Act made money laundering itself a criminal act, so banks also need to establish policies and train employees to keep such acts from occurring. These efforts largely focus on requiring banks to know their customers well and to document transactions carefully in the event that subsequent events prove that money laundering has occurred.

Banks are used by criminals for drug money laundering in a variety of ways. The main problem in the 1970s was the delivery of large amounts of drug-related cash that was being deposited into commercial banks. For example, without clear rules to keep records that might later demonstrate the trail from cocaine or heroin to the money and subsequent laundered financial assets such as bank accounts and investments, law enforcement was truly limited in its ability to produce evidence about such activities. Once the BSA was written and implemented, banks were required to take the first big step toward helping law enforcement deal with the problem. In particular, they were required to file Currency Transaction Reports (CTRs) when customers made cash transactions of $10,000 or more and Currency and Monetary Instrument Reports (CMIRs) for transfers of cash or monetary instruments into or out of the United States, again for transactions of $10,000 or more. Bank clients were required to file Foreign Bank Account Reports (FBARs) when they had bank accounts overseas valued at more than $5,000 (later changed to $10,000).

Next the narcotics traffickers and their money laundering accomplices had to find other ways to move the money and convert it into better cleaned forms, thus smurfing of large quantities of money in small portions into many banks became a solution for the criminals. While this was a bit more complicated than simply dragging bags and boxes of cash into banks, it still did not noticeably slow down the launderers. This strategy was attacked with a reduction in the minimum reporting requirement under the BSA to $3,000 instead of $10,000 (later returned to $10,000). Also, structuring transactions to evade the reporting requirements (for example, making 20 deposits of $9,000 in cash instead of one deposit of $180,000 in cash) was made a crime in 1986.

Another way to clean the money was (and is) to physically ship it offshore to a banking haven such as Panama, Nassau, or the Cayman Islands and to deposit it there, where the rules are much less strict. Then the funds can be wire transferred to a U.S. bank and used just as in the previous methods. If the funds are smuggled out of the United States and remain in bank accounts there, pursuit by the U.S. authorities is very difficult. But when the funds are brought back to the United States through some electronic means, the trail is once again possible to attack by U.S. law enforcement. This led in 1996 to greater reporting requirements on banks with respect to wire transfers and other electronic funds transfers under the BSA.

Separate from the BSA, the 1986 Money Laundering Control Act (MLCA) made it a crime to launder money, whether or not BSA reporting rules are violated. This means that, since 1986, money launderers have broadly been forced to find better ways to hide their activities, because even without violating BSA rules, they still can be prosecuted. This step does not directly stop money laundering, since the narcotics traffickers still need to get their money into usable forms such as bank accounts and securities investments. However, it puts pressure on the criminals to find alternative mechanisms for their money laundering activities.

Perhaps the easiest way to look at the kinds of responses banks need to undertake so that they can avoid money laundering activity is to follow the two key legislative initiatives: the BSA and the MLCA.

POLICIES TO COMPLY WITH THE BANK SECRECY ACT

The easiest way to understand a bank's responsibilities under the BSA is to look at the reporting requirements for financial transactions and then to note the handful of key additional concerns. The three main reporting forms are discussed, noting aspects that have led to problems for banks and recommending ways to deal with them; additional concerns are then addressed.

Currency Transaction Report CTR (Form 4789)

Under the current law, the U.S. Treasury requires that every bank must file CTRs for cash transactions that meet the stated criteria. The form is reproduced as Figure 16.1.

Bank executives have been prosecuted for conspiring with customers to structure transactions so that no CTRs are filed (*United States v. Hayes*, 827 F 2d. 469 [9th Circuit, 1987]). Financial institutions themselves may be prosecuted for repeatedly failing to file CTRs, as was the case with the Bank of Boston and several other money center banks, which were fined more than a million dollars each for hundreds or thousands of instances of failure to file CTRs in the early 1980s. If the failure to file is construed as a "pattern of illegal activity," the financial institution can even be prosecuted on criminal grounds (*United States v. St. Michael's Credit Union*, 880 F. 2d 579 [1st Circuit, 1989]).

Currency or Monetary Instrument Report CMIR (Form 4790)

This form is required to be filed by individuals carrying, mailing, or shipping into or out of the United States any monetary instrument valued at $10,000 or more. Monetary instruments include cash, checks, money orders, and other similar cash-like instruments. As institutions, banks are explicitly excluded from this requirement for their normal activities—but bankers, when they travel, are not. Also, banks are only excluded from the requirement for mailing or shipping monetary instruments to customers "with respect to overland shipments of currency or monetary instruments shipped to or received from an established customer maintaining a deposit relationship with the bank, in amounts which the bank may reasonably conclude do not exceed amounts commensurate with the customary conduct of the business, industry, or profession of the customer concerned"[1] (Form 4790 Instructions). In other instances, banks must file the CMIR just as individuals do. Bank shipments of monetary instruments between branches or other affiliates also are exempt from the filing requirement. The CMIR is reproduced as Figure 16.2 here.

Looking at the legal case history, it is clear that prosecutions for failure to file CMIRs are almost exclusively related to individuals, not to financial institutions.

Foreign Bank Account Report FBAR (Form TDF 90-22.1)

For completeness, the final form that was developed to implement the BSA is presented. In fact, the report is required to be filed by individuals (and com-

Figure 16.1
CTR Form 4789

Form **4789**	**Currency Transaction Report**	
(Rev. October 1995) Department of the Treasury Internal Revenue Service	▶ Use this 1995 revision effective October 1, 1995. ▶ For Paperwork Reduction Act Notice, see page 3. ▶ Please type or print. *(Complete all parts that apply—See instructions)*	OMB No. 1545-0183

1 Check all box(es) that apply:

a ☐ Amends prior report   **b** ☐ Multiple persons   **c** ☐ Multiple transactions

Part I Person(s) Involved in Transaction(s)

Section A—Person(s) on Whose Behalf Transaction(s) Is Conducted

2 Individual's last name or Organization's name	**3** First name	**4** M.I.

5 Doing business as (DBA)	**6** SSN or EIN

7 Address (number, street, and apt. or suite no.)	**8** Date of birth M M D D Y Y

9 City	**10** State	**11** ZIP code	**12** Country (if not U.S.)	**13** Occupation, profession, or business

14 If an individual, describe method used to verify identity:

a ☐ Driver's license/State I.D.   **b** ☐ Passport   **c** ☐ Alien registration   **d** ☐ Other ....

e Issued by: **f** Number:

Section B—Individual(s) Conducting Transaction(s) (if other than above).
If Section B is left blank or incomplete, check the box(es) below to indicate the reason(s):

a ☐ Armored Car Service   **b** ☐ Mail Deposit or Shipment   **c** ☐ Night Deposit or Automated Teller Machine (ATM)

d ☐ Multiple Transactions   **e** ☐ Conducted On Own Behalf

15 Individual's last name	**16** First name	**17** M.I.

18 Address (number, street, and apt. or suite no.)	**19** SSN

20 City	**21** State	**22** ZIP code	**23** Country (if not U.S.)	**24** Date of birth M M D D Y Y

25 If an individual, describe method used to verify identity:

a ☐ Driver's license/State I.D.   **b** ☐ Passport   **c** ☐ Alien registration   **d** ☐ Other ....

e Issued by: **f** Number:

Part II Amount and Type of Transaction(s). Check all boxes that apply.

26 Cash In $ _____ .00   **27** Cash Out $ _____ .00   **28** Date of Transaction   M M D D Y Y

29 ☐ Foreign Currency _____ (Country)   **30** ☐ Wire Transfer(s)   **31** ☐ Negotiable Instrument(s) Purchased

32 ☐ Negotiable Instrument(s) Cashed   **33** ☐ Currency Exchange(s)   **34** ☐ Deposit(s)/Withdrawal(s)

35 ☐ Account Number(s) Affected (if any):   **36** ☐ Other (specify)

Part III Financial Institution Where Transaction(s) Takes Place

37 Name of financial institution	Enter Federal Regulator or BSA Examiner code number from the instructions here. ▶ [ ]

38 Address (number, street, and apt. or suite no.)	**39** SSN or EIN

40 City	**41** State	**42** ZIP code	**43** MICR No.

Sign Here ▶	**44** Title of approving official	**45** Signature of approving official	**46** Date of signature M M D D Y Y
	47 Type or print preparer's name	**48** Type or print name of person to contact	**49** Telephone number ( )

Cat. No. 42004W

Form **4789** (Rev. 10-95)

184

Figure 16.1 (continued)

Multiple Persons

(Complete applicable parts below if box 1b on page 1 is checked.)

Part I Person(s) Involved in Transaction(s)

Section A—Person(s) on Whose Behalf Transaction(s) Is Conducted

2 Individual's last name or Organization's name			3 First name		4 M.I.
5 Doing business as (DBA)			6 SSN or EIN		
7 Address (number, street, and apt. or suite no.)			8 Date of birth	M M D D Y Y	
9 City	10 State	11 ZIP code	12 Country (if not U.S.)	13 Occupation, profession, or business	

14 If an individual, describe method used to verify identity:
a ☐ Driver's license/State I.D. b ☐ Passport c ☐ Alien registration d ☐ Other ....
e Issued by: f Number:

Section B—Individual(s) Conducting Transaction(s) (if other than above).

15 Individual's last name			16 First name		17 M.I.
18 Address (number, street, and apt. or suite no.)			19 SSN		
20 City	21 State	22 ZIP code	23 Country (if not U.S.)	24 Date of birth	M M D D Y Y

25 If an individual, describe method used to verify identity:
a ☐ Driver's license/State I.D. b ☐ Passport c ☐ Alien registration d ☐ Other ....
e Issued by: f Number:

Part I Person(s) Involved in Transaction(s)

Section A—Person(s) on Whose Behalf Transaction(s) Is Conducted

2 Individual's last name or Organization's name			3 First name		4 M.I.
5 Doing business as (DBA)			6 SSN or EIN		
7 Address (number, street, and apt. or suite no.)			8 Date of birth	M M D D Y Y	
9 City	10 State	11 ZIP code	12 Country (if not U.S.)	13 Occupation, profession, or business	

14 If an individual, describe method used to verify identity:
a ☐ Driver's license/State I.D. b ☐ Passport c ☐ Alien registration d ☐ Other ....
e Issued by: f Number:

Section B—Individual(s) Conducting Transaction(s) (if other than above).

15 Individual's last name			16 First name		17 M.I.
18 Address (number, street, and apt. or suite no.)			19 SSN		
20 City	21 State	22 ZIP code	23 Country (if not U.S.)	24 Date of birth	M M D D Y Y

25 If an individual, describe method used to verify identity:
a ☐ Driver's license/State I.D. b ☐ Passport c ☐ Alien registration d ☐ Other ....
e Issued by: f Number:

Figure 16.2
Currency and Monetary Instrument Report Form 4790

(U.S. Customs Use Only)		DEPARTMENT OF THE TREASURY UNITED STATES CUSTOMS SERVICE	Form Appro OMB No. 15
Control No.		**REPORT OF INTERNATIONAL TRANSPORTATION OF CURRENCY OR MONETARY INSTRUMENTS**	▶ This form is to be filed United States Customs ▶ For Paperwork Reducti Notice and Privacy Act see back of form.
31 U.S.C. 5316; 31 CFR 103.23 and 103.25 ▶ ease type or print.			

Part I FOR INDIVIDUAL DEPARTING FROM OR ENTERING THE UNITED STATES

1. NAME *(Last or family, first, and middle)*	2. IDENTIFYING NO. *(See instructions)*	3. DATE OF BIRTH *(Mo./Day/Yr.)*
4. PERMANENT ADDRESS IN UNITED STATES OR ABROAD		5. OF WHAT COUNTRY ARE CITIZEN/SUBJECT?
6. ADDRESS WHILE IN THE UNITED STATES		7. PASSPORT NO. & COUNTRY
8. U.S. VISA DATE	9. PLACE UNITED STATES VISA WAS ISSUED	10. IMMIGRATION ALIEN NO. *(If a*

11. CURRENCY OR MONETARY INSTRUMENT WAS: *(Complete 11A or 11B)*

A. EXPORTED		B. IMPORTED	
Departed From: *(City in U.S.)*	Arrived At: *(Foreign City/Country)*	From: *(Foreign City/Country)*	At: *(City in U.S.)*

Part II FOR PERSON SHIPPING, MAILING, OR RECEIVING CURRENCY OR MONETARY INSTRUMENTS

12. NAME *(Last or family, first, and middle)*	13. IDENTIFYING NO. *(See instructions)*	14. DATE OF BIRTH *(Mo./Day/Yr.)*
15. PERMANENT ADDRESS IN UNITED STATES OR ABROAD		16. OF WHAT COUNTRY ARE YOU A CITIZEN/SUBJECT?
17. ADDRESS WHILE IN THE UNITED STATES		18. PASSPORT NO. & COUNTRY
19. U.S. VISA DATE	20. PLACE UNITED STATES VISA WAS ISSUED	21. IMMIGRATION ALIEN NO. *(If a*

22. CURRENCY OR MONETARY INSTRUMENTS	23. CURRENCY OR MONETARY INSTRUMENTS	NAME AND ADDRESS	24. IF THE CURRENCY OR MONETARY INSTRUMEN MAILED, SHIPPED, OR TRANSPORTED COM BLOCKS A AND B.
DATE SHIPPED	☐ Shipped To ▶		A. Method of Shipment *(Auto, U.S. Mail, Public Carrier, etc.)*
DATE RECEIVED	☐ Received From ▶		B. Name of Transporter/Carrier

Part III CURRENCY AND MONETARY INSTRUMENT INFORMATION (SEE INSTRUCTIONS ON REVERSE)(To be completed by everyor

25. TYPE AND AMOUNT OF CURRENCY/MONETARY INSTRUMENTS		Value in U.S. Dollars	26. IF OTHER THAN U.S. CUF IS INVOLVED, PLEASE CON BLOCKS A AND B. *(SEE S INSTRUCTIONS)*
Coins	☐ A. ▶ $		A. Currency Name
Currency	☐ B. ▶		
Other Instruments *(Specify Type)* ↗	☐ C. ▶		B. Country
(Add lines A, B and C)	TOTAL AMOUNT ▶ $		

Part IV GENERAL - TO BE COMPLETED BY ALL TRAVELERS, SHIPPERS, AND RECIPIENTS

27. WERE YOU ACTING AS AN AGENT, ATTORNEY OR IN CAPACITY FOR ANYONE IN THIS CURRENCY OR MONETARY INSTRUMENT ACTIVITY? *(If "Yes" complete A, B and C)*		☐ Yes	☐ No
PERSON IN WHOSE BE-HALF YOU ARE ACTING ▶	A. Name	B. Address	C. Business activity, occupation, or p

Under penalties of perjury, I declare that I have examined this report, and to the best of my knowledge and belief it is true, correct and complete.

28. NAME AND TITLE	29. SIGNATURE	30. DATE

(Replaces IRS Form 4790 which is obsolete.)

Customs Form 4790 (031

panies) concerning their own bank or securities accounts overseas, and banks are exempt from the requirement with respect to their institutional accounts overseas. Figure 16.3 reproduces the FBAR. (Note the statements on the form relating to account holders rather than to financial institutions.)

Additional Concerns of Banks with Respect to the Bank Secrecy Act

Beyond the three basic forms required under the BSA, banks need to file the Suspicious Activity Report (SAR), described below, in appropriate circumstances. This report was not included in the BSA implementation, but in 1996, it was added to the arsenal of tools used to pursue violators of both the BSA and the 1992 Annunzio–Wylie Act.

POLICIES TO COMPLY WITH THE ANNUNZIO–WYLIE ACT

The 1992 Annunzio–Wylie Act contained a large number of additional penalties and other rules to toughen the anti-money laundering stance of the U.S. government. The act called for the forfeiture of a financial institution's license to operate when convicted of money laundering and for greater financial penalties for convicted money launderers. It also called for banks to make a greater effort to help reduce money laundering by requiring them to report "suspicious transactions" that might indicate money laundering and to keep more detailed records of electronic funds transfers (especially wire transfers) so the sender, receiver, and any intermediaries could be better identified and prosecuted if money laundering were to take place. In both of these areas, the act called for this record keeping and reporting but subsequently left it to the U.S. Treasury to determine the specific forms and reporting mechanisms.

Suspicious Activity Report (SAR)

The Annunzio–Wylie Act stated that "The Secretary of the Treasury may require any financial institution, and any director, officer, employee, or agent of any financial institution, to report any suspicious transaction relevant to a possible violation of law or regulation" (138 Congressional Record H 11942, *H12046). This assignment of responsibility did not immediately lead to a new reporting form but rather to an effort by the U.S. Treasury to design a vehicle for making such reports. This effort eventually resulted in the SAR. After three years of requiring banks to use alternative reporting instruments (beginning with the IRS Criminal Referral Form) and receiving recommendations from banks and regulators, the U.S. Treasury implemented the SAR. The form is reproduced here as Figure 16.4.

This form is much more directly related to law enforcement interests than the

Figure 16.3
FBAR Form TDF 90–22.1

Department of the Treasury	REPORT OF FOREIGN BANK AND FINANCIAL ACCOUNTS	FinCEN
TD F 90-22.1 SUPERSEDES ALL PREVIOUS EDITIONS	Do **NOT** file with your Federal Tax Return	1
		OMB No. 1505-0063

1 Filing for Calendar Year Y Y Y Y	2 Type of Filer a ☐ Individual b ☐ Partnership c ☐ Corporation d ☐ Fiduciary	3 Taxpayer Identification Number

Part I   Filer Information

4 Last Name or Organization Name	5 First Name	6 Middle Initial

7 Address (Number, Street, and Apt. or Suite No.)	8 Date of Birth M M D D Y Y Y Y

9 City	10 State	11 Zip/Postal Code	12 Country	13 Title (Not necessary if reporting a personal account)

14 Are these account jointly owned? a ☐ Yes b ☐ No	15 Number of joint owners	16 Taxpayer Identification Number of joint owner (if known)

17 Last Name or Organization Name	18 First Name	19 Middle Initial

Part II   Information on Financial Accounts

20 Number of Foreign Financial Accounts in which a financial interest is held	21 Type of account a ☐ Bank b ☐ Securities c ☐ Other _____

22 Maximum value of account a ☐ Under $10,000 c ☐ $100,000 to $1,000,000 b ☐ $10,000 to $99,999 d ☐ Over $1,000,000	23 Account Number or other designation

24 Name of Financial Institution with which account is held	25 Country in which account is held

26 Does the filer have a financial interest in this account? a ☐ Yes b ☐ No If no, complete boxes 27-35.	27 Last Name or Organization Name of Account Owner

28 First Name	29 Middle Initial	30 Taxpayer Identification Number

31 Address (Number, Street, and Apt. or Suite No.)	32 City

33 State	34 Zip/Postal Code	35 Country	

36 Signature	37 Date M M D D Y Y Y Y

This form should be used to report a financial interest in, signature authority, or other authority over one or more financial accounts in foreign countries, as required by the Department of the Treasury Regulations (31 CFR 103). No report is required if the aggregate value of the accounts did not exceed $10,000. **SEE INSTRUCTIONS FOR DEFINITION.** File this form with:

U.S. Department of the Treasury, P.O. Box 32621, Detroit, MI 48232-0621.

Figure 16.4
Suspicious Activity Report (SAR)

Suspicious Activity Report	FRB: FR 2230 OMB No. 7100-0212 FDIC: 6710/06 OMB No. 3064-0077 OCC: 8010-9,8010-1 OMB No. 1557-0180 OTS: 1601 OMB No. 1550-0003 NCUA: 2362 OMB No. 3133-0094 TREASURY: TD F 90-22.47 OMB No. 1506-0001
ALWAYS COMPLETE ENTIRE REPORT	Expires September 30, 1998

1 Check appropriate box:
a ☐ Initial Report   b ☐ Corrected Report   c ☐ Supplemental Report

Part I   Reporting Financial Institution Information

2 Name of Financial Institution	3 Primary Federal Regulator
	a ☐ Federal Reserve d ☐ OCC
4 Address of Financial Institution	b ☐ FDIC e ☐ OTS
	c ☐ NCUA

5 City	6 State	7 Zip Code	8 EIN or TIN

9 Address of Branch Office(s) where activity occurred	10 Asset size of financial institution $ .00

11 City	12 State	13 Zip Code	14 If institution closed, date closed (MMDDYY) ___/___/___

15 Account number(s) affected, if any
a _____
b _____

16 Have any of the institution's accounts related to this matter been closed?
a ☐ Yes   b ☐ No   If yes, identify _____

Part II   Suspect Information

17 Last Name or Name of Entity	18 First Name	19 Middle Initial

20 Address	21 SSN, EIN or TIN (as applicable)

22 City	23 State	24 Zip Code	25 Country	26 Date of Birth (MMDDYY) ___/___/___

27 Phone Number - Residence (include area code) ( )	28 Phone Number - Work (include area code) ( )

29 Occupation

30 Forms of Identification for Suspect:
a ☐ Driver's License   b ☐ Passport   c ☐ Alien Registration   d ☐ Other _____

e Number _____   f Issuing Authority _____

31 Relationship to Financial Institution:
a ☐ Accountant   d ☐ Attorney   g ☐ Customer   j ☐ Officer
b ☐ Agent   e ☐ Borrower   h ☐ Director   k ☐ Shareholder
c ☐ Appraiser   f ☐ Broker   i ☐ Employee   l ☐ Other

32 Is insider suspect still affiliated with the financial institution? a ☐ Yes If no, specify { c ☐ Suspended e ☐ Resigned b ☐ No { d ☐ Terminated	33 Date of Suspension, Termination, Resigna- tion (MMDDYY) ___/___/___	34 Admission/Confession a ☐ Yes b ☐ No

189

Figure 16.4 (continued)

| Part III | Suspicious Activity Information | 2 |

35 Date of suspicious activity (MMDDYY)

____ / ____ / ____

36 Dollar amount involved in known or suspicious activity

$ _____ .00

37 Summary characterization of suspicious activity:

a ☐ Bank Secrecy Act/Structuring/ Money Laundering
b ☐ Bribery/Gratuity
c ☐ Check Fraud
d ☐ Check Kiting
e ☐ Commercial Loan Fraud
f ☐ Consumer Loan Fraud

g ☐ Counterfeit Check
h ☐ Counterfeit Credit/Debit Card
i ☐ Counterfeit Instrument (other)
j ☐ Credit Card Fraud
k ☐ Debit Card Fraud
l ☐ Defalcation/Embezzlement

m ☐ False Statement
n ☐ Misuse of Position or Self-Dealing
o ☐ Mortgage Loan Fraud
p ☐ Mysterious Disappearance
q ☐ Wire Transfer Fraud

r ☐ Other

38 Amount of loss prior to recovery (if applicable)
$ _____ .00

39 Dollar amount of recovery (if applicable)
$ _____ .00

40 Has the suspicious activity had a material impact on or otherwise affected the financial soundness of the institution?

a ☐ Yes   b ☐ No

41 Has the institution's bonding company been notified?

a ☐ Yes   b ☐ No

42 Has any law enforcement agency already been advised by telephone, written communication, or otherwise? If so, list the agency and local address.

Agency _____

43 Address

44 City

45 State

46 Zip Code

| Part IV | Witness Information |

47 Last Name

48 First Name

49 Middle Initial

50 Address

51 SSN

52 City

53 State

54 Zip Code

55 Date of Birth (MMDDYY)

____ / ____ / ____

56 Title

57 Phone Number (include area code)
(   )

58 Interviewed

a ☐ Yes b ☐ No

| Part V | Preparer Information |

59 Last Name

60 First Name

61 Middle Initial

62 Title

63 Phone Number (include area code)
(   )

64 Date (MMDDYY)

____ / ____ / ____

| Part VI | Contact for Assistance (If different than Preparer Information in Part V) |

65 Last Name

66 First Name

67 Middle Initial

68 Title

69 Phone Number (include area code)
(   )

70 Agency (If applicable)

Figure 16.4 (continued)

| Part VII | Suspicious Activity Information Explanation/Description | 3 |

Explanation/description of known or suspected violation of law or suspicious activity. This section of the report is **critical**. The care with which it is written may make the difference in whether or not the described conduct and its possible criminal nature are clearly understood. Provide below a chronological and **complete** account of the possible violation of law, including what is unusual, irregular or suspicious about the transaction, using the following checklist as you prepare your account. If necessary, continue the narrative on a duplicate of this page.

a **Describe** supporting documentation and retain for 5 years.

b **Explain** who benefited, financially or otherwise, from the transaction, how much, and how.

c **Retain** any confession, admission, or explanation of the transaction provided by the suspect and indicate to whom and when it was given.

d **Retain** any confession, admission, or explanation of the transaction provided by any other person and indicate to whom and when it was given.

e **Retain** any evidence of cover-up or evidence of an attempt to deceive federal or state examiners or others.

f **Indicate** where the possible violation took place (e.g., main office, branch, other).

g **Indicate** whether the possible violation is an isolated incident or relates to other transactions.

h **Indicate** whether there is any related litigation; if so, specify.

i **Recommend** any further investigation that might assist law enforcement authorities.

j **Indicate** whether any information has been excluded from this report; if so, why?

For Bank Secrecy Act/Structuring/Money Laundering reports, include the following additional information:

k **Indicate** whether currency and/or monetary instruments were involved. If so, provide the amount and/or description.

l **Indicate** any account number that may be involved or affected.

Paperwork Reduction Act Notice: The purpose of this form is to provide an effective and consistent means for financial institutions to notify appropriate law enforcement agencies of known or suspected criminal conduct or suspicious activities that take place at or were perpetrated against financial institutions. This report is required by law, pursuant to authority contained in the following statutes. Board of Governors of the Federal Reserve System: 12 U.S.C. 324, 334, 611a, 1844(b) and (c), 3105(c) (2) and 3105(a). Federal Deposit Insurance Corporation: 12 U.S.C. 93a, 1818, 1881-84, 3401-22. Office of the Comptroller of the Currency: 12 U.S.C. 93a, 1818, 1881-84, 3401-22. Office of Thrift Supervision: 12 U.S.C. 1463 and 1464. National Credit Union Administration: 12 U.S.C. 1756(a), 1786(q). Financial Crimes Enforcement Network: 31 U.S.C. 5318(g). Information collected on this report is confidential (5 U.S.C. 552(b)(7) and 552a(k)(2), and 31 U.S.C. 5318(g)). The Federal financial institutions regulatory agencies and the U.S. Departments of Justice and Treasury may use and share the information. Public reporting and recordkeeping burden for this information collection is estimated to average 36 minutes per response, and includes time to gather and maintain data in the required report, review the instructions, and complete the information collection. Send comments regarding this burden estimate, including suggestions for reducing the burden, to the Office of Management and Budget, Paperwork Reduction Project, Washington, DC 20503 and, depending on your primary Federal regulatory agency, to Secretary, Board of Governors of the Federal Reserve System, Washington, DC 20551; or Assistant Executive Secretary, Federal Deposit Insurance Corporation, Washington, DC 20429; or Legislative and Regulatory Analysis Division, Office of the Comptroller of the Currency, Washington, DC 20219; or Office of Thrift Supervision, Enforcement Office, Washington, DC 20552; or National Credit Union Administration, 1775 Duke Street, Alexandria, VA 22314; or Office of the Director, Financial Crimes Enforcement Network, Department of the Treasury, 2070 Chain Bridge Road, Vienna, VA 22182.

previous BSA forms that have been discussed. That is, the SAR requires the filing institution to identify both the people and/or institutions involved in the relevant activity and the reason the activity is suspect. It is filed directly with the Financial Crimes Enforcement Network, which gives a higher priority to processing and evaluating these reports than the CTRs or other BSA reports.

The SARs have brought another wrinkle of complexity to banks' need to help the government in the effort to reduce money laundering. By putting the banks into the position of reporting suspected money laundering activities rather than just record keeping, the government has created a potential liability for the banks with respect to their obligation to protect client information. The principle of bank secrecy is intended to preserve the clients' Fourth Amendment right of privacy; the SAR creates a difficult requirement for banks to help enforcement agencies spot potential money laundering activity and still try to protect their clients' right to privacy.

The implementation of SARs brought with it the explicit protection for banks that provide such information to law enforcement so that they may be exempt from prosecution under the right to privacy rules. This concept, known as a "safe harbor provision," appears as follows in the Act:

Liability for disclosures.—Any financial institution that makes a disclosure of any possible violation of law or regulation or a disclosure pursuant to this subsection or any other authority, and any director, officer, employee, or agent of such institution, shall not be liable to any person under any law or regulation of the United States or any constitution, law, or regulation of any State or political subdivision thereof, for such disclosure or for any failure to notify the person involved in the transaction or any other person of such disclosure. (Section 1517 (3))

This protection does not simply exempt banks from protecting clients' right to privacy when suspicious activity is uncovered, as subsequent court cases have shown. For example, in *Lopez v. First Union National Bank of Florida* (U.S. Court of Appeals, 11th Circuit, 96–4931) and in *Coronado v. BankAtlantic Bancorp* (97-4238), the court held that the two banks may be held liable for disclosing information about their clients' checking accounts to federal authorities. In the Lopez case, the bank may have been liable because it divulged the client account information on only a verbal instruction of federal law enforcement authorities, without a warrant for that information, as required by the Electronic Communications Privacy Act. In the Coronado case, the bank disclosed information about 1,100 accounts when it found suspicious activity in only some unidentified accounts in the group. The court held that the bank may be liable for disclosing the information to federal authorities because "there must be some good faith basis for believing there is a nexus between the suspicion of illegal activity and the account or accounts from which information is disclosed."

The court pointed out that the safe harbor provision for banks under the law (31 U.S. Code Section 5318 (g)(3)) supplies "an affirmative defense to claims against a financial institution for disclosing an individual's financial records or account-related activity. Financial institutions are granted immunity from liability for three different types of disclosure:

1. A disclosure of any possible violation of law or regulation,
2. A disclosure pursuant to paragraph 5318 (g) itself, or
3. A disclosure pursuant to any other authority."

In each of the cases cited above, the bank's situation fell outside of the three areas that are granted immunity from liability.

The American Bankers Association drafted its list of recommended Privacy Principles for banks in 1997. These principles may be used by banks as part of their individual statements of policies to avoid money laundering activity. The eight principles are:

1. *Recognition of a customer's expectation of privacy.* This could be accomplished, for example, by making available privacy guidelines and/or by providing a series of questions and answers about financial privacy to those customers.

2. *Use, collection, and retention of customer information.* Financial institutions should collect, retain, and use information about individual customers only where the institution reasonably believes it would be useful (and allowed by law) to administering that organization's business.

3. *Maintenance of accurate information.* Financial institutions should establish procedures so that a customer's financial information is accurate, current, and complete in accordance with reasonable commercial standards.

4. *Limiting employee access to information.* Financial institutions should limit employee access to personally identifiable information to those with a business reason for knowing such information. Financial institutions should educate their employees so that they will understand the importance of confidentiality and customer privacy.

5. *Protection of information via established security procedures.* Financial institutions should maintain appropriate security standards and procedures regarding unauthorized access to customer information.

6. *Restrictions on the disclosure of account information.* Financial institutions should not reveal specific information about customer accounts or other personally identifiable data to unaffiliated third parties fo their independent use, except for the exchange of information with reputable information reporting agencies to maximize the accuracy and security of such information or in the performance of bona fide corporate due diligence.

7. *Maintaining customer privacy in business relationships with third parties.* If personally identifiable customer information is provided to a third party, the financial institutions should insist that the third party adhere to similar privacy principles that provide for keeping such information confidential.

8. *Disclosure of privacy principles to customers.* Financial institutions should devise methods of providing a customer with an understanding of their privacy policies. . . . Each financial institution should create a method for making available its privacy policies. (*Source*: www.aba.com/About +ABA/ABA_PrivPrinPublic.htm)

Rules on Wire Transfers and Other Electronic Transfers

The Annunzio–Wylie Act also called for banks to produce more detailed records of wire transfers and other electronic funds transfers that could be used in money laundering activities. In Section 1515 Part (a), the act states that,

> Whenever the Secretary [of the U.S. Treasury] and the Board of Governors of the Federal Reserve System determine that the maintenance of records, by insured depository institutions, of payment orders which direct transfers of funds over wholesale funds transfer systems has a high degree of usefulness in criminal, tax, or regulatory investigations or proceedings, the Secretary and the Board shall jointly prescribe regulations to carry out the purposes of this section with respect to the maintenance of such records. (138 Congressional Record H 11942, *H12045)

This wording does not prescribe a specific reporting vehicle, so the U.S. Treasury subsequently had to design one. This process took four years and resulted in the rules on funds transfers and remittal of funds, effective May 28, 1996.

These rules are laid out in 31 CFR Part 103, as promulgated by the Federal Reserve and FinCEN. They basically call for financial institutions (entities subject to the BSA reporting requirements) to record the true name and address of orginators and senders as well as recipients and beneficiaries of electronic funds transmittals.

Training Requirements Imposed by the Annunzio–Wylie Act

Banks are required to train their personnel in the rules on money laundering and to have in place a system to avoid criminal use of the bank for money laundering. The act states that,

> (1) In order to guard against money laundering through financial institutions, the Secretary may require financial institutions to carry out anti-money laundering programs, including at a minimum:
> (a) the development of internal policies, procedures, and controls,
> (b) the designation of a compliance officer,
> (c) an ongoing employee training program, and
> (d) an independent audit function to test programs.
> (2) Regulations.—The Secretary may prescribe minimum standards for programs established under paragraph (1).

As of May 1998, the U.S. Treasury Secretary had not provided minimum standards for policies and training programs in financial institutions. Banks must conclude from the court cases and the pronouncements of U.S. Treasury Department officials that every one of the four items listed above must be covered, but that the detailed method used by a given bank may differ from those used by other banks.

Payable through Accounts

In the early 1990s, U.S. law enforcement agencies found that one financial service offered by U.S. banks for their foreign client banks—the "payable through account"—was being used for money laundering purposes. This discovery led to efforts by the enforcement agencies to better understand the use of such accounts to further money laundering schemes and by lawmakers and rule makers in the United States to define new regulations that would reduce this problem.

The basic idea of the payable through account is that a U.S. bank can offer an account to a foreign bank so the foreign bank's clients in turn may use the U.S. account as their own checking account. The foreign clients can write checks that are payable through the U.S. bank, even though the foreign account holder is not a registered client of the U.S. bank.

The payable through account became popular in the early 1990s as a product that U.S. banks could sell their foreign bank clients to serve their customers' growing interest. Namely, as the economies of many emerging markets were opened to international financial transactions, companies and individuals wanted to have funds in the United States and the ability to make payments in U.S. dollars. Holding a checking account in a U.S. bank would serve this need, but the logistics of setting up such an account were somewhat onerous for many potential clients. By allowing a local bank (say, in Ecuador) to open a U.S. account and then permit its customers to use that account to write their own checks, this logistical problem was solved simply. The non-U.S. bank earns a fee from its clients for providing the service; the U.S. bank earns a fee for offering the payable through account to its non-U.S. client bank; and the foreign customer obtains the access to dollar payments that was the desire that started the whole process.

This arrangement clearly presents the opportunity for abuse if foreign clients are involved in an illegal activity and if they are not known to the U.S. bank. Figure 16.5 shows how a payable through account could be used by a narcotics trafficker without knowledge of the U.S. bank, whose checks are involved.

The narcotics trafficker must become a signatory account holder in the (non-U.S.) bank, under whatever rules hold in that country. Then the non-U.S. bank opens an account at the U.S. bank in its own name, with multiple signatory users of the account. The U.S. bank presumably has adequate knowledge of the non-U.S. bank to offer it the checking account, but the U.S. bank does not necessarily know anything about the signatories.

This practice was first criticized by the FDIC in 1995 (FDIC Financial Institutions Letters, April 7, 1995), when it offered guidelines to U.S. banks on this subject. The guidelines called for U.S. banks to "know the customer" to the extent of requiring foreign banks to identify the ultimate users of the payable through accounts and to verify their credibility, just as with any domestic client permitted to hold an account with the U.S. bank. Specifically, the FDIC said:

Figure 16.5
Using the Payable through Account in Money Laundering

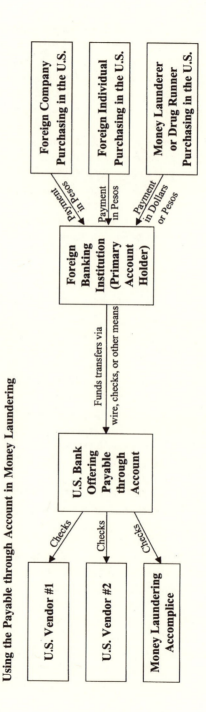

Because of the possibility of illicit activities being conducted through payable through accounts at U.S. banking entities, we believe that it is inconsistent with the principles of safe and sound banking for U.S. banking entities to offer payable through account services without developing and maintaining policies and procedures designed to guard against the possible improper or illegal use of their payable through account facilities by foreign banks and their customers.

These policies and procedures must be fashioned to enable each U.S. banking entity offering payable through account services to foreign banks to identify sufficiently the ultimate users of its foreign bank customers' payable through accounts, including obtaining (or having the ability to obtain) in the United States substantially the same type of information on the ultimate users as the U.S. banking entity obtains for its domestic customers. This may require a review of the foreign bank's own procedures for identifying and monitoring sub-account holders, as well as the relevant statutory and regulatory requirements placed on the foreign bank to identify and monitor the transactions of its own customers by its home country supervisory authorities. In addition, U.S. banking entities should have procedures whereby they monitor account activities conducted in their payable through accounts with foreign banks and report suspicious or unusual activity in accordance with applicable FDIC criminal referral regulations. (www.fdic.gov/news/news/financial/1995/fil9530.html)

The payable through account also became the target of congressional legislation, appearing as part of House Bill 2896 for a "Foreign Money Laundering Deterrence and Anticorruption Act" in 1999. This act requires the kinds of reporting and surveillance that appear in the FDIC guidelines. In addition, the act requires U.S. banking institutions to not open accounts for foreign users unless the foreign entity identifies every account user, or if the foreign entity has shares that are publicly traded. If the foreign institution is in a jurisdiction not recognized by the U.S. authorities as possessing adequate comprehensive supervision, or if the foreign institution is not a licensed banking organization, then a payable through account may not be opened.

As the twenty-first century begins, U.S. legislation and compliance rules continue to attack the activities of money launderers, pushing banks and other financial intermediaries to help in the effort to identify and eliminate the various steps in the laundry process.

NOTES

I thank Michael Crowe, Esq., for his excellent research assistance in preparing this chapter.

1. See, for example, *United States v. Bank of New England*, 821 F. 2d. 844 (1st Circuit 1987), in which it was held that the bank could be prosecuted for failing to aggregate multiple transactions totaling more than $10,000 in one day.

Chapter 17

Conclusions and Government Policy Recommendations

There is no question that "better" government policies and/or increased efforts at enforcement will not end the laundering of drug money in the United States or anywhere else. The lessons that could be drawn from the experiences of the past 30 years under the Bank Secrecy Act (BSA) are that increased policy efforts do lead to reaction by the narcotics money launderers and that such efforts have indeed made it more difficult for them to carry out the laundering. By raising the cost and risk of money laundering, legislative and enforcement efforts have had an impact on the desired direction.

But eliminating drug money laundering implies eliminating drug trafficking—a hopeless task by anyone's estimation. Without passing too far into the realm of psychology or biology, one can see that throughout history, people have always used drugs, from alcohol to narcotics to psychedelics. Assuming that this human preference will continue, then drug consumption will continue as well. And if any drugs are made illegal, then the sellers of these drugs will necessarily keep their business from being recorded and will put it into the underground market. Hence, drug trafficking will continue, and laundering the funds involved will continue, through one avenue or another.

An obvious solution would be to legalize the drugs and to tax their sales, as is done today with alcohol. This alternative often has been proposed with marijuana, which is perceived to be a less harmful, less addictive narcotic than cocaine. Whatever the arguments and emotions involved, the idea of legalizing additional drugs would surely lead to greater consumption, as long as the price declined from its contraband level.[1] If taxes were used to raise prices back to prelegalization levels, then entrepreneurs (drug traffickers) would revert to the underground market to evade taxes, and the problem would remain. With alcohol, after Prohibition ended, estimated consumption grew dramatically.[2] This lesson probably would preclude advocates of legalization from asserting that taxes could limit consumption to near-current levels. The positive side of this solution is that, under this arrangement, at least the law enforcement costs would be eliminated or greatly reduced.[3]

If society takes the stand that it is worth discouraging people from using or overusing or abusing drugs, then some degree of legislative prohibition is called for, and some level of enforcement effort is likewise required. This combination leads to an outcome very similar to where we are today. When shocking examples of drug abuse or criminal activity related to drugs surface in the press, then lawmakers are likely to seek additional rules to cut down on the amount of such activity, and we will see renewed efforts to strengthen the law and its enforcement to reduce drug trafficking and related money laundering.

This may be obvious, but it emphasizes the fact that, unless societal characteristics change dramatically, the drug money laundering problem will not go away. Given the impossibility of law enforcement to completely monitor every person and every activity, then regardless of the strictness of the rules and the severity of enforcement efforts, launderers will take risks and will find ways to escape capture. Drug trafficking and money laundering *will* continue.

It is estimated that law enforcement in the United States currently captures about 35 percent of the cocaine trafficking activity[4] and at best about 10 percent of the related money laundering. If law enforcement efforts were doubled, conservative estimates say that the amount of the total activity that would be caught is around an additional half of the current percentage, say a total of 50 percent of drug trafficking and maybe one-sixth of the money laundering. This process could go on increasingly, up until the point where the entire national government budget would be spent on anti-drug and anti-money laundering enforcement, with the likely result that another percentage would be caught—but probably leaving well more than half of the total money laundering still in operation. As long as the demand for the drugs remains, and the drugs remain illegal, the problem will remain.

PAYING FOR THE LAW ENFORCEMENT COSTS

An interesting feature of the law enforcement effort is that it has become partly self-sustaining. In 1986, Congress gave U.S. government enforcement agencies a powerful tool in the Asset Forfeiture Fund, which was established in the U.S. Justice Department. The basic concept was to return to the enforcement agency the proceeds of successful asset forfeiture prosecutions to help with additional work in that area. At that time, U.S. Justice Department agencies such as the DEA and the U.S. Customs Office were included, since the IRS and other U.S. Treasury agencies did not have asset forfeiture responsibilities. Subsequently, such authority was granted to the additional U.S. Treasury agencies, and they were placed under the U.S. Justice Department forfeiture fund.

In 1992, the U.S. Treasury agencies were assigned a separate asset forfeiture fund. Thus, the DEA and FBI, agencies under the U.S. Justice Department, share in asset forfeitures from one fund, and U.S. Customs and the IRS, both under the U.S. Treasury Department, share from another. In either case, the agencies can pursue legal cases against money launderers, and in the event of successful prosecutions, they are allowed to retain a percentage of forfeited assets for financing additional anti-money laundering efforts.

To a certain extent, the asset forfeiture funds encourage cooperation between the enforcement agencies, since successful prosecutions make more money available for them. This is especially true since local law enforcement agencies that become involved in asset forfeitures are eligible for sharing the forfeited assets along with the federal agencies. Perhaps the only downside is the operation of two separate funds, which is mostly an overlap of record keeping and administration. It would be more sensible and more efficient to have a single fund and to use the assets that are forfeited more for law enforcement and less for administration.

The numbers involved in these Asset Forfeiture Funds are not trivial. In 1997, there was approximately $750 million forfeited in asset prosecutions, related to money laundering, health care fraud, food stamp fraud, smuggling, and other crimes. These funds were then used to support law enforcement at the federal and local levels, significantly though not exclusively related to the problem of money laundering. This support goes a long way toward funding the government's anti-money laundering efforts and, importantly, relieves the burden on taxpayers.

CONFLICTING POLICY GOALS

Government policy is also aimed at achieving a wide range of goals—economic, social, political, cultural, and otherwise. These multiple targets often cause conflict in policy making, as is certainly evidenced in the money laundering arena.

For one thing, anti-money laundering efforts have caused a strong backlash by financial institutions that have essentially been roped into service as assistants to law enforcement agencies in identifying and reporting money laundering activity. This makes banking business more costly and more complicated, as banks seek to comply with these rules. Each time new money laundering legislation is passed, it creates grounds for possible conflict between the U.S. Justice Department, trying to enforce that law, and the Federal Reserve (and possibly the U.S. Treasury), trying to ensure that banks operate efficiently and protect customers' interests.

In one context, a territorial dispute between the U.S. Justice Department and the U.S. Treasury Department disallowed a potentially major anti-money laundering weapon from being used in the early 1990s. The U.S. Justice Department proposed to use the argument that money launderers' purchase of dollars in Latin American foreign exchange black markets should be cause for forfeiting the funds, since purchasing the dollars in this way was illegal according to the Latin American country's laws. If the dollars were purchased illegally, they should be subject to forfeiture, according to this reasoning. Or, in slightly more legalistic jargon, the U.S. government should not enforce (black market) exchange contracts that were carried out in violation of the Latin American country's laws.

The initial weakness of the argument, as asserted by the U.S. Treasury Department, was that the United States could not reasonably be expected to recognize the exchange controls or capital controls of other countries, given the many situations in which the United States did not agree with such controls. Under this logic, the funds obtained from black market transactions that entered the U.S. market would have to be treated as any other funds entering the country. That is, if it could be proven that they were proceeds from narcotics trafficking (or some other specified, unlawful in the U.S. activity), then they could be forfeited, but not otherwise.

The U.S. Justice Department's argument was bolstered by resorting to an international treaty as well. The United States belongs to the International Monetary Fund (IMF), as do the relevant Latin American countries (e.g., Colombia, Mexico, Peru, Bolivia, Venezuela, Brazil). According to Article VIII, Section 2(b), of the Articles of Agreement of the IMF, if one member country upholds the freedom of capital market transactions, then that country is obligated to support the freedom of capital market transactions involving other countries that likewise are IMF members and which subscribe to Article VIII, Section 2(b).[5] Since the United States and Colombia are both IMF members, and since both subscribe to Article VIII, Section 2(b), the United States should therefore enforce the Colombian laws on foreign exchange transactions in support of the IMF treaty.

Although the logic may appear a bit arcane, the net result is that the United States should support Colombia's effort to operate a regulated foreign exchange market as long as Colombia subscribes to Article VIII, Section 2(b). If transactions take place in violation of Colombia's foreign exchange rules, then the United States would be obligated to find such transactions illegal, and then to deny ownership by claimants of funds resulting from such transactions. If the funds were proceeds from narcotics transactions, then the United States would have the right to confiscate and forfeit assets produced from these transactions.

The U.S. Treasury Department was consulted on this issue before the U.S. Justice Department took an official position, and it was vehemently opposed to the position. The U.S. Treasury recognized the importance of U.S. support for the IMF and for countries that follow exchange regimes that permit open capital flows. However, the U.S. Treasury Department argued that Colombia's foreign exchange rules at that time (1990) did not permit open access to foreign exchange, and that an attempt to support the restrictive Colombian laws would only hinder the free flow of capital (to the United States), which the U.S. Treasury did not want to restrict. The goal of opening up current account transactions

(e.g., money flows and payments for exports and imports) was more important
as a policy goal to the U.S. Treasury than was the support of Colombian (or
Peruvian, or Argentine, etc.) law.

The U.S. Treasury viewpoint won the day, and so the U.S. Justice Department
was deprived of a potentially powerful tool for enforcement of anti-money laundering law.

Interestingly, almost all of the Latin American countries opened up their foreign exchange markets during the early 1990s. Argentina, Bolivia, Brazil, Colombia, and Peru all passed laws and policies that today allow domestic residents
to invest overseas and to buy and sell dollars freely. By 1999, the U.S. government seemed to be changing its position on the foreign exchange black market
issue and at that point was debating once again whether to declare black market
funds forfeitable due to their being in violation of foreign country laws.

THE BROAD CONTEXT

It is practically impossible to make policy recommendations without drawing
up first a huge number of assumptions about additional policy constraints, pri-
orities among government goals, and even people's willingness to support one
or another policy regime.

For example, to me, the most obvious steps to take in the immediate term
would speak to the most costly aspect of the problem. If we include the narcotics
traffic within our scope, then measures of the costs and benefits of this activity
can be seen under four headings:

1. *Health costs*, due primarily to the rehabilitation costs of drug addicts. These costs
   include federal and local government programs of rehabilitating drug abusers.

2. *Lost work*, or lost productivity, due to drug addiction and even death from drug abuse.
   This also is due to the illegal drug trafficking in which people are harmed and killed
   (and property is damaged) by Mafia-type activity.

3. *Law enforcement costs*, in which the efforts of the various enforcement agencies are
   counted (including their efforts to deal with money laundering), as are the costs of
   maintaining prisons for offenders and the operation of the court system.

4. *Increased income* from the activities of the drug traffickers, who generate new income
   that would not have existed otherwise (including that from money laundering).

It turns out that the largest economic impact by far is the cost of lost work,
estimated nationally at about $U.S. 70 billion in 1992. Law enforcement costs,
though certainly not negligible, were estimated at about $U.S. 29 billion. Health
care costs likewise were quite significant, but much smaller than the estimates
of lost income/production due to lost work. Health care expenditures from drug
abuse were estimated at about $U.S. 10 billion in 1992.[6] The increased income
generated from drug trafficking is difficult to define, because it is difficult to
judge how much the earnings of the traffickers and launderers would have been

in the absence of this activity. Certainly one could argue that there is some value added from the activity, otherwise the people would have chosen alternative, more profitable activities. However, the net economic impact is far less than their trafficking or laundering earnings, due to the lost opportunity to earn income in other (legal) activities. In any event, total illegal drug spending in the United States was estimated at $U.S. 57 billion in 1997; assuming that this business is 100 percent more profitable than alternatives for the participants leads to an estimate of about $U.S. 28 billion of incremental income generated in 1997.[7]

Notice that this discussion has moved away from money laundering to considering the underlying activity that generated the money. This really is necessary, since a policy to deal with the one activity has to take into account the other. Anti-money laundering enforcement costs are a small part of this picture, but the whole picture is needed to see how such costs fit in.

If the most significant part of the whole picture is the cost of lost work, then this should be attacked most directly and forcefully. These costs can be reduced by convincing more people not to abuse drugs—so an increased educational effort is fundamental. Also, any additional effort to reduce consumption, such as by making it more costly, would help. This could include increasing the penalties for getting caught.

Interestingly, the enforcement costs could be reduced dramatically by going in the opposite direction. That is, if drug consumption and selling were legalized, this would bring most of the activity into the above-ground market, would increase government tax revenue, and would eliminate the criminalization of an industry that will exist in any event. Law enforcement costs could be dropped close to zero. This happy outcome, however, ignores the much greater cost of increased consumption causing greater health problems and more lost work. Or, if taxes were set so high as to keep the price of cocaine, marijuana, and heroin about the same, then black markets for these drugs would spring up by those seeking to evade the taxes, and the law enforcement costs would remain. In fact, the increased consumption also could add to enforcement costs by producing greater crime by addicts seeking to pay for their consumption. In all, it is not clear that legalization would dramatically decrease the law enforcement costs associated with narcotics trafficking.

Thus, on the enforcement cost side, it is reasonably clear that the legalization of some or all narcotic drugs would produce some welcome reduction. Unfortunately, on the health care side, the cost of additional lost work and lost lives due to addiction and drug abuse would, under most scenarios, far outweigh these savings.

The net result, from an economic point of view, is to justify the effort to fight drug money laundering as part of the effort to reduce consumption and the associated health costs. Overall, the effort to fight the traffickers and launderers needs to be matched with efforts to inform people about the costs of drug abuse, which also could reduce consumption. In the final analysis, there is no doubt that people will continue to seek out drugs as they have throughout history, thus no effort to stop consumption can be completely successful.

The idea of legalizing, say, marijuana, could potentially work if taxes on the sale of marijuana were raised high enough to keep the price similar to its existing level, and if some of the tax revenue went into an educational campaign to convince people not to consume it (and if raising the tax on marijuana did not push suppliers back into the black market to evade taxes). Judging from the results of repealing Prohibition on alcohol consumption, which increased very significantly, this does not appear to be a likely scenario.

The repeal of Prohibition, which lasted from 1922 until 1931 in the United States, did not produce clear-cut results. That is, consumption of alcoholic beverages most likely increased quite significantly upon repeal of the eighteenth Amendment to the U.S. Constitution, but this point has been hotly debated. The debate arises because enforcement of the Prohibition laws became so lax by the end of the 1920s that it was not really effective in reducing alcohol consumption. While most analyses show some degree of reduced consumption, some authors assert that consumption even reached the pre-Prohibition level by 1930. Warburton[8] estimated that consumption dropped initially to 40 percent of the pre-war level, but then grew to two-thirds of that level by 1930. Jellinek[9] estimated that alcohol consumption dropped to less than one-fourth of the pre-war level and never grew dramatically up until 1927. Gerstein[10] used various sources to show that alcohol consumption probably did not return to its pre-war level until the 1940s. Figure 17.1 shows Gerstein's broad conclusion. The net result is that many factors intervened, not the least of which was the Great Depression, to negate efforts to precisely fix the upsurge in alcohol consumption after Prohibition was repealed. It does appear that consumption decreased during Prohibition, especially during the early years, and that it increased after repeal, though only gradually due to initial supply limits and to the depression.

This entire discussion is not altogether dissimilar from the debate on tobacco consumption. With the government seeking to force tobacco companies to pay for the health costs of smokers, the parallel to having narcotics "drug companies" pay for similar costs of their consumers is clear. What is not clear is the comparison of the net cost of legalizing drugs and trying to operate a regulatory system that does not cause higher overall costs, contrasted to the net cost of criminalizing tobacco sales and consumption and trying to enforce that ban. In both instances, the key issue is the health and lost work costs. Judging at least from the repeal of Prohibition, the increase in alcohol consumption was significant and quite costly in lost work, rehabilitation, and deaths.

FOREIGN POLICY

Another facet of the narcotics money laundering issue that presents a major government policy challenge is the international extension of such policies. That is, when the United States pursues money launderers (and drug traffickers),

Figure 17.1
Time Trend of U.S. Consumption of Absolute Alcohol, Per Capita Drinking Age Population, 1830–1977

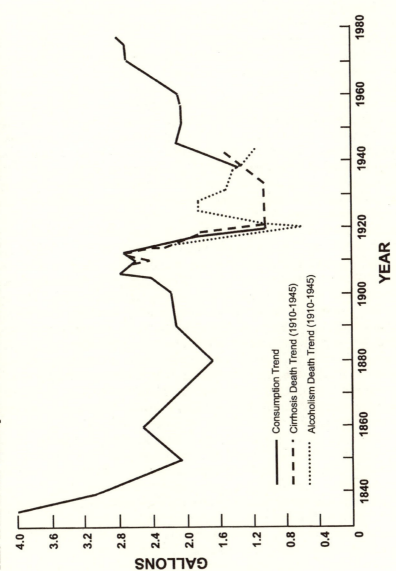

Note: Data points are less dense and less reliable prior to 1900. All estimates adjusted to reflect population 15 years and older.
Source: Reprinted with permission from Dean Gerstein, "Alcohol Use and Consequences," in Mark Moore and Dean Gerstein (eds.), *Alcohol and Public Policy: Beyond the Shadow of Prohibition* (Washington, D.C.: National Academy Press, 1981), p. 105. Copyright 1981 by the National Academy of Sciences. Courtesy of the National Academy Press, Washington, D.C.

frequently that pursuit leads to foreign jurisdictions, such as the Andean countries. The U.S. government typically seeks to pursue the criminals (under U.S. law) wherever they go, and this means into other countries. In some cases, this presents a problem in that the legal offense in the United States is not classified as an offense in the other country. In other cases, the person or funds are identified, and the other country agrees that an offense exists, but there is no mechanism that requires the other country to deliver the person (i.e., to extradite him or her) or the funds to the U.S. government. These problems at least are now dealt with on a systematic basis under the United Nations forum on drug abuse, and within the various fora that have been created in the Americas—but of course the degree of cooperation is imperfect.

Another direction in which U.S. foreign policy has moved to deal with the drug problem has been to try to cut off the supply of narcotics by attacking coca production in Bolivia, Peru, and Colombia. This effort has led to initiatives such as financial support for host country crop eradication programs and military buildup to fight narcotics traffickers. This policy has met with varying degrees of success, though nothing substantial. That is, the amount of coca production has not declined (according to U.S. government estimates) over the past decade, and the number of narcotics traffickers extradited can be counted on one hand.

The anti-supply policy also has led to programs for crop replacement—trying to replace coca with alternative crops. This policy has likewise produced limited results, mainly because no alternative crop has been found that could produce even one-tenth of the profitability of coca, and because the farmers are so isolated and independent that they are quite difficult to work with in the first place. As the Andean countries found more of a domestic drug consumption problem in the 1990s, their governments pushed for alternative crop production, so perhaps this line of attack will be more successful in the years ahead.

One clearly counterproductive policy has been the U.S. initiative to "decertify" countries that do not demonstrate adequate efforts to fight drug trafficking. Once decertified, a country is subject to sanctions such as a reduction in U.S. foreign aid and possible tariff penalties or other import restrictions. This policy has been a tremendous failure in Latin America, where South American countries see the hypocrisy of U.S. decertification of Colombia—which spent possibly 10 times as much per capita in fighting the drug traffickers and lost thousands of lives to armed conflict with them during the past decade—while the United States continues to be the premier consumer of the drugs, with relatively little effort spent in fighting consumption.

The policy is viewed as even more misguided when comparing Mexico to Colombia. Mexico has never been decertified, probably because of its much greater economic and strategic links to the United States, but clearly Mexico's governmental efforts to deal with narcotics trafficking and money laundering are far inferior to Colombia's. Repeatedly throughout the mid- and late 1990s, top Mexican government officials were found guilty of participating in narcotics trafficking, of laundering drug money, and of taking bribes from drug traffickers. From the head of anti-drug enforcement to the head of the national police force to possibly even the brother of the president, Mexican leaders were involved in the problem rather than the solution. To hold up Mexico as a positive example of the war on drugs and to criticize Colombia in the same context is nonsense.

The logical answer to this problem is to drop the explicit policy of certification. It serves no real purpose except to polarize opinion, mostly against the United States. U.S. economic policies can be used to reward or penalize countries that pursue policies consistent with U.S. interests without the additional lightning rod of certification policy. Certification of foreign governments' efforts to deal with the drug problem can be done internally within the U.S. government and used in subsequent economic policy decisions without publicizing the results and creating a divisive atmosphere.

POLICY DIRECTION

While none of the policy prescriptions discussed earlier shows any possibility of solving the overall problem, several positive steps can be taken with respect to drugs and money laundering.

Drugs

First, the effort to educate people to the real costs of drug use and abuse must be increased. Since the health costs (and lost work) are the greatest ones involved in the drug trafficking and related money laundering, they should be attacked initially. This effort can be pursued at the national level through the "Drug Czar's" office and locally through many initiatives as more people see the full picture. Success at reducing consumption through this means will have the most significant impact on the problem.

Second, the efforts to encourage other countries to support U.S. efforts to reduce drug trafficking and related money laundering can be continued with the carrot-and-stick policies that already exist (especially foreign aid policy). This effort can be enhanced by pursuing much of the effort through multilateral fora such as the United Nations.

Money Laundering

Narrowing the focus to merely the funds and not the drugs, money laundering policy can be improved by developing additional tools to attack the money as well as the launderers. Even recognizing that once new policies are developed to cope with known laundering techniques additional techniques will have to be developed, it is still worth establishing those policies.

The basic tools of record keeping and proactively moving to identify suspicious kinds of financial activities are the logical and appropriate ones to develop further. With the level of computerization of the United States today, it is not an impossible task to define additional kinds of (electronic) documentation that can be used in transactions and then later used to track down money laundering activity.

Since the banking system is used for most of the volume of money laundering today, additional reporting requirements to pursue suspicious activities of clients are certainly called for. This does not mean a wholesale witch-hunt for all financial information imaginable, but rather a careful effort by enforcement agencies to identify the kinds of documentation that would really enable them to capture laundered funds, and then to implement rules that produce the documentation.

One tool that undoubtedly would simplify the pursuit of laundered money is the principle that funds moved through illegal foreign exchange markets should be subject to forfeiture because they constitute proceeds of illegal transactions. At present, the rules call for forfeiture of such funds only as they can be traced to narcotics trafficking (or another specified unlawful activity). By widening the net and not requiring the drug link, prosecutions would be simpler and more easily substantiated. This also would alert users of foreign exchange black markets that the risk of using such illegal means to obtain or sell foreign exchange is much higher.

This policy has its drawbacks as well. By making funds moved through a foreign exchange black market subject to forfeiture in the United States, such a policy would open the way to possible overextension of law enforcement to pursue any users of these markets. While one may applaud the effort, it could produce a backlash against the United States in the many countries around the world where underground economies flourish, and where foreign exchange black markets are illegal but widely tolerated. Most government policy makers would probably approve of using this forfeiture policy to pursue narcotics traffickers, while many probably would not want to see the heavy-handed pursuit of all users of black markets. Even today, the black markets often are used as an "overflow" mechanism when economic crises call for foreign exchange restrictions and some otherwise legitimate businesses are attracted into using these markets to obtain dollars at any cost.

Money laundering is a fascinating subject. In the broad scope of activities covered in this book, only the tip of the iceberg has been seen. Drug money laundering is certainly important, but we have just begun to understand some of the ways in which the funds are laundered, even as new methods are constantly being invented. And other sources of "specified unlawful activity," such as illegal gambling, prostitution, bribery, and the whole area of unreported financial transactions that feeds into money laundering, remain to be discussed— elsewhere.

NOTES

1. Logically, consumption would increase even at the same price of the drugs, since legalizing consumption would attract more consumers who previously abstained because it was a criminal activity.

2. Actually, studies on alcohol consumption after Prohibition show somewhat varied results, depending on differing assumptions of consumption during Prohibition. On the one hand, a number of studies have found that the (illegal and unreported) consumption of alcoholic beverages increased significantly after the first three years of Prohibition, to the point where consumption may have approached pre-Prohibition levels. On the other hand, some studies have found that the consumption of alcohol dropped dramatically under Prohibition and only increased to about two-thirds of its pre-Prohibition level by 1931. See Clark Warburton, *The Economic Results of Prohibition* (New York: Columbia University Press, 1932).

3. Even this assertion requires some major assumptions. With greater consumption of legalized narcotics, greater addiction could lead to higher levels of robberies and other crimes by addicts seeking to pay for their consumption.

4. U.S. Department of State, *International Narcotics Control Strategy Report, 1997* (Washington, D.C.: U.S. GPO, March 1998).

5. The section reads, "Exchange contracts which involve the currency of any member and which are contrary to the exchange control regulations of that member maintained or imposed consistently with this Agreement shall be unenforceable in the territories of any member." International Monetary Fund, *Articles of Agreement* (Washington, D.C., July 22, 1944). Amended on April 1, 1978. Article VIII, Section 2(b).

6. National Institute on Drug Abuse, National Institutes of Health, "Economic Costs of Drug Abuse in the United States, 1992" (Washington, D.C.), http://www.nida.nih.gov/EconomicCosts/Table1_1.html.

7. A 1994 statement by federal anti-drug officials revealed that $U.S. 29 billion had been earned by narcotics traffickers in the previous year. See David A. Andelman, "Trouble by the Ton," *San Diego Union-Tribune*, September 25, 1994, p. G4.

8. Warburton, *The Economic Results of Prohibition*.

9. E.M. Jellinek, "Recent Trends in Alcoholism and Alcohol Consumption," *Quarterly Journal of Studies on Alcohol* 8 (1947–48), pp. 1–42.

10. Dean Gerstein, "Alcohol Use and Consequences," in Mark Moore and Dean Gerstein (eds.), *Alcohol and Public Policy: Beyond the Shadow of Prohibition* (Washington, D.C.: National Academy Press, 1981).

Appendix

The Forty Recommendations of The Financial Action Task Force on Money Laundering

INTRODUCTION

1. The Financial Action Task Force on Money Laundering (FATF) is an inter-governmental body whose purpose is the development and promotion of policies to combat money laundering—the processing of criminal proceeds in order to disguise their illegal origin. These policies aim to prevent such proceeds from being utilised in future criminal activities and from affecting legitimate economic activities.

2. The FATF currently consists of 26 countries.[1] and two international organisations.[2] Its membership includes the major financial centre countries of Europe, North America and Asia. It is a multi-disciplinary body—as is essential in dealing with money laundering—bringing together the policy-making power of legal, financial and law enforcement experts.

3. This need to cover all relevant aspects of the fight against money laundering is reflected in the scope of the forty FATF Recommendations—the measures which the Task Force have agreed to implement and which all countries are encouraged to adopt. The Recommendations were originally drawn up in 1990. In 1996 the forty Recommendations were revised to take into account the experience gained over the last six years and to reflect the changes which have occurred in the money laundering problem.[3]

---

[1] Reference in this document to "countries" should be taken to apply equally to "territories" or "jurisdictions." The twenty-six FATF *member countries* and governments are: Australia, Austria, Belgium, Canada, Denmark, Finland, France, Germany, Greece, Hong Kong, Iceland, Ireland, Italy, Japan, Luxembourg, the Kingdom of the Netherlands, New Zealand, Norway, Portugal, Singapore, Spain, Sweden, Switzerland, Turkey, United Kingdom, and the United States.

[2] The two international organisations are: the European Commission and the Gulf Cooperation Council.

[3] During the period 1990 to 1995, the FATF also elaborated various *Interpretative Notes* which are designed to clarify the application of specific Recommendations. Some of these Interpretative Notes have been updated in the Stocktaking Review to reflect changes in the Recommendations.

4. These forty Recommendations set out the basic framework for anti-money laundering efforts and they are designed to be of universal application. They cover the criminal justice system and law enforcement; the financial system and its regulation, and international co-operation.

5. It was recognised from the outset of the FATF that countries have diverse legal and financial systems and so all cannot take identical measures. The Recommendations are therefore the principles for action in this field, for countries to implement according to their particular circumstances and constitutional frameworks allowing countries a measure of flexibility rather than prescribing every detail. The measures are not particularly complex or difficult, provided there is the political will to act. Nor do they compromise the freedom to engage in legitimate transactions or threaten economic development.

6. FATF countries are clearly committed to accept the discipline of being subjected to multilateral surveillance and peer review. All member countries have their implementation of the forty Recommendations monitored through a two-pronged approach: an annual self-assessment exercise and the more detailed mutual evaluation process under which each member country is subject to an on-site examination. In addition, the FATF carries out cross-country reviews of measures taken to implement particular Recommendations.

7. These measures are essential for the creation of an effective anti-money laundering framework.

A. GENERAL FRAMEWORK OF THE RECOMMENDATIONS

1. Each country should take immediate steps to ratify and to implement fully, the 1988 United Nations Convention against Illicit Traffic in Narcotic Drugs and Psychotropic Substances (the Vienna Convention).

2. Financial institution secrecy laws should be conceived so as not to inhibit implementation of these recommendations.

3. An effective money laundering enforcement program should include increased multilateral co-operation and mutual legal assistance in money laundering investigations and prosecutions and extradition in money laundering cases, where possible.

B. ROLE OF NATIONAL LEGAL SYSTEMS IN COMBATING MONEY LAUNDERING

Scope of the Criminal Offence of Money Laundering

4. Each country should take such measures as may be necessary, including legislative ones, to enable it to criminalise money laundering as set forth in the Vienna Convention. Each country should extend the offence of drug money laundering to one based on serious offences. Each country would determine which serious crimes would be designated as money laundering predicate offences.

5. As provided in the Vienna Convention, the offence of money laundering should apply at least to knowing money laundering activity, including the concept that knowledge may be inferred from objective factual circumstances.

6. Where possible, corporations themselves—not only their employees—should be subject to criminal liability.

Provisional Measures and Confiscation

7. Countries should adopt measures similar to those set forth in the Vienna Convention, as may be necessary, including legislative ones, to enable their competent authorities to confiscate property laundered, proceeds from, instrumentalities used in or intended for use in the commission of any money laundering offence, or property of corresponding value, without prejudicing the rights of bona fide third parties.

Such measures should include the authority to: (1) identify, trace and evaluate property which is subject to confiscation; (2) carry out provisional measures, such as freezing and seizing, to prevent any dealing, transfer or disposal of such property; and (3) take any appropriate investigative measures.

In addition to confiscation and criminal sanctions, countries also should consider monetary and civil penalties, and/or proceedings including civil proceedings, to void contracts entered into by parties, where parties knew or should have known that as a result of the contract, the State would be prejudiced in its ability to recover financial claims, e.g., through confiscation or collection of fines and penalties.

C. ROLE OF THE FINANCIAL SYSTEM IN COMBATING MONEY LAUNDERING

8. Recommendations 10 to 29 should apply not only to banks, but also to non-bank financial institutions. Even for those non-bank financial institutions which are not subject to a formal prudential supervisory regime in all countries, for example bureaux de change, governments should ensure that these institutions are subject to the same anti-money laundering laws or regulations as all other financial institutions and that these laws or regulations are implemented effectively.

9. The appropriate national authorities should consider applying Recommendations 10 to 21 and 23 to the conduct of financial activities as a commercial undertaking by businesses or professions which are not financial institutions, where such conduct is allowed or not prohibited. Financial activities include, but are not limited to, those listed in the attached annex. It is left to each country to decide whether special situations should be defined where the application of anti-money laundering measures is not necessary, for example, when a financial activity is carried out on an occasional or limited basis.

Customer Identification and Record-Keeping Rules

10. Financial institutions should not keep anonymous accounts or accounts in obviously fictitious names: they should be required (by law, by regulations, by agreements between supervisory authorities and financial institutions or by self-regulatory agreements among financial institutions) to identify, on the basis of an official or other reliable identifying document, and record the identity of their clients, either occasional or usual, when establishing business relations or conducting transactions (in particular opening of accounts or passbooks, entering into fiduciary transactions, renting of safe deposit boxes, performing large cash transactions).

In order to fulfill identification requirements concerning legal entities, financial institutions should, when necessary, take measures:

(i) to verify the legal existence and structure of the customer by obtaining either from a public register or from the customer or both, proof of incorporation, including information concerning the customer's name, legal form, address, directors and provisions regulating the power to bind the entity.

(ii) to verify that any person purporting to act on behalf of the customer is so authorised and identify that person.

11. Financial institutions should take reasonable measures to obtain information about the true identity of the persons on whose behalf an account is opened or a transaction conducted if there are any doubts as to whether these clients or customers are acting on their own behalf, for example, in the case of domiciliary companies (i.e. institutions, corporations, foundations, trusts, etc., that do not conduct any commercial or manufacturing business or any other form of commercial operation in the country where their registered office is located).

12. Financial institutions should maintain, for at least five years, all necessary records on transactions, both domestic or international, to enable them to comply swiftly with information requests from the competent authorities. Such records must be sufficient to permit reconstruction of individual transactions (including the amounts and types of currency involved if any) so as to provide, if necessary, evidence for prosecution of criminal behaviour.

Financial institutions should keep records on customer identification (e.g. copies or records of official identification documents like passports, identity cards, driving licenses or similar documents), account files and business correspondence for at least five years after the account is closed.

These documents should be available to domestic competent authorities in the context of relevant criminal prosecutions and investigations.

13. Countries should pay special attention to money laundering threats inherent in new or developing technologies that might favour anonymity, and take measures, if needed, to prevent their use in money laundering schemes.

Increased Diligence of Financial Institutions

14. Financial institutions should pay special attention to all complex, unusual large transactions, and all unusual patterns of transactions, which have no apparent economic or visible lawful purpose. The background and purpose of such transactions should, as far as possible, be examined, the findings established in writing, and be available to help supervisors, auditors and law enforcement agencies.

15. If financial institutions suspect that funds stem from a criminal activity, they should be required to report promptly their suspicions to the competent authorities.

16. Financial institutions, their directors, officers and employees should be protected by legal provisions from criminal or civil liability for breach of any restriction on disclosure of information imposed by contract or by any legislative, regulatory or administrative provision, if they report their suspicions in good faith to the competent authorities, even if they did not know precisely what the underlying criminal activity was, and regardless of whether illegal activity actually occurred.

17. Financial institutions, their directors, officers and employees, should not, or, where appropriate, should not be allowed to, warn their customers when information relating to them is being reported to the competent authorities.

18. Financial institutions reporting their suspicions should comply with instructions from the competent authorities.

19. Financial institutions should develop programs against money laundering. These programs should include, as a minimum:

1. the development of internal policies, procedures and controls, including the designation of compliance officers at management level, and adequate screening procedures to ensure high standards when hiring employees;
2. an ongoing employee training programme;
3. an audit function to test the system.

Measures to Cope with the Problem of Countries with No or Insufficient Anti-Money Laundering Measures

20. Financial institutions should ensure that the principles mentioned above are also applied to branches and majority owned subsidiaries located abroad, especially in countries which do not or insufficiently apply these Recommendations, to the extent that local applicable laws and regulations permit. When local applicable laws and regulations prohibit this implementation, competent authorities in the country of the mother institution should be informed by the financial institutions that they cannot apply these Recommendations.

21. Financial institutions should give special attention to business relations and transactions with persons, including companies and financial institutions, from countries which do not or insufficiently apply these Recommendations. Whenever these transactions have no apparent economic or visible lawful purpose, their background and purpose should, as far as possible, be examined, the findings established in writing, and be available to help supervisors, auditors and law enforcement agencies.

Other Measures to Avoid Money Laundering

22. Countries should consider implementing feasible measures to detect or monitor the physical cross-border transportation of cash and bearer negotiable instruments, subject to strict safeguards to ensure proper use of information and without impeding in any way the freedom of capital movements.

23. Countries should consider the feasibility and utility of a system where banks and other financial institutions and intermediaries would report all domestic and international currency transactions above a fixed amount, to a national central agency with a computerised data base, available to competent authorities for use in money laundering cases, subject to strict safeguards to ensure proper use of the information.

24. Countries should further encourage in general the development of modern and secure techniques of money management, including increased use of checks, payment cards, direct deposit of salary checks, and book entry recording of securities, as a means to encourage the replacement of cash transfers.

25. Countries should take notice of the potential for abuse of shell corporations by money launderers and should consider whether additional measures are required to prevent unlawful use of such entities.

Implementation and Role of Regulatory and Other Administrative Authorities

26. The competent authorities supervising banks or other financial institutions or intermediaries, or other competent authorities, should ensure that the supervised institutions have adequate programs to guard against money laundering. These authorities should co-operate and lend expertise spontaneously or on request with other domestic judicial or law enforcement authorities in money laundering investigations and prosecutions.

27. Competent authorities should be designated to ensure an effective implementation of all these Recommendations, through administrative supervision and regulation, in other professions dealing with cash as defined by each country.

28. The competent authorities should establish guidelines which will assist financial institutions in detecting suspicious patterns of behaviour by their customers. It is understood that such guidelines must develop over time, and will never be exhaustive. It is further understood that such guidelines will primarily serve as an educational tool for financial institutions' personnel.

29. The competent authorities regulating or supervising financial institutions should take the necessary legal or regulatory measures to guard against control or acquisition of a significant participation in financial institutions by criminals or their confederates.

D. STRENGTHENING OF INTERNATIONAL COOPERATION

Administrative Cooperation

Exchange of General Information

30. National administrations should consider recording, at least in the aggregate, international flows of cash in whatever currency, so that estimates can be made of cash flows and reflows from various sources abroad, when this is combined with central bank information. Such information should be made available to the International Monetary Fund and the Bank for International Settlements to facilitate international studies.

31. International competent authorities, perhaps Interpol and the World Customs Organisation, should be given responsibility for gathering and disseminating information to competent authorities about the latest developments in money laundering and money laundering techniques. Central banks and bank regulators could do the same on their network. National authorities in various spheres, in consultation with trade associations, could then disseminate this to financial institutions in individual countries.

Exchange of Information Relating to Suspicious Transactions

32. Each country should make efforts to improve a spontaneous or "upon request" international information exchange relating to suspicious transactions, persons and corporations involved in those transactions between competent authorities. Strict safeguards should be established to ensure that this exchange of information is consistent with national and international provisions on privacy and data protection.

Other Forms of Cooperation

Basis and Means for Cooperation in Confiscation, Mutual Assistance and Extradition

33. Countries should try to ensure, on a bilateral or multilateral basis, that different knowledge standards in national definitions—i.e., different standards concerning the intentional element of the infraction—do not affect the ability or willingness of countries to provide each other with mutual legal assistance.

34. International co-operation should be supported by a network of bilateral and multilateral agreements and arrangements based on generally shared legal concepts with the aim of providing practical measures to affect the widest possible range of mutual assistance.

35. Countries should be encouraged to ratify and implement relevant international conventions on money laundering such as the 1990 Council of Europe Convention on Laundering, Search, Seizure and Confiscation of the Proceeds from Crime.

Focus of Improved Mutual Assistance on Money Laundering Issues

36. Cooperative investigations among countries' appropriate competent authorities should be encouraged. One valid and effective investigative technique in this respect is controlled delivery related to assets known or suspected to be the proceeds of crime. Countries are encouraged to support this technique, where possible.

37. There should be procedures for mutual assistance in criminal matters regarding the use of compulsory measures including the production of records by financial institutions and other persons, the search of persons and premises, seizure and obtaining of evidence for use in money laundering investigations and prosecutions and in related actions in foreign jurisdictions.

38. There should be authority to take expeditious action in response to requests by foreign countries to identify, freeze, seize and confiscate proceeds or other property of corresponding value to such proceeds, based on money laundering or the crimes underlying the laundering activity. There should also be arrangements for coordinating seizure and confiscation proceedings which may include the sharing of confiscated assets.

39. To avoid conflicts of jurisdiction, consideration should be given to devising and applying mechanisms for determining the best venue for prosecution of defendants in the interests of justice in cases that are subject to prosecution in more than one country. Similarly, there should be arrangements for coordinating seizure and confiscation proceedings which may include the sharing of confiscated assets.

40. Countries should have procedures in place to extradite, where possible, individuals charged with a money laundering offence or related offences. With respect to its national legal system, each country should recognise money laundering as an extraditable offence. Subject to their legal frameworks, countries may consider simplifying extradition by allowing direct transmission of extradition requests between appropriate ministries, extraditing persons based only on warrants of arrests or judgements, extraditing their nationals, and/or introducing a simplified extradition of consenting persons who waive formal extradition proceedings.

Annex to Recommendation 9: List of Financial Activities Undertaken by Business or Professions Which Are Not Financial Institutions

1. Acceptance of deposits and other repayable funds from the public.
2. Lending.
3. Financial leasing.
4. Money transmission services.
5. Issuing and managing means of payment (e.g., credit and debit cards, cheques, traveller's cheques and bankers' drafts . . .).
6. Financial guarantees and commitments.
7. Trading for account of customers (spot, forward, swaps, futures, options . . .) in:

    (a) money market instruments (cheques, bills, CDs, etc.);

    (b) foreign exchange;

    (c) exchange, interest rate and index instruments;

    (d) transferable securities;

    (e) commodity futures trading.

8. Participation in securities issues and the provision of financial services related to such issues.
9. Individual and collective portfolio management.
10. Safekeeping and administration of cash or liquid securities on behalf of clients.
11. Life insurance and other investment related insurance.
12. Money changing.

    Including inter alia

    —consumer credit

    —mortgage credit

    —factoring, with or without recourse

    —finance of commercial transactions (including forfaiting)

Selected Bibliography

Adam, Courtenay. "The Buck Never Stops." *The Banker* (November 1994), pp. 88–89.

Adams, James Ring, and Douglas Frantz. *A Full Service Bank: How BCCI Stole Billions.* New York: Pocket Books, 1992.

Aggarwal, Raj. "The Nature of Currency Black Markets: Empirical Test of Weak and Semistrong Form Efficiency." *International Trade Journal* 5, no. 1 (Fall 1990), pp. 1–24.

Alert Publications. "The Citibank-Salinas Affair." *Money Laundering Alert* (April 1996), pp. 5–8.

Alvarez, E.H. "Economic Development, Restructuring and the Illicit Drug Sector in Bolivia and Peru: Current Policies." *Journal of Interamerican Studies and World Affairs* 37, no. 3 (1995), pp. 25–49.

Andelman, D.A. "The Drug Money Maze." *Foreign Affairs* 73, no. 4 (1994), pp. 95–108.

Andelman, David A. "Troubled by the Ton." *San Diego Union-Tribune*, September 25, 1994, p. G4.

Bagley, Bruce M., and William Walker III. *Drug Trafficking in the Americas.* Coral Gables, Fla.: North/South Center Press, 1995.

A Banker's Guide to Avoiding Problems (pamphlet). Washington, D.C.: Office of the Controller of the Currency, 1989.

Bhandari, Jagdeep, and Bernard Decaluwe. "A Framework for the Analysis of Legal and Fraudulent Trade Transactions in Parallel Exchange Markets." *Weltwirtschaftliches Archiv* 122, no. 2 (June 1986), pp. 233–253.

Borrero, Oscar. "La Finca Raiz y la Economia Subterranea." *Camacol Seminario*, November 8, 1989.

Bray, W., and C. Dollery. "Coca Chewing and High Altitude Stress: A Spurious Correlation." *Current Anthropology* 24, no. 3 (1993), pp. 269–282.

Briceño, Juan, and Javier Martinez. "El Ciclo Operativo del Trafico Ilicito de la Coca y Sus Derivados: Implicaciones en la Liquidez del Sistema Financiero." In Federico

Leon and Ramiro Castro de la Mata, *Pasta Basica de Cocaina*. Lima, Peru: CEDRO, 1989, pp. 216–279.

Caballero Argaez, Carlos. "La Economia de la Cocaina, Algunos Estimativos para 1988." *Coyuntura Economica* 18, no. 3 (September 1988), pp. 179–183.

Campondónico, Humberto. "La Politica del Avestruz." In Diego Garcia-Sayan (ed.), *Coca, Cocaina, y Narcotrafico*. Lima, Peru: Comision Andina de Juristas, 1989, pp. 225–257.

Canto, Victor. "Monetary Policy, Dollarization, and Parallel Market Exchange Rates: The Case of the Dominican Republic." *Journal of International Money and Finance* 4, no. 4 (September 1985), pp. 507–521.

Clark, T., and J.J. Tigue. *Dirty Money*. London: Millington Books, 1975.

Clawson, Patrick, and Rensselaer W. Lee III. *The Andean Cocaine Industry*. New York: St. Martin's Press, 1996.

Connolly, Michael, and Dean Taylor. "The Exact Timing of the Collapse of an Exchange Rate Regime and Its Impact on the Relative Price of Traded Goods." *Journal of Money, Credit, and Banking* 16, no. 2 (May 1984), pp. 194–207.

Cowitt, Philip, Carolyn Edwards, and Elliot Bryce (eds.). *World Currency Yearbook* (various editions). Brooklyn, N.Y.: Currency Data & Intelligence, 1990, 1996.

Cuevas, Angela. *La Otra Cara del Dolar*. Bogotá: Tercer Mundo, 1986.

Culbertson, W. Patton. "Empirical Regularities in Black Markets for Currency." *World Development* 17, no. 12 (December 1989), pp. 1907–1919.

De Franco, M., and Godoy, R. "The Economic Consequences of Cocaine Production in Bolivia." *Journal of Latin American Studies* 24 (1992), pp. 375–406.

De Soto, Hernando. *El Otro Sendero*. Lima, Peru: Instituto de Libertad y Democracia, 1986.

Dinges, John. *Our Man in Panama*. New York: Random House, 1990.

Dornbusch, Rudiger et al. "The Black Market for Dollars in Brazil." *Quarterly Journal of Economics* 98, no. 1 (February 1983), pp. 25–40.

Drug Enforcement Administration (DEA). *National Narcotics Intelligence Consumers Committee Report* (various annual issues). Washington, D.C.: DEA, 1988–97.

Ehrenfeld, Rachel. *Evil Money*. New York: HarperCollins, 1992.

Estevez, Dolia. "Mexico: Asilo de Preferencia de los Narcodolares." *El Financiero Internacional*, March 18, 1998, p. 32.

Financial Action Task Force (FATF). *Report on Money Laundering Typologies*. Paris: FATF, February 10, 1999.

Financial Crimes Enforcement Network (FinCEN). "Court Interprets 'Safe Harbor' Provision." *FinCEN Advisory* 1, no. 8 (February 1997).

Financial Crimes Enforcement Network (FinCEN). "Preparing Suspicious Activity Reports (SARs)." *FinCEN Advisory*, no. 5 (August 1996).

Gerstein, Dean. "Alcohol Use and Consequences." In Mark Moore and Dean Gerstein (eds.), *Alcohol and Public Policy: Beyond the Shadow of Prohibition*. Washington, D.C.: National Academy Press, 1981.

Gomez, Hernando Jose. "El Tamaño del Narcotráfico y su Impacto Económico." *Economía Colombiana*, nos. 226–227 (February–March 1990), pp. 8–17.

Greenwood, Jeremy, and Kent Kimbrough. "Foreign Exchange Controls in a Black Market Economy." *Journal of Development Economics* 26, no. 1 (June 1987), pp. 129–143.

Grosse, Robert. "Colombia's Black Market in Foreign Exchange." *World Development* 20, no. 3 (1992), pp. 1193–1207.

Grosse, Robert. *Foreign Exchange Black Markets in Latin America*. New York: Praeger, 1994.

Grosse, Robert. "Global Corporate Strategy: Citibank's Acquisition of Confia in Mexico." Glendale, AZ: Thunderbird Case Clearinghouse, 2000.

Grosse, Robert. "Mexico's Black Market in Foreign Exchange and Its Relation to Narcotics Money Laundering." *Journal of Money Laundering Control* (August 1999).

Grosse, Robert. "Peru's Black Market in Foreign Exchange." *Journal of Interamerican Studies and World Affairs* 33, no. 3 (Fall 1991), pp. 135–165.

Gugliotta, Guy, and Jeff Leen. *Kings of Cocaine*. New York: Simon & Schuster, 1989.

International Currency Analysis. *World Currency Yearbook*. New York: International Currency Analysis, 1991. (Formerly *Pick's World Currency Yearbook*.)

International Monetary Fund (IMF). *Direction of Trade Yearbook, 1990*. Washington, D.C.: IMF, 1990.

Intriago, Charles. *Money Laundering Alert*. Miami, Fla.: Alert Global Media (published monthly).

Jellinek, E.M. "Recent Trends in Alcoholism and Alcohol Consumption." *Quarterly Journal of Studies on Alcohol* 8 (1947–48), pp. 1–42.

Jones, Christine, and Michael Roemer. "The Behavior of Parallel Markets in Developing Countries." In Michael Roemer and Christine Jones (eds.), *Markets in Developing Countries: Parallel, Fragmented, and Black*. San Francisco: International Center for Economic Growth, 1991, pp. 15–27.

Kalmanovitz, Salomon. "La Economía del Narcotráfico en Colombia." *Economía Colombiana*, nos. 226–227 (February–March 1990), pp. 18–28.

Karchner, Cliff. *Illegal Money Laundering: A Strategy & Resource Guide for Law Enforcement Agencies*. Washington, D.C.: Police Executive Resources, 1988.

Kempe, Frederick. *Noriega: Toda la Verdad*. Mexico City: Grijalbo, 1990.

Kochan, Nick, with Bob Whittington and Mark Potts. *Dirty Money: The Inside Story of the World's Sleaziest Bank*. Washington, D.C.: National Press Books, 1992.

Koveos, Peter, and Bruce Siefert. "Purchasing Power Parity and Black Markets." *Financial Management* 14, no. 3 (Autumn 1985), pp. 40–46.

"KYC—Or Else." *Businessweek*, July 21, 1997.

Lindauer, David. "Parallel, Fragmented, or Black? Defining Market Structure in Developing Economies." *World Development* 17, no. 12 (December 1989), pp. 1871–1880.

MacDonald, Scott B. *Mountain High, White Avalanche: Cocaine Power in the Andean States and Panama*. Washington, D.C.: Center for Strategic and International Studies, 1989.

Mermelstein, Max. *The Man Who Made It Snow*. New York: Simon & Schuster, 1990.

Michaely, Michael. "A Geometric Analysis of Black Market Behavior." *American Economic Review* 44, no. 4 (September 1954), pp. 627–637.

Money Laundering Alert. "KYC." 1997 article.

Morales, Edmundo. *Cocaine: White Gold Rush in Peru*. Tucson: University of Arizona Press, 1989.

Munroe, Kirk. "Money Laundering: Problems for International Private Banking." *Review of Banking & Financial Services*, January 27, 1993, pp. 9–17.

Nadelman, E.A. "Drug Prohibition in the United States: Costs, Consequences, and Alternatives." *Science* 245 (1989), pp. 939–947.

Naylor, R.T. *Bankers, Bagmen, and Bandits.* New York: Black Rose, 1990.

Nelson, Richard, Paul Schultz, and Robert Slighton. *Structural Change in a Developing Economy.* Princeton, N.J.: Princeton University Press, 1971.

Nowak, Michael. "Quantitative Controls and Unofficial Markets in Foreign Exchange: A Theoretical Framework." *IMF Staff Papers* 21, no. 3 (September 1984), pp. 404–481.

Pitt, Mark. "Smuggling and the Black Market for Foreign Exchange." *Journal of International Economics* 16, no. 4 (May 1984), pp. 243–257.

Plombeck, Charles Thelen. "Confidentiality and Disclosure: The Money Laundering Control Act of 1986 and Banking Secrecy." *The International Lawyer* (Spring 1988), pp. 69–98.

Possamai, Mario. *Money on the Run.* Toronto: Penguin, 1992.

Powis, Robert. *The Money Launderers.* Chicago: Probus, 1992.

Roark, Garland. *The Coin of Contraband.* Garden City, N.Y.: Doubleday, 1984.

Robinson, Jeffrey. *The Laundrymen.* New York: Arcade, 1996.

Rodriguez, Hector Mario. *Los Piratas de la Bolsa.* Bogotá: Peyre, 1988.

Roemer, Michael, and Christine Jones (eds.). *Markets in Developing Countries.* San Francisco: International Center for Economic Growth, 1991.

Sarmiento, Eduardo. "Economía del Narcotráfico." In Carlos Gustavo Arrieta, Luis Javier Orjuela, Eduardo Sarmiento Palacio, and Juan Gabriel Tokatlian (eds.), *Narcotráfico en Colombia* (2nd ed.). Bogotá: Universidad de los Andes, 1991.

Shiekh, Munir. "Black Market for Foreign Exchange, Capital Flows, and Smuggling." *Journal of Development Economics* 3, no. 1 (March 1976), pp. 9–26.

Steiner, Roberto. "Colombia's Income from the Drug Trade." *World Development* 26, no. 6 (1998), pp. 1013–1031.

Tokatlian, Juan, and Bruce Bagley (eds.). *Economía y Política del Narcotráfico.* Bogotá: Universidad de los Andes, 1990.

Torres, Craig, Joel Millman, and Dianne Solis. "Raul's World: Cash, Connections—and Corruption?" *Wall Street Journal*, August 7, 1996, p. A10.

Truell, Peter, and Larry Gurwin. *False Profits.* Boston: Houghton Mifflin, 1992.

U.S. Department of State. *Economics of the Narcotics Industry.* Washington, D.C.: U.S. State Department, 1994. (Report on joint State Department–CIA Conference, November 21–22, 1994.)

U.S. Department of State. *International Narcotics Control Strategy Report* (various annual issues). Washington, D.C.: U.S. GPO, 1989–98.

U.S. Department of State. *National Narcotics Intelligence Consumer Commission Report.* Washington, D.C.: U.S. Department of State. (Annual since 1986.)

Urrutia, Miguel. "Análisis Costo-Beneficio del Tráfico de Drogas para la Economía Colombiana." *Coyuntura Económica* (October 1990), pp. 115–126.

Walter, Ingo. *Secret Money.* London: Unwin Hyman, 1989.

Warburton, Clark. *The Economic Results of Prohibition.* New York: Columbia University Press, 1932.

Welling, Sarah N. "Smurfs, Money Laundering, and the Federal Criminal Law: The Crime of Structuring Transactions." *Florida Law Review* 41 (1989), pp. 287–339.

Index

About the Author

ROBERT E. GROSSE is Director of Research at Thunderbird, The American Graduate School of International Management. He holds a B.A. from Princeton and a doctorate from the University of North Carolina, both in international economics. He has taught international finance in MBA programs at the University of Miami, the University of Michigan, and the Instituto de Empresa (Madrid, Spain), as well as in various universities in Latin America. He has published numerous studies on financial and managerial strategies of international firms and on government–business relations.